We Passed This Way

A Coast-to-Coast Bicycle Trip
with Historical Reflections

We Passed This Way

A Coast-to-Coast Bicycle Trip
with Historical Reflections

By Dick Swinnerton

EASY BREAK, FIRST TIME PUBLISHING
CUPERTINO

To Mary Anna

For always being there

CONTENTS

In the summer of 1992, Roger Wedel and I were returning from Palo Alto, California, to our homes in Cupertino on one of our many Saturday-morning bicycle rides. The conversation turned to something we had begun discussing more and more seriously: a coast-to-coast ride. "Let's do it in the summer of '94," one of us proposed. We could both retire by then, so why not kick off retirement with something special? "Okay," we agreed, "let's do it!"

Kirby Miller and Ken Witthaus wanted to join us, but the group narrowed to three when Ken was diagnosed with prostate cancer just a few months before our departure. Ken is doing fine now and is back to active cycling, as well as other important things in life.

Riding a bicycle across the country was not always my life's ambition. I remember delivering newspapers on a bike as a kid and thinking, "When I have my own car, I'm never going to ride a bicycle again, at least not uphill." Well, that's another indication of one of the few certainties in life: things change. Why would middle-aged guys want to ride bicycles at all? Yes, it's great exercise and an environmentally sound form of transportation, but it's much more than that. Cyclists are drawn to it for the freedom to go where they can't in a car, such as trails through parks and bike lanes during rush-hour traffic. They love to feel the wind and smell the fresh air on a long downhill run. Some take pride in completing a long, tough ride, and most like to stop to enjoy the scenery, read an information sign, or talk to other people that are moving under their own power. And one of the ultimate rides in America is coast-to-coast. For Roger, Kirby, and me it was all of the above, plus a chance to do something monumental in our lives, while seeing the country in more depth than ever before. Our wives and families were supportive. "Do it, Dad!" was the advice I kept getting from each of my four grown children. So why do it? We just knew we wanted to, and, in 1992 when we made the final decision to go, there was no turning back.

In the late 1970s we began biking actively, riding nearly every week, either to and from work or with family or friends on weekends. Cycling became a principal source of exercise and a reason to be outdoors. But cycling is more than riding. It entails an efficient machine that needs care and special clothing to wear; it is something to do alone or with hundreds of other cyclists on a group tour; it is a way to spend time with our kids, most of whom have quickly become strong riders and push us to ride harder and further; it is an excuse to stop at our favorite cafés for breakfast--after all, we pedal hard to get there and deserve it. Cycling is a cause to support, for more and better bike lanes and trails, for access to bridges and trains. It is races to follow. It is dreaming of the ultimate ride.

Reactions varied when other people heard our plans. Some were in awe, some were envious, while others just questioned our sanity. A non-cycling friend commented when hearing of our plans, "There has to be an easier way to get there." Another asked, "Why would three guys in their mid-fifties, of supposedly sound mind, want to pedal bicycles over three thousand miles, on seats about as comfortable as fence rails?" We paid little attention to the few nay sayers and never seriously analyzed "why." We had been cycling actively for the past fifteen years, so the decision to do it was not a sudden impulse; rather it was a natural next step in our lives. Who knows all the reasons why? We just wanted to do it.

Planning for the trip began in September, 1992, with rambling discussions of where to stay (camping or motels), what type of support to have (self-contained or with an accompanying van), and whether to go it on our own or with a commercial tour group. The option of doing it on our own with van/sag wagon support quickly won out. My wife Mary Anna agreed to drive our van and provide logistical support for the entire trip. Roger's wife Lynn and Kirby's wife Mary Dean would also join us for various parts of the trip. Other decisions were hammered out over the next year and a half, usually by unanimity but sometimes only by simple majority (we had no provision for filibuster). We all appreciated the value of good planning, but Roger, in particular, was the planning bulldog. He wanted it all laid out in great detail, and so it was.

Our route was planned to avoid the highest mountains and largest cities, see a few sites, and visit friends and relatives along the way. Summer was the time, so north was the location. We wanted to follow sections of the old Oregon Trail because of our interest in history and because those pioneers knew the best way to get across the western mountains. Boston became our destination, as Kirby and Roger had personal ties there and because of its historic ring. The location of the Erie Canal across upstate New York made it another anchor for our route, the least hilly way across the eastern mountains. Our path between Casper, Wyoming, and the Erie Canal would be a fairly straight line, linking the locations of friends and relatives and avoiding the cities.

Our pace was to be modest by cross-country biking standards-- fifty to seventy miles per day, with a rest day every six or seven days. In summary, it was a practical route, with modest social and historic overtones. It was designed primarily to get us there efficiently, not necessarily to provide daily, life-enhancing experiences.

We were wrong. As the trip began, we thought that reaching the Atlantic Ocean would be the highlight of our trip, but instead it became just another of many memorable days. Dipping our front wheels into the Atlantic on August 10, 1994, was the final milestone, but the experience was anti-climactic compared to other highlights:

- Walking in the Oregon Trail's ruts and talking about life on the trail with a living-history mother at the Blue Mountain Crossing;
- Enjoying conversation and coffee at the local cafés with cowboys in Oregon, farmers in Iowa, and professors in Massachusetts;
- Experiencing the chores, fun, frustrations, and richness of life on an Idaho ranch;
- Finding places in small towns that could read our laptop computer software and print out the weekly newsletter;
- Reliving the Plains Indian Wars at restored eighteenth-century forts in Wyoming and Nebraska;
- Discovering real Americana in Le Mars, Iowa, on the Fourth of July;
- Riding the Elroy-Sparta trail in Wisconsin with my son Matt and his family and enjoying the bicycle-friendly towns along the way;
- Being absorbed in German/Mennonite culture in Kitchener, Ontario;
- Seeing the Erie Canal, learning of its role in the westward migration, and riding on the restored towpath;
- Riding along the "Battle Road" between Lexington and Concord, Massachusetts, our country's birthplace and a fitting conclusion of our trip.

As soon as I let myself relax a little from the push to get to Boston, these people, places, and experiences allowed me to appreciate our beautiful and ever-changing "American tapestry." The "threads" are simply people, past and present. The colors and materials of the threads are determined by our differences, which are in turn enriched by our histories, traditions, habits, hopes, and heartaches and shaped by the physical makings of our country--climate, landscape, and economy, to name just a few. These "threads" are seldom noted in the current newspaper or nightly news, but they play such an integral role in making our system of freedom, democracy, diversity, and capitalism work. As I mention people and places throughout this book that sparked my awareness of our "American tapestry," I hope the reader can also feel the beauty and strength of these threads.

Visiting historical sites was an objective from the start. As we took time to stop and read roadside markers, visit historic sites, and read about places we passed by, our nation's history and its effect on contemporary life came alive. Our experience was enriched by understanding who else had "passed this way." People who are long gone were the first threads in the tapestry that exists today.

There are easier ways to travel from coast to coast than by bike, but for cyclists there is no greater American adventure. And for anyone, there is no better way to see, understand, and appreciate our great country than to get off the interstate highways and to slow down along the backroads. It was well worth the head winds, mosquitoes, hills, traffic, and bumpy roads along the way. Indeed it was the most fulfilling experience of our lives.

1

THE OREGON COAST

Wet sand stuck to the tires as we wheeled our bicycles across the beach toward the breakers. Wind and rain slowed our pace as we carried them the last hundred feet for the ceremonial dipping of the rear wheels in the Pacific Ocean. Three of us, Roger Wedel, Kirby Miller, and myself, were trudging across the beach near Astoria, Oregon, on that blustery day, May 28, 1994. Our spirits were high despite the lousy weather, as we were about to start a grand adventure that would end too soon, seventy-five days later, near Boston, Massachusetts.

We chose Astoria as our beginning point for geographic and historic reasons. A summer trip meant a northerly route, and the nearby Columbia River had carved a notch through the Cascade and Coast Mountain Ranges on its way to the Pacific, the only such water route through the northwestern mountains. In addition, Lewis and Clark had reached the Pacific Ocean nearby.

Astoria's Roots

Near the site of Lewis and Clark's Pacific-coast encampment, the town of Astoria would later be established, the first permanent American settlement west of the Mississippi. John Jacob Astor, one of the wealthiest men in America in his time, started the Pacific American Fur Company there in 1811. Though taken over by the British during the War of 1812, the area returned to American jurisdiction in 1846. Astoria can be rightfully proud of its heritage as America's first foothold on the Pacific coast, a highly appropriate spot to begin a cross-country bicycle adventure.

We stayed at the Crest Motel near Astoria on the 27th. That evening, I walked out on the motel's back lawn where I could see the Columbia River and its confluence with the Pacific Ocean at Cape Disappointment. Though filled with anticipation about our own unfolding adventure, I couldn't help but be in awe of the scene and think about Lewis and Clark and the others who have passed this way, influencing what Oregon and the United States have become.

At one time the Columbia River was thought to be the western terminus of the Northwest Passage across North America. Lewis and Clark followed it from eastern Washington to the Pacific Ocean near Astoria, and the Oregon Trail followed it from eastern Oregon through the Cascades to the Willamette Valley. The river route would also be our "passage" through those mountains.

🚲 🚲 🚲

Fur and the Northwest Passage

The northwest coastal area of America (now the states of Washington and Oregon) was one of the last major coastal areas in the world to be explored by Europeans. The great distances across the Pacific Ocean or around South America, the northwesterly winds out of Alaska, and the heavy fog along the coast were all barriers to marine exploration.

Since Columbus's voyages to the Americas, several European nations wanted to develop colonies there and find more direct routes across the continent to Asia, a land with rich trading potential. There was widespread belief that somewhere through the American continent a great waterway connected the Atlantic and Pacific Oceans. It came to be known as the "Northwest Passage."

The Spanish periodically explored the northwest coast by sea from their Pacific Ocean ports in Mexico for 175 years, beginning in 1542. They were seeking the Northwest Passage and attempting to expand their empire. Although they were unsuccessful in both objectives, their explorers have been honored with geographic feature names: the Strait of Juan de Fuca between the United States and Canada and Heceta Head on the Oregon coast. Many don't know that de Fuca was actually a Greek mariner by the name of Apostolos Valerianus, who changed his name when he was hired by the Spanish.

The Russians, interested primarily in furs, hired an experienced Danish mariner, Vitus Bering, to sail across the North Pacific from Siberia to America in the late 1700s. When he reached Alaska he found highly prized sea otters in abundance. Because he was able to communicate and trade with the coastal tribes who trapped the otters, his successful voyages vastly enhanced Russia's profitable fur trade with China. The Russians established permanent settlements in Alaska and worked their way down the coast seeking more sea otters, raising anxiety among the Spanish regarding their claims in the Northwest. There was even concern that Russia might be in possession of the Northwest Passage. But Russia was overextended and the sea otters nearly extinct, so she soon withdrew from North America.

Discovering the Columbia River

The English and American mariners were becoming frequent visitors to the Northwest coast by the late 1700s. In 1778, Captain Cook, while on a voyage seeking the Northwest Passage, was the first to trade with Indians in that area, but he found no great river or passage. In 1788, the British missed it again as Captain John Meares attempted to cross the treacherous Columbia River bar. He gave up and never entered the river but left a permanent mark, naming the northern promontory Cape Disappointment, the name it still bears today. Captain Robert Gray, an American fur trader sailing out of Boston, also explored the northwest coast. His travels include some penetration of the Strait of Juan de Fuca.

In 1792, he accidentally encountered British Captain George Vancouver off the coast of Washington. Vancouver was also seeking Juan de Fuca's Strait, so Gray gave him directions to the strait and then headed south. This time the weather was clear as Gray sailed by Cape Disappointment and into the mouth of the Columbia River. (It's interesting to note that Gray's voyage from Boston to present-day Astoria had the same termini as our bike trip.) He traded with the Clatsop and Chinook tribes for furs and named the river Columbia after his ship of that name. Gray went ashore, claimed the region for the United States, and buried some American coins as proof of his visit. This event became the most important of Gray's life, as it permanently marked the course of the British empire. The British would contest ownership of the Oregon Country (Oregon, Washington, Idaho, and parts of Montana and British Columbia) for another fifty years, but Gray's discovery gave the United States a legitimate claim. The Columbia River was also to become the western terminus of America's overland version of the Northwest Passage. The only problem, as Lewis and Clark and others found out later, was a barrier between the east- and west-flowing rivers called the Rocky Mountains.

We awoke on the morning of May 28th to gray skies, light wind, drizzle, and temperatures in the fifties. We wondered whether this was real rain or northwest "liquid sunshine" that would soon burn-off. (It proved to be the former.) Roger was feeling as lousy as the weather-- seemed like a touch of stomach flu. Were these bad omens? We debated about delaying a day but found there were no rooms available in Astoria's inns over the Memorial Day weekend. Roger looked as bad as he felt but quietly said, "Let's go!"

Our son Mike and his family were the first to arrive in Astoria on the 27th, and they scouted out the starting-point possibilities. Actually, the starting point was an ethical issue. We debated about how to make the "coast-to-coast" title official. For convenience, one might stretch the definition and start near Portland, as the nearby Columbia River has a little tidal action and salinity. I felt that was stretching it too far and suggested we start at Astoria, still ten miles inland. Roger and Kirby concurred as it would save the ten-mile round-trip to the actual ocean, and no one would know the difference. I made the mistake of mentioning this dilemma to my son Matt, an active cyclist who wants to take such a trip someday, and he ridiculed me to no end. "Dad, if you are going to ride coast to coast, over three thousand miles, do it right. Start at the ocean!" So we did the right thing; thus Mike was looking for the right spot *on the ocean*. He found it at Fort Stevens State Park.

Japanese Shell Fort Stevens in World War II

Fort Stevens was built during the Civil War, but it is most famous for being fired upon by a Japanese submarine on June 21, 1942. The sixteen shells landed harmlessly on the beach and in the woods behind the fort. The American troops manned their guns and prepared for the order to return fire. But the order never came, as the first salvo had done no harm, and the officers were reluctant to betray the location of the U.S. guns. No second salvo ever arrived. It was a frightening time for Astorians and for the troops at Fort Stevens which guarded the strategic entrance to the Columbia River. The Japanese had just invaded two islands in the Aleutian chain in Alaska and had shelled a petroleum installation in Santa Barbara, California, and a lighthouse on Vancouver Island, British Columbia. There was fear of an invasion somewhere in the Pacific Northwest, but that fear subsided after the defeat of the Japanese Imperial Navy at the Battle of Midway. Fort Stevens was closed as a military base after World War II. Later it was converted to a state park--a perfect spot for initiating a cross-country bicycle ride.

Our caravan heading to the beach that blustery morning included the following crowd: the cyclists, sag wagon support team and part-time riders Mary Anna Swinnerton and Lynn Wedel, well-wisher and part-time supporter Mary Dean Miller, and some Swinnerton family from Seattle (daughter Juli, son Mike, daughter-in-law Robbi, and grandson Andy). It meant a lot to us to have family there to share in the celebration. We had toasted Mike and Robbi as well as the cyclists the night before, as Mike's birthday and the birth of their daughter, Mari, would be in June, while we were on the trip. After a couple of wrong turns in the fog and rain we finally found the place on the beach that Mike had in mind. The location was fine, as we could drive right up to the dunes next to the ocean, but the weather was a downer. We cyclists were struggling in the worsening wind and rain to don rain gear and to get our bikes checked out and loaded with water bottles and utility bags. The supporters and well-wishers were taking pictures, moving to and from cars and under umbrellas. They were no doubt saying under their breath, "Can't you guys move a little faster?" Finally we headed down to the surf for the ceremonial dipping of the rear wheels. I did not bother to take pictures under those conditions, but others did. Fortunately, Robbi Swinnerton had a Polaroid camera, so we had instant pictures of the send-off. Lynn, a die-hard photographer, even set up her tripod to get a group photo next to the skeletal remains of an old shipwreck.

At 9:30 a.m. Pacific Standard Time we were on our way! Juli chose to ride with us on the first day. It was great to have her along as she has always been as much a pal as a daughter and wanted to be a part of our adventure. Because she loves to talk, the first couple of miles flew by; before we knew it a sign announced the location of Fort Clatsop, the winter home for the Lewis and Clark party. We wondered why they had come so far.

America Extends to the Pacific Ocean

By the early 1800s the stage was set for America to extend her boundary to the Pacific Ocean, as the Louisiana Purchase had already doubled her size. The Oregon Country was desirable because it provided access to the Pacific without treading on Spanish territory in California. President Jefferson commissioned the Lewis and Clark expedition to explore and solidify U.S. claims to the territory. The eight-thousand-mile, two-and-a-half-year expedition from St. Louis to Astoria and back is considered the most arduous, important, and well-documented expedition in American history. They reached the Pacific in November 1805 via the Columbia River. "The grandest and most pleasing prospects which my eyes ever surveyed," wrote Clark on January 8, 1806. The voyagers built Fort Clatsop near Astoria's future site and wintered there. Anxious to return home, they left early the following spring and arrived back in St. Louis on September 23, 1806. Although not the continuous waterway that was originally envisioned, the Northwest Passage was found. The maps and journals of Lewis and Clark would show Americans an overland route to the Pacific.

The send-off group met us for breakfast near Astoria, and then Mike, Robbi, and Andy headed home to Seattle. The hot breakfast fueled us for the initial climb out of Astoria, and we were off again.

2

UP THE COLUMBIA

(Days 1-3)

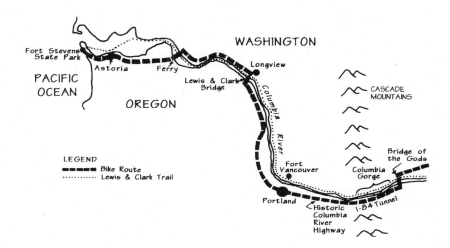

The trip up the Columbia River from Astoria to Umatilla, Oregon, provided a most amazing change in landscape and culture. In just three hundred miles, we rode from ocean beach and rain forest to high desert. We passed farmlands, lumber mills, port cities, a spectacular gorge through the Cascade Mountains, waterfalls, freeways, railroads, three major dams, tugboats, barges, state parks, and a nearby Indian reservation. The rest of the trip remained fascinating, but nothing topped the variety of that first week up the Columbia.

We gained a lot of experience with our wardrobes on the first few days, as the weather ranged from cool and wet to warm and sunny. Our basic cycling clothes proved very effective on warm days. The tight-fitting, colorful polyester shirts and shorts lowered wind resistance, enhanced visibility, and diminished perspiration. The stiff-soled shoes reduced fatigue by distributing the pedal pressure on our feet. Our rain gear worked well also. We had water-repellent jackets and pants as well as the neoprene booties. The rain gear was not perfect; a little water leaked in during heavy rains and some perspiration was unavoidable, but we were always comfortable and thankful to have it. Helmets and gloves (warm and cold weather) completed our wardrobe.

Perhaps our spirits were just naturally high on those first few days, but I remember no complaints about the weather. Even Roger was moderately upbeat, despite feeling ill and having the opinion that rain was something to appreciate from indoors. Kirby was really soaking it up as this was his first visit to the Columbia River country. Being a Pacific Northwest "junkie," I loved it all, rain or shine. Mary Anna and Lynn found that sag wagon duty was more demanding than expected: keeping track of us, finding lodging, checking the route ahead, writing a newsletter, buying food, helping with camp chores, learning to think like us, and, most of all, getting us to Boston in one piece.

Oregon's Route 30 between Astoria and Rainier (across the river from Longview, Washington) has two major hills. The first one is just east of Astoria--one heck of a way to start our trip. Juli was never crazy about hills, and I knew from our training rides that my rightful place was in the rear, so we were comfortable riding together behind Roger and Kirby. We got to the top in our own way. Once one masters the gears on a multi-speed bike and learns to be patient, hills are much less threatening. We just had to learn what pace we could tolerate and keep plugging along. My pace was simply a bit slower than Roger's and Kirby's. And having Juli along on that first day eased whatever minor embarrassment being last might have caused.

Climbing that first hill brought back memories of my first serious hill-climbing with Bob Fox near our home in Cupertino in the late 1970s. Bob gave us the idea for a cross-country bicycle trip. He had completed some longer bike tours, and a cross-country ride was one of his dreams. He convinced Roger, Kirby, and me that we could learn to ride over fifty miles a day--in the mountains--and enjoy it. And we did, most of the time. His infectious enthusiasm soon had us sharing his dream.

I remember his first invitation to ride around the reservoir (the Stevens Creek Reservoir in the hills behind our home). How could I refuse? As we were both in our early forties, our manhood was at stake. When he arrived that Saturday morning he took a look at my old, no-name ten-speed bike and just shook his head. "You're not going to make it on that thing," he said with a friendly smirk. "You need to get a much larger freewheel." "A larger what?" I asked, reluctant to show my cycling ignorance. He explained that the cluster of gears on the rear wheel is called a "freewheel," and it comes in various sizes. The smaller-diameter clusters, like mine, are for racing and flat-land riding, while the larger "granny-gears," like his, are for touring and hill-climbing. I listened apprehensively but chose to give it a try anyway. Although it was only a six-hundred-foot climb, and I was in reasonably good shape, I was able to ride merely the first hundred feet and walked the rest of the way. Bob pedaled up that hill with ease. The biking bug had bitten, so that afternoon I got a granny-gear cluster and began a whole new relationship with the bicycle. Roger and Kirby soon joined us on our rides. While Bob was not ready to retire in 1994 and was able to join us on this adventure for only one day in Wisconsin, his spirit was always with us.

That first hill was also a reminder of the motel manager's comments the night before. As we checked in he asked us about our trip. The van, with five bikes (the three riders' plus Lynn's and Mary Anna's) and a storage box on top, was an indication that we might be doing some serious biking. As I described our overall plans, with more detail about the Oregon portion, his only comment was, "Are you going up Cabbage Hill?" No doubt I looked puzzled and asked, "I don't know. Where is it?" "It's between Pendleton and La Grande. It's the way up to Dead Man's Pass. You know, Cabbage Hill, it's really something! You're going to ride your bikes up that hill?" I finally got the geography straight and admitted that we probably were going up Cabbage Hill, one way or the other. He shook his head, apparently wondering about our judgment, but wished us well.

Hills are not so bad, but flat is much better. We had driven over the two hills on the way to Astoria and wondered about alternate routes. So the sag crew went to work right away the next morning and found a route that would avoid the second hill. It included a ferry ride across the Columbia River to Puget Island, thence by bridge to Cathlamet, Washington. They found it to be a very pleasant detour and waved us down as we reached the bottom of the first hill.

The ferry ride was a nice change from the highway. It reminded me of ferry rides I'd had as a kid, crossing Chesapeake Bay on our way to vacations on the eastern shore of Maryland. Later, the Washington State ferries transported me to work when Mary Anna and I lived on Bainbridge Island near Seattle in the 1960s. Small ferries, like the eight-car vessel we were riding across the Columbia, are the most fun, though, as you are outdoors and close to the water, the engine, and the captain. You feel like you are wearing the ferry rather than just riding on it.

Puget Island

Puget Island was named after a Lieutenant Peter Puget, who sailed under Lieutenant George Vancouver during his exploration of the Northwest in 1792. After hearing from Gray about his discovery of the Columbia, Vancouver decided to investigate. He successfully crossed the bar into the mouth of the Columbia and sent a longboat upriver to explore the entrance of the Columbia Gorge. They identified and named Mount Hood and other geographic features, as well as Puget Island. Vancouver also claimed the Oregon Country (for Britain), feeling that his deeper explorations made his claim stronger than Gray's.

The ride across Puget Island and on to Cathlamet is a cyclist's dream, flat and nearly traffic-free, a great diversion from Oregon's Route 30. We had a detailed plan for the entire trip, thanks to Roger's urging, but we were also open to better opportunities that came along, usually discovered by the sag crew. This was the first of many such changes that would enhance our trip. Cathlamet was a delightful old river town and a great spot for a break. Juli decided that thirty miles was enough, so she drove on with Mary Dean Miller to confirm our reservations at a Longview motel.

The road from Cathlamet to Longview was close to the Columbia River that carries a lot of marine traffic. Ships loaded with grain and timber products were headed downriver and out to sea. Others, with names like Hyundai and Mitsubishi painted in large letters on their sides, were coming upriver to Portland and other ports along the Columbia. It was an amazing contrast to have lush forests and farms on one side of the road and on the other side, ocean-going ships that you could almost reach out and touch.

Roger was beginning to tire, so Mary Anna and Lynn drove about five miles ahead, waited for us, and debated about how much further we would ride. They repeated this procedure a few times, until after fifty-five miles Roger had enough. So fourteen miles short of Longview, we loaded into the van and drove into town. This was the only time on the trip that Roger was the first rider to want to quit for the day. We noted the exact spot and would return to it the next morning, as we were determined to ride the entire route. This was a good beginning. We had cycled fifty-five miles in wet weather after a late start and with one sick cyclist. Our only mishap was Juli being hit by the remains of a hamburger tossed from a passing pickup truck. (This was the only such incident we had on the entire trip.) Juli's great temperament and coolness under fire prevailed (characteristics that serve her well as a junior high school teacher). She did not even mention the incident until our next break.

Longview and the Washington Territory

Longview, Washington, has a special place in northwestern history. It was there in 1852 that Cowlitz Valley and Puget Sound settlers met and agreed to pursue the creation of a separate territory north of the Columbia River. Their wish was granted, and the Washington Territory was established by Congress the following year.

Intermittent showers on the second day's ride to Troutdale, Oregon, allowed us more opportunities to practice our rain gear routine.

From Longview, we crossed the Columbia back to Oregon via the Lewis and Clark Bridge. This was the first of many enjoyable bridge rides. We were thrilled to stop in the middle and observe the river traffic and countryside from high above. The view from the Lewis and Clark Bridge was dominated by ships and docks covered with mountains of large, freshly cut logs. Most of the logs were stacked in piles called "cold decks"; others were being loaded on ships for transport to far-away mills, most likely in Japan or other Asian countries.

Logging in the Northwest

Lumber mills and cold decks have long been a familiar sight in the Pacific Northwest. Seeing the logs and ships was a reminder of the history and current controversy in Washington and Oregon regarding old-growth forests, timber, and exporting.

Harvesting trees for lumber has been a major industry in the Northwest since the mid-1800s. The first sawmill was built by the British at Fort Vancouver in 1827, and within fifty years, there were hundreds more. The tree most associated with the Northwest is the Douglas fir, named for the Scotsman and naturalist David Douglas. He came to the Northwest in 1825 to inventory the trees in the region and send specimens back to England. Disembarking near the mouth of the Columbia River, he spent several years examining the forests of Oregon, Washington, and California. His records were influential in spawning the lumber industry. Over the next century, millions of board feet of timber were harvested to build ships, houses, railroad ties, bridges, and mining tunnels.

The early northwestern loggers were much like the western cattlemen, working in small groups with very little restraint. They went where the timber was, initially within close proximity to water for transportation purposes. The forests were originally all public domain, an "open range" for loggers, and there was minimal regulation regarding where and how much to cut.

As logging activity accelerated after 1900, the federal government recognized the need to manage some of the publicly owned forests for the long-term benefit of all. President Theodore Roosevelt established the national forests to be managed under the principles of multiple-use with timber harvested on a sustained-yield basis, which means that the annual volume of cut timber was not to exceed the annual growth in a given forest. While most of the receipts from timber sales were returned to the federal treasury, some were returned to the local counties in lieu of taxes to support public schools and road construction. Timber was also managed in balance with the other forest resources: water, wildlife, range, and recreation.

Railroad companies also got into the forest management business. Land grants were provided along the railway corridors as part of the federal government's construction subsidy. Some of these forest lands are still owned and managed by the railroads. Others were sold to private timber companies or reverted to government ownership if railroads were not built.

World War II and the post-war housing boom stimulated increased demand for wood products, and a growing urban population had more leisure time to spend in the forests. They often did not understand the science of sustained-yield harvest or multiple-use forest management. Even if they did understand, many didn't like it, as they valued the pristine forests most highly and considered logging to be in conflict with those values. An environmental movement was taking root.

The post-war economic boom extended overseas; the exploding Japanese economy required far more timber than they had at home. They began to outbid U.S. firms for national forest timber, and the raw logs were shipped to Japan for processing. Another dilemma was evolving--exporting was a plus for the U.S. balance of payments but a minus for the Northwest's lumber mills and mill workers.

Controversies over the economic and environmental values of the northwest forests have intensified in recent years. The spotted owl, as an endangered species, was used effectively by environmentalists to retard timber harvesting. Many loggers had to find other occupations. However, the number of Douglas fir logs on that dock in Longview for overseas shipment indicated that the timber industry is still very much alive.

The seventy-five miles to Troutdale on the second day was longer than any of us had cycled in one day before. Although Roger had not fully recovered from his stomach bug when we left Longview, we found out that he was plenty tough as we rode east and south on Route 30. He had always been physically active, having run a marathon in the 1970s and continually run or biked ever since. He was fifty-five when we dipped our wheels in the Pacific and had just retired as a heat-transfer engineer from a down-sizing Lockheed Missiles and Space Division. As the youngest of our group, he should have been tough.

Mid-morning we noticed a man and woman cycling ahead of us. As we caught up to them and stopped to compare notes, we found they were training for the Seattle-to-Portland ride, an annual tour event that involves hundreds of cyclists. These were the first of many touring cyclists that we would meet as we pedaled eastward.

After crossing the St. Johns Bridge over the Willamette River near Portland, Lynn joined us for the afternoon ride. She had little difficulty keeping up and no doubt stimulated Roger to keep cranking.

To get around Portland, we followed a route recommended by the Oregon Department of Transportation on their *Oregon Bicycling Guide* map. This was a great ride through quiet neighborhoods and parks, with no significant hills. We gave the bicycling map good marks so far. The final ten miles into Troutdale was terrific, a paved bike trail along the Columbia River. The sun was out and all was right with the world.

Stumptown and Fort Vancouver

Portland is a major metropolitan area of over one million people, the largest city in Oregon. It is a major seaport and winner of the "Most Livable City" award in 1976 and 1977. Its rose gardens and parks are world-famous. It even had a world championship NBA basketball team in the 1976-77 season. Vancouver, Washington, just across the Columbia River, is now largely a bedroom community for Portland. Such was not always the case.

Fort Vancouver was established as a major fur trading post in 1825 by the British Hudson's Bay Company. It was located on the north side of the Columbia River because the British felt that the river would ultimately become the international boundary, and they wanted to be on the correct side. Fort Vancouver was the primary outpost of European civilization in the Pacific Northwest for the next twenty years. Though its leader, Dr. John McLoughlin, was loyal to the crown, he was always hospitable to American explorers and pioneers and thus contributed to the Americanization of both Oregon and Washington. In 1848, after the final decision on the U.S.-Canada border, the Hudson's Bay Company moved its headquarters to British Columbia, Canada. Most of the American pioneers settled in the fertile Willamette Valley to the south, positioning Portland to become the major city it is today. Dr. McLoughlin, head of Fort Vancouver, became one of those American pioneers. After being fired by the British for being too friendly to the Americans, he moved to Oregon City, Oregon, and became a leading American citizen.

Portland was originally named "Stumptown" for the tree stumps that littered the site. In 1844, the city was laid out by A.L. Lovejoy and Francis W. Pettygrove on the banks of the Willamette River, just south of its confluence with the Columbia River. Lovejoy and Pettygrove recognized the need for a more palatable name, and they debated what it should be. Lovejoy, from Boston, and Pettygrove, from Portland, Maine, each wanted to name it after their hometown. They flipped a coin and Pettygrove won, so Portland it was. (Somehow, Boston, Oregon, does not have a ring to it.)

We pedaled into Troutdale about 7:00 p.m. Roger was still not feeling great, but he hadn't complained or held us back, and that last ten miles on the bike path along the Columbia lifted all of our spirits. My brother Jerry drove down from his home in Grandview, Washington, and met us at the motel. We had a great visit over dinner at a nearby truck stop and were impressed by the telephones in each booth. The booth phones have apparently become a standard fixture in the better truck stops, allowing the drivers to keep in touch there, as well as on the road with their CB radios.

We discovered the first of what would be many of "Roger's Rules" that evening at the truck stop. (We got to know each other pretty well during seventy-five days together.) We all have our idiosyncrasies, and I kept track of them, occasionally bringing them up for friendly debate. Roger's were named "Roger's Rules," Kirby had "Kirby's Commandments," and I spouted "Dick's Dictates." Roger's list was the most lengthy and colorful and thus got the most attention. Unlike the rest of us, Roger had no ice cream on his pie, not because of his illness but because it was contrary to,

Roger's Rule No. 1 - "Never have ice cream on pie."

The rest of us were utterly amazed and in unanimous disagreement with this rule. I even claimed that Roger was probably the only one in the world with such a rule. But he stood his ground, claiming that ice cream simply detracts from the flavor of the pie. He was strengthened in his resolve later on the trip, when he found one other kindred soul who eats pie only in its naked form.

After breakfast the next morning, we bid good-bye to Jerry and Mary Dean Miller. Jerry drove home, while Mary Anna took Mary Dean to the Portland airport for her return flight to California. This was a sad time for her and Kirby, as they would not see each other until she rejoined us in Michigan about eight weeks later.

Lynn cycled with us again on day three for a beautiful fifteen-mile ride on the historic Columbia River Highway to Multnomah Falls, where she would be picked up by Mary Anna. The old highway follows the Sandy River for a few miles then climbs about seven hundred feet to a spectacular overlook of the Columbia Gorge. Lynn's plan from the start was to ride only in dry weather and on flat or downhill terrain. She broke her "no uphill" rule that morning.

The view from Crown Point is awesome. The Columbia River slices through the Cascade Mountain's snow-covered volcanic peaks. Mount Hood, on the Oregon side, and Mount Adams, on the Washington side, frame the gorge, each exceeding ten thousand feet in elevation. Vegetation is lush on the west side of the Cascades, with rainfall at the crest exceeding one hundred inches per year. The Douglas fir trees are over 150 feet tall and so thick that we could not see the ground below when looking down on them from Crown Point. The old highway then descends through rugged cuts in the basalt cliffs, into the forest and past several gorgeous waterfalls. Multnomah, at six hundred feet, is the tallest and most popular of the falls. We took a break there to enjoy the falls, take pictures, and wait for Mary Anna. The wait was longer than expected, so three of us biked on. Mary Anna was held up by the Memorial Day traffic, but finally came to Lynn's rescue and soon thereafter to ours as well.

A Highway through the Columbia Gorge in 1915

The historic Columbia River Highway is very impressive today and should be on the must-see list for anyone visiting the Portland area. Shortly after its completion in 1915, it was considered a world-class engineering achievement that was also known for its sensitivity to one of the most dramatic landscapes in North America. Teddy Roosevelt once said, "You have in the Columbia Highway the most remarkable engineering in the United States which for scenic grandeur is not equaled anywhere."

The Columbia River Gorge had been a commercial transportation corridor for nearly twelve thousand years, but it was never an easy one. Three areas of falls or cascades impeded water travel, whether by Indian canoes or white man's steamboats. For the Oregon Trail pioneers, this was arguably the most hazardous portion of the trip. By the 1860s commercial travel was available through the gorge by a combination of steamboats on the flat water and short rail lines around the rapids. A continuous rail line was completed in the 1880s. Locks were built around the most dangerous falls and cascades in the 1890s, allowing steamboats to travel unimpeded from Portland to Lewiston, Idaho.

The highway was envisioned as a way to free travelers from timetables and allow them to start and stop at will. It was proposed by many early northwesterners, the most influential of whom was Samuel C. Hill, a Washingtonian. Even though he was a lawyer for the Northern Pacific Railroad, Hill could see the utility of the personal motor car. He understood the importance of high quality roads to the growth of automobile transportation. He arranged financing for the highway and hired the premier highway engineer of the day, Samuel C. Lancaster, to design it and oversee its construction.

Lancaster was a spiritual man, as well as a talented engineer, and he was dedicated to building roads that allowed people to see and appreciate the natural world as well as get them to their destination. Upon overlooking the site as survey work began, he said, "Standing here I realize the magnitude of my task and the splendid opportunity presented. Instinctively, there came a prayer for strong men and that we might have the sense to do the right thing in the right way...so as not to mar what God had put there...." It appeared to us as we cycled down toward the falls that Lancaster's prayer had been answered.

Just a couple of miles beyond Multnomah Falls the historic highway merges with I-84. Bicycling on the interstate highways is legal outside metropolitan areas in Oregon and in most other western states. Also, I-84 was recommended by the *Oregon Bicycling Guide* as the "most suitable" route through the Columbia Gorge. So we cautiously wheeled onto the freeway, very mindful of the heavy holiday traffic. Within a few minutes things got scary as a sign told us that a tunnel lay ahead. "Surely there must be accommodations for bikes," we said, as the tunnel entrance came into view. Not so! There is no shoulder and the sidewalk is only about two feet wide--barely wide enough to walk with our bikes. With hearts pounding, we walked along within an arm's length of the trucks barreling by at 70 mph. The last hundred yards were the worst as the tunnel sidewalk slopes toward the roadway and was covered with mud.

We emerged from the tunnel a bit shaky and were slow to remount our bikes. We'd had more than enough of I-84. Though the freeway in the open air appeared benign compared to the tunnel, we quickly decided to find another route. While studying our maps (other than the *Oregon Bicycling Guide*), Mary Anna and Lynn drove up with uncanny timing. At the next exit near the town of Cascade Locks there was a bridge across the Columbia to the Washington side. The "Bridge of the Gods," as it was called, was truly a godsend for us that day. The toll booth folks must have sensed our distress as they waived us through without collecting the seventy-five-cent bicycle toll. Although the beautiful old steel bridge was fun to ride across it was too narrow for us to stop, so picture-taking was delayed until we reached a viewpoint on the other side.

A Bridge Site with a Past

This site and the Bridge of the Gods have had an interesting past. This was where the British at Fort Vancouver met pioneer wagons and ferried them on to the fort after they had portaged around the cascades. Later, one of the most important battles in northwestern Indian history took place there in 1856. Kamiakin, the powerful chief of the Yakima nation in Central Washington, was leading an uprising that he hoped would remove the white man from the Northwest. A small fort stood in the way on the Washington side of the river. Kamiakin felt that capturing the fort would clear their way to invade Oregon. A small band of whites stopped him, holding out at the blockhouse for three days. Troops from Fort Vancouver (a U.S. fort by that time) arrived by boat just in time and defeated the Indians. Those troops were led by Lieutenant Phil Sheridan, who later gained fame during the Civil War.

Locks were completed around the cascades in 1896. During construction, the town of Whiskey Flat grew up on the Oregon side to support the construction workers. There were many saloons in town but no churches, until William Hoskins, a stonecutter, started a Sunday school. After construction was completed, the town was renamed "Cascade Locks."

The Bridge of the Gods was completed in 1926, and a year later it had a famous visitor, Charles Lindbergh. Immediately following his solo flight across the Atlantic, he toured America in the Spirit of St. Louis. *While on a flight from Seattle to Portland, Lindbergh detoured across the Cascade Mountains and flew down the Columbia Gorge and under the bridge.*

I was especially perturbed by the tunnel experience and the *Oregon Bicycling Guide*. Having used and produced maps for nearly forty years as a summer aide and civil engineer with the U.S. Forest Service and later as a manager/cartographer with the U.S. Geological Survey, I was the "map guy" for the group. I was supposed to know a good map from a bad one. Well, so much for experience. There is no substitute for doing my homework; in this case I should have checked other sources. After the trip I notified the Oregon Department of Transportation of our frightening experience in the tunnel. They reported that a tunnel bypass is under development for cyclists and other non-motorized users and that an improved bicycling guide is available.

The tunnel scare highlighted our safety concerns. We had prepared well for most conditions, and the brightly colored clothing, helmets, and rear-view mirrors all helped. The route was planned to avoid major cities and heavy traffic. Hazardous road surfaces, such as pavement cracks that could grab a bike tire, were rare and could usually be seen far enough in advance to be avoided. Riding on the same road with large trucks and recreation vehicles was a challenge, but after a couple of days we also learned how to deal with them. Truck drivers knew how massive they appeared to us and how much wind they generated when they passed, so if traffic conditions allowed, they usually swung well to the left and gave us a friendly honk as they passed. RV drivers were something else as they usually didn't budge from their lane regardless of how close they were to us, so we pulled far to the right when we saw them coming.

The effect of wind from the passing trucks and RV's varied greatly. If there was a cross wind from the left, the trucks on our left intercepted it momentarily, throwing us off stride; then the wind they generated would hit us--a double whammy. If two trucks were passing near us, it was a triple whammy, so we slowed down. Once or twice we even stopped and got off our bikes. A cross wind from the right was hardly a problem; in fact, at times it seemed to counteract the wind generated by the truck. Head winds and tail winds had moderate effect, and, of course, the impact varied with the wind velocity. Based on the conditions, we soon were able to predict pretty well what our actions should be: 1) ignore it/no problem; 2) stop pedaling and hold on tight; 3) stop and get off the road; or, 4) in the case of RV's passing nearby, stop, get off the road, and lay down and hide.

What a pleasant change to be on the Washington side of the Columbia. Washington's SR14 is a quiet two-lane road with a wide shoulder and great views of the river and gorge. And as Roger pointed out, "By riding on the river side of the road we can enjoy the scenery without having to look across lanes of traffic." The next twelve miles through Stevenson to Home Valley were great, a time to unwind from the tunnel nightmare. The weather was good and the sag team found a campground equipped with showers, having no mosquitoes, and situated next to the river, meeting all of our camping criteria.

The showers were pretty minimal, but their quality did not discourage Kirby from singing. He sings classical music in a highly regarded chorus as well as in the shower and other places. It was a miracle that Kirby was with us at all as he was still recovering from a near-fatal cycling accident when we made plans for the trip. His wife Mary Dean was apprehensive at first but, seeing his determination, gradually became supportive. Kirby was fifty-eight when we started the trip. An acoustical physicist, he had recently retired from GTE Sylvania and was starting a consulting business, but he was ready to put his business on hold and join us.

After setting up camp, we returned to Stevenson for dinner. The gas station attendant gave us the following options for places to eat: "The place across the road is fast but so-so; the Spar Tree, a couple of blocks away, has good food, but if it's crowded you may have to wait awhile, depending on who's cooking; the fancy place, further down the road, is expensive and I don't like their food." We opted for the Spar Tree and the food was fine, fast, and inexpensive (about $4.00 for a full meal). With those prices, we knew we were a long way from California. After dinner, Kirby found an ice cream store whose two-scoop cones held about a pint of ice cream. We had to ask for dishes to hold the overflow.

The only problem at the campground, which we discovered later that night, was that the Burlington-Northern railroad track was hidden in the woods within fifty yards of our tents. Actually, it wasn't as bad as it sounds. Although the first train woke us up, the steady rumble was soothing after awhile, and it was exciting to see the trains up close the next morning. There was a nostalgia and friendliness about them that we would anticipate and appreciate for the remainder of the trip.

3

SAGEBRUSH IN WASHINGTON

(Days 4-6)

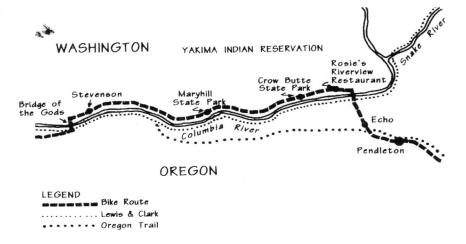

WASHINGTON   YAKIMA INDIAN RESERVATION

Rosie's
Riverview
Restaurant

Crow Butte
State Park

Maryhill
State Park

Stevenson

Bridge of
the Gods

Snake River

Echo

Columbia River

Pendleton

OREGON

LEGEND
▬▬▬▬▬▬ Bike Route
············· Lewis & Clark
• • • • • • Oregon Trail

From Home Valley we began to notice the effects of the dramatic change in rainfall from the west side to the east side of the Cascade Mountains. Vegetation changes from rain forest and ferns near Multnomah Falls to scattered pines and sagebrush. The Cascades soak up the moisture from the clouds as they come in from the ocean, and the result is dramatic; annual rainfall drops from over one hundred to about ten inches in the fifty miles from the crest to the eastern base of the Cascades. It's like walking through a wall between two different worlds.

SR14 is a little hilly, but the traffic and road conditions were great and winds had been modest, which was unusual for the Columbia Gorge. Near White Salmon, Washington, we saw some wind surfers on the river. Hood River, Oregon, (just across the river) is considered the wind surfing capital of the world.

In just the few days that we had been on the trip, we began to form some habits that would remain with us. Kirby always liked to have a small, cold breakfast before we started, while Roger and I preferred to get going, then stop for a hot breakfast in an hour or so. We decided to compromise and do both. We called the second (real) breakfast "B-2." That morning B-2 was at Bingen, Washington, which is famous for being the first white settlement in Klickitat County and, based on our experience, for having great blueberry pancakes. Roger was finally feeling good, so he joined us in the pancake feast. After we finished our stacks, the café's cook (who played classical music in the kitchen) brought out extra pancakes "on the house" to use up the batter. While we were finishing our last cup of coffee, the owner stopped by to talk about our trip. "Are you going up Cabbage Hill?" he asked.

Another habit we formed was looking for milkshakes or preferably, from Kirby's standpoint, malts. We usually had them for an afternoon break, often for lunch, and sometimes Kirby even had one for breakfast. Thus we learned and lived,

Kirby's Commandment No. 1 - "A malt a day is minimal for survival."

That afternoon we could see The Dalles Dam and across the river, the city of The Dalles, Oregon. Later we learned that the site has been known as The Dalles for centuries. The Celilo Falls, which was covered by the lake behind the dam, had been a highly productive fishing area for the Yakima and other local tribes for thousands of years. The Dalles was a trading center for many of the Indian tribes and the early white fur traders. It later became the overland terminus of the Oregon Trail. At that point the pioneers had to float or portage through the Columbia Gorge. (The Barlow Road was eventually carved out over the Cascade Mountains and became the route of choice for many immigrants.)

Dams Tame the Columbia

The fifteen dams on the Columbia River were built between 1930 and 1980 as part of America's love affair with large public works. The benefits of transportation, flood control, irrigation, and electric power generation far outstripped the direct costs of construction and operation. Washington's and Oregon's apple and grain production would be only a fraction of their current level without diverted water and efficient barge transportation. Both of these products are exported, thus contributing to the nation's trade balance as well as the local economy. On the other hand, the dams have had a devastating effect on migrating fish populations and the people in the fishing industry. Americans are just beginning to understand all of the long-term costs, as well as benefits, of dam construction.

With the light traffic and sparse population along SR14 we began developing some consistent riding habits. Kirby and Roger were the stronger riders, Kirby a bit stronger in the wind (despite his upright riding position due to a back condition) and Roger a bit stronger on the hills. So before too long, the two of them would usually pull away. I would eventually catch them on a long downhill run or they would wait for me at the top of a hill. Thus, our first nicknames were born: Kirby was "The Horse" or "Wind Slayer"; Roger was "Hill Stalker"; and I was "Shot Gun" or "Tail Gunner." More nicknames emerged as our personalities and riding habits were more fully revealed. Also, we soon learned,

Roger's Rule No. 2 - "Stop only at the top of a hill."

Roger felt that stopping in a flat area was okay, but he would never stop at the bottom of a hill or on the way up because he would lose momentum. If he stopped on the way up, the hill had conquered him; if he made it without stopping, he had conquered the hill. Kirby and I had no argument with that one, just noted it for future reference.

Other riding habits we formed were our stopping preferences. We called our rest stops "butt-breaks." Roger liked to ride fast and almost never stop. (Another nickname for Roger and the one that stuck was "Iron Butt.") I think Roger also had an iron bladder. Kirby liked to ride fast and stop often, while I liked to ride slow and stop often. Kirby and I won out on this one, and we agreed to stop every ten miles or every hour, whichever came first. There was also the question of the type of break. The "micro-butt-break" was not even stopping but just standing on our pedals during a strong tail wind or downhill run. The "mini-butt-break" was stopping but not getting off our bikes, just standing on solid ground for a few minutes. The preferred "maxi-butt-break" entailed stopping, getting off our bikes, drinking, snacking, and seeing to other necessities.

Neither could we agree about how to keep our bikes erect while taking maxi-butt-breaks or other longer stops. Roger and Kirby had kickstands on their bikes, the type that are usually found on bikes used by children or other casual riders. I explained, "Real cyclists do not have a kickstands on their bikes as they are an unnecessary dead weight, sometimes hazardous, and definitely not stylish." I went on to describe the three ways real cyclists support their bikes in lieu of kickstands: 1) lean it against a firm object, such as a wall, guard rail, or sign post; 2) lean it against a curb with the pedal toward the rear and locked on the top of the curb; or 3) find a rock about the height of a curb and lock the pedal on top of it as described above.

These methods are all superior to using kickstands, which are unreliable in soft ground, with additional weight on the bikes (like our utility bags), or in a strong wind. One can easily be over-confident about the effectiveness of a kickstand, leave the bike unattended for a moment, and then suddenly hear the spine-tingling sound of the bike crashing to the ground. With no kickstand, the cyclist selects the appropriate method to assure the bike's stability and knows he/she will not be embarrassed if other real cyclists pass by. Finally, if the worst conditions prevail, the bike must be laid on the ground anyway, with or without a kickstand. So,

Dick's Dictate No. 1 - "Never have a kickstand on a touring bike."

This tongue-in-cheek debate raged on throughout our trip with Roger being particularly adamant in his defense of the kickstand. Funny, he was so logical about most things, but when it came to kickstands, he seemed to go strictly with his emotions.

Where to ride on the roadway was another issue we debated. With the light traffic on SR14 we had some options. Being the oldest at fifty-nine and most cautious, I preferred to stay on the shoulder, unless there was no one in sight in either direction. Roger, being the youngest and most opportunistic, chose to ride on the smoothest pavement--the roadway itself--as long as passing vehicles had room to get around. The roadway was usually smoother, either because traffic had worn down the roughness or because the shoulder was not repaved when the roadway was. Roger would eventually move to the shoulder when traffic was heavy. Kirby tended to do some of both. We had some serious discussions about this but could not reach agreement. As we neared the Atlantic Ocean near Boston over two months later, we still had the same habits; it's tough for old guys to change. So,

Roger's Rule No. 3 - "Ride on the smoothest part of the roadway."

Dick's Dictate No. 2 - "Ride on the shoulder if traffic is in sight."

Also, during our restaurant breakfasts we soon learned another:

Roger's Rule No. 4 - "Never buy juice at a restaurant."

Here, Roger's rationale was purely economic: "Don't pay premium prices for juice at a restaurant; buy it in bulk at the grocery store." It was beginning to look like "Iron Butt" Wedel had metal in more than one place in his body.

Camping conditions were ideal again the next night. We stayed at Maryhill State Park, located on the Columbia River and at the bottom of a five-mile downhill run. The irrigated park and surrounding orchards were a green oasis in what had become a desert landscape. The campsites were spacious and the company stimulating. We met a lone cyclist, Jeff Bossart, who was on his way to San Francisco via Missoula, Montana, and Anchorage, Alaska. Jeff had just completed his masters degree in social work from the University of North Carolina, and, as this was his second cross-country bike trip, we enjoyed comparing notes.

Jeff was riding a mountain bike with four fully-loaded panniers (cargo bags). Kirby, Roger, and I were using touring bikes--skinny-tired road bikes with multiple speeds, lugs for attaching panniers, and underslung handlebars. We chose touring bikes, as racing bikes were too light to carry the variety of gear (rain gear, food, tools, and spare inner tubes) that we needed. Mountain bikes, heavier and having fatter tires, are more rugged and comfortable on rough surfaces and necessary for excessive loads but are less efficient over long distances. So for us, with moderate loads, touring bikes were the best bet.

We all had similar components on our bikes, up to twenty-one speeds to make hill-climbing easier. But we had two different systems to secure our feet to the pedals. Roger and I had the old-fashioned toe clips, while Kirby had a snap-on system similar to ski bindings. His system provided a firmer connection but took some getting used to. Roger and I were comfortable with our well worn, but still usable, old toe clips. Each system allows some lifting as well as pushing action on the pedals, thus increasing efficiency. We each had racks to hold panniers, pumps, two water bottles, and speedometers. Kirby had extra heavy-duty touring tires, while Roger and I had thorn-resistant plastic strips called "Mr. Tuffy" that were placed between the tire and tube. We had fourteen flat tires between us on the trip, and without such protection there would no doubt have been many more.

Just before we left, Roger was given some low-profile bars that attached to the handlebars. I was impressed with them and also ordered a set. By resting our forearms on the cushioned pads attached to the bars, our profiles and wind resistance were lowered, and the stress on our hands and wrists was reduced. We had a little less control of the bikes when using the profile bars, so it was best not to use them in congested areas. They were a great help, though, on those quiet rural roads where we would spend most of our time, and especially when fighting head winds. Kirby's back bothered him if he bent over for too long, so he stayed with the standard handlebars.

That night the famous winds of the Columbia Gorge returned, and our tents were nearly blown down. By unzipping all of the tent's openings and holding on for dear life, we managed to stay in one place, more or less.

As the five-mile downhill ride to the park was a stub off of SR14 we easily concluded that carrying our bikes back up the hill on the van the next morning was perfectly ethical. Jeff Bossart came to the same conclusion, welcomed our assistance, and was the first one up the hill, agreeing to meet us at Crow Butte State Park that night. We thought we would surely catch him along the route as he was carrying such a heavy load.

We would be leaving the Columbia Gorge the next day--and the nearby Yakima Indian reservation.

Kamiakin and the Yakimas

American Indians have lived in or near the Columbia Gorge for about twelve thousand years. For most of that period, the tribes of the Yakima nation fished in the river and freely roamed an area of nearly thirty thousand square miles in central Washington. Most of the Yakima people now live on the 2000-square mile Yakima reservation just north of the Columbia Gorge. Their story in many ways parallels that of other American Indian tribes, especially after their encounter with the white man. History has often presented the Indians as simply a stumbling block to the great westward movement of the white man, but fortunately a more balanced record has been documented by some contemporary historians. The Yakima people indeed passed this way, and their story is worth repeating here.

Fish have migrated up the Columbia River and have been the main food supply for the Yakima for thousands of years. More fish were caught than were needed, thus providing commodities for trading with other tribes. Celilo Falls (near present-day The Dalles) became one of the favorite fishing and trading sites along the river; thousands of Indians set up temporary housing around the falls during fishing season. It was also a sacred site for many of the tribes.

In the early 1700s, the Shoshone Indians of western Montana traveled over the Rockies and introduced horses to the Yakima for the first time. The Shoshones had acquired horses by trading with tribes to the south who had acquired them from the Spanish in the seventeenth century. Some horses were left behind when the Spanish were driven out of northern New Mexico by the Pueblo Indians in 1650. Horses thrived in the wild with the Indians, and they contributed greatly to increased mobility and communication among the tribes.

European and American goods arrived in the Columbia basin in the late 1700s. Metal cooking and eating utensils and glass objects appeared at the Celilo Falls trading grounds, as they had moved across the trade routes from the East and soon thereafter upriver from the Pacific coast. White man's diseases moved through those same Indian trade routes; smallpox and measles killed Indians in the West even before the whites arrived.

The Yakima met the Lewis and Clark expedition at Celilo Falls in 1805--their first encounter with the white man and a peaceful one. They traded with the voyagers, helped them portage around the falls, and remained on peaceful terms with whites for the next fifty years.

The 1850s brought a dramatic increase in white migration to the Yakima country. For the first time, the Indians were a problem to the whites. Originally, the white man needed the Indian to help him survive, then as a trading partner, and finally as a convert to Christianity. But the white pioneers eventually saw the Indians in a different light, when they coveted Indian land. In the 1840s, the Oregon Trail pioneers passed by Yakima country on their way to the Willamette Valley, but in 1853 the first wagon train went up the Yakima Valley. That same year, forty percent of the Yakima population died of smallpox, and in 1854 an Army survey crew led by Captain George B. McClellan laid out routes for a road and a railroad through the Yakima Valley. The seeds of conflict were being sown.

In order to strengthen their positions, the Nez Perce, Umatilla, Cayuse, Walla Walla, and Yakima tribes formed a confederation. In 1855, Isaac I. Stevens, territorial governor of Washington, took action to move those tribes onto reservations. He arranged for a conference to begin on May 29, 1855, near Fort Walla Walla, Washington. The treaty, signed on June 9th by most tribal leaders, provided for the Indians to move onto the designated reservations in exchange for cash and continuous federal benefits of food, shelter, health care, training, and education. Chief Kamiakin signed for the Yakima.

Within weeks after the treaty was signed, white settlers broke it. They trespassed on Indian land, grazed their cattle, and planted crops where they had no right to do so. Miners on their way to the gold fields in northeast Washington also trespassed and harassed the Indians. Some miners were killed by the Indians in retaliation, and, in September of 1855, widespread hostilities erupted.

Kamiakin led the Yakima and was instrumental in arranging alliances with several other tribes. The Indians triumphed in many of the early battles. Kamiakin's defeat at Cascade Locks was one of the turning points of the war, however, forcing the Indians to surrender in September, 1858. Most of the Yakima then gradually moved onto the reservation and began a new life, but Kamiakin refused to comply. He escaped to Canada, where he lived in exile until his death at age seventy-three.

Some of the reservation lands were later taken by the government for railroads. There was also a period when Indians sold some of their lands to white settlers, thus further reducing the size of the reservation.

Today, the approximately eight thousand people of the Yakima nation are led by fourteen elected leaders. Their economy is based primarily on timber and agriculture. They manage lumber mills, a furniture factory, cattle ranches, and farms and are adapting to the white man's world and taking advantage of educational and technological opportunities. A modern cultural center in Toppenish is a celebration of their proud history and strong desire to preserve their heritage.

After being nearly blown away the previous night at Maryhill State Park, we were anxious to ride with that westerly wind. This would be our strongest, all-day tail wind of the trip--20 to 25 mph. It was probably the best pure cycling day of the trip: wide, smooth shoulders on the road, little traffic, a cool, sunny day, and that fabulous wind. At one point, Roger announced that the wind was pushing him at a speed of 13 mph, without pedaling. We learned to calculate the tail wind speed using the "spit test." We would simply spit sidewise, then check our speedometers. If the spit blew ahead of us the wind speed was exceeding our biking speed. We then adjusted our biking speed (if possible) until the spit seemed to move with us. Of course, we were careful about where this test was performed.

Roger rated segments of our route from one-star to five-star (see Appendix). It was a subjective rating that considered the road surface, shoulder, traffic, and scenery, but he did not consider the highly variable factors of wind and rain. This segment from Maryhill to Crow Butte State Park got a four-star rating. But had he considered the wind and cool, sunny weather, it surely would have earned five stars.

After Lynn and Mary Anna delivered us to the top of the hill, they broke camp, did the laundry (we guys took on the laundry chores later), and then took time to explore the nearby Maryhill Museum of Art. It was built to be the home of Samuel C. Hill, the father of the historic Columbia River Highway. Hill unsuccessfully attempted to develop an agricultural colony for his fellow Quakers at the Maryhill site. As his wife refused to live there, it was used only for special occasions and eventually converted to a museum. It now houses Rodin sculptures, Indian baskets, and Russian icons. Queen Marie of Romania gave the icons in appreciation to Hill for his peacemaking efforts during World War I. She came to Maryhill for the dedication of the museum, with much local fanfare. The museum was definitely worth a visit, one of the many surprises along the route.

We stopped for lunch at a café in Roosevelt and got unpleasant expressions from a couple of men who were wearing coveralls. Roger said hello to one of them as he was leaving. He just scowled and grunted in response. We had heard that some local folks in the West and Midwest are unfriendly to bicyclists, so we were a little concerned. However, in hindsight we realized our concern was unnecessary. The owner was very friendly, referring to us as her "boys" and wishing us a safe trip. We later learned that Roosevelt has a huge landfill nearby, and apparently the uniformed men were refuse workers. Trash was hauled there by train (the Burlington Northern tracks were still nearby) from as far away as Seattle.

The wind continued after lunch, and we soon arrived at Crow Butte State Park for our third straight night of camping. But we had not caught up to Jeff; apparently, the additional bulk of his loaded panniers also served as a sail in the tailwind, for we never saw him until we pulled into the park. His pace may also have had something to do with his younger legs. Crow Butte is another beautiful Washington state park, with large campsites, an immaculate irrigated lawn, and riverside location.

When camping, our first order of business was selecting a site. At Crow Butte, the process was classic. We had learned by then that Lynn had the highest campsite standards among us, and at Crow Butte she had the opportunity to really show her stuff. She and Mary Anna had arrived in the van just ahead of us. Jeff had just arrived also and had not yet picked a site, so the stage was set to watch the expert at work. Roger suggested we just relax and watch Lynn "do her thing." Jeff and Kirby may have not yet fully trusted Lynn's judgment, so they joined her in the search. Mary Anna waited in the van for the signal from Lynn. As only a couple of the campground's fifty sites were occupied, this would take awhile. The campground was on a gradual slope from the entrance down to the river, and Roger and I could see it all from our comfortable observation post.

Lynn started by visiting with the camp hosts at the bottom of the hill. They described an additional site selection criteria: no camping on the grass because tent pegs might puncture the irrigation pipes. We were to set up our tents only on the gravel, as the campground was designed primarily for RV's. Based on the previous night's experience, Lynn also wanted protection from the wind. We needed enough space for four small tents and two picnic tables. So she and her team started out, meticulously inspecting site after site as they worked their way up the hill. Every now and then I would whisper, "I think she found it," but Roger would calmly counter with, "No, it's too soon." After seeing all of the most likely sites, the team had a conference. Mary Anna drove up the hill to the conference site, thinking that was it. She had just pulled into the site's parking area when Lynn started back down the hill, followed by her trusty team. That was not it--yet--and the search went on for another twenty to thirty minutes, marching up the hill and down the hill and up the hill again. Mary Anna understood the process by that time and stayed put until Lynn finally waved us on. That afternoon at Crow Butte I learned what Roger knew all too well, that Lynn also has rules:

Lynn's Law No. 1 - "Fully examine all campsites before selecting one."

After setting up camp, the hosts stopped by with a couple more rules: don't drive on the grass and don't spill water on the gravel. Despite the restrictions, we had a great time at Crow Butte, including good visits with Jeff and walks along the river. I would go out of my way to stay there again because of the beauty and serenity of the place.

It was Thursday, June 2nd, the sixth day, and we were four riders again. Jeff rode with us on our last stretch of Washington SR14 and across the Columbia River to Umatilla, Oregon. He then headed northeast to Missoula, Montana, while we turned southeast toward Pendleton, Oregon.

Our B-2 in Paterson, Washington, was another memorable one. The van arrived as we were being served coffee (hot chocolate for Kirby) and cinnamon rolls at Rosie's Riverview Restaurant. We got the initial odd look from a customer, no doubt a response to our biking attire which was out of place in that ranching, railroading, and truck-driving country. But the atmosphere quickly warmed when Rosie arrived with coffee. She was very friendly and full of questions about our trip. She had lived in that area all of her life and had never been east of Umatilla, which was just across the river. After feasting on Rosie's rolls we asked about biking on the I-82 highway bridge across the Columbia. She explained how to get onto the bike lane, which we might never have found on our own. "Turn off SR14 at Plymouth. Take a right, then a left, then through a tunnel under the highway and back up to the bike trail." I don't know how she ever knew; she probably hadn't been on a bike for thirty years. But lucky for us, her directions were perfect. We took pictures of Rosie and her husband George, and while saying our good-bye's she asked, "Are you going to ride up Cabbage Hill?"

We parted with Jeff after lunching together in Umatilla but got back in touch with him later. (He fell and broke a collar bone just beyond the Alaskan border and had to modify his trip. He now lives and works in the Seattle area.)

As we crossed the Columbia River and re-entered Oregon, I glanced upstream and realized that Lewis and Clark and their crew had passed by here on their way to the Pacific Ocean.

The afternoon ride to Pendleton had some highs and lows. The road conditions, scenery, and culture were terrific, but Roger was feeling lousy again, partly due to dehydration. After resting in the shade and pouring some water on his head he was much improved. The van's timing was perfect again, showing up with more water when our bottles were nearly dry. From then on we were more cautious about carrying and drinking plenty of water.

County Road 1300 (old Highway 30) follows the Umatilla River from Echo to Pendleton, one of my favorite stretches of the entire trip, worth four stars. Echo was the site of the first Indian agency in the area. Fort Henrietta was built there in 1855 and had the first frame building the Oregon Trail emigrants had seen since leaving Wyoming. The railroad came through in the 1880s, making Echo a major railhead for local ranchers. Currently off the interstate highway and experiencing quieter times, it has retained the look and hospitality of the Old West.

The Umatilla Valley is about a mile wide, with low basalt bluffs on both sides and irrigated ranches along the river. We were in Union Pacific Railroad country. The tracks meander up the valley in harmony with the river and the road, each one occasionally crossing the other. Long freight trains rambled by, but there was almost no traffic on the road, a scene that city cyclists dream about. We even saw a picturesque lumber mill near Pendleton, with all the wonderful smells associated with freshly cut wood. This was another time when I thought to myself, "Thanks, God, for letting me do this."

4

ALONG THE OREGON TRAIL

(Days 7-11)

Echo and the trip up the Umatilla Valley was our first sighting of remnants of the Oregon Trail. We had been near the trail from Troutdale to The Dalles, Oregon, but it was mostly a water route at that stage. Near Echo we saw and touched some actual ruts made by the wagons. We would roughly follow the trail for the next one thousand miles through Oregon and much of Idaho and Wyoming. Seeing those ruts was like being introduced to a very special friend that we immediately liked and soon grew to love and respect as we began to understand its history.

Wagons West to Oregon

"Come on out to the Oregon Country!" That cry was heard by farmers all over the Midwest in the early 1840s. Missionaries had been to Oregon evangelizing the Indians. and they were back home on the lecture circuit encouraging Americans to join them out west. Oregon Immigration Societies were formed in Indiana, Illinois, Ohio, Michigan, and Missouri to help stimulate interest. Jason Lee, a Methodist, and Marcus Whitman, a

Presbyterian, were especially active. Narcissa Whitman journeyed with her husband to Oregon, and as the first white woman to settle there, she proved that families could thrive there as well. Her enthusiastic letters were widely circulated and helped convince many families to pack up and head west.

Pioneers knew little of Oregon, that mysterious land west of the Rocky Mountains, between California and Alaska. It was not even part of their country yet, being jointly claimed by Great Britain and the United States. A few trappers and traders had been there and Indians, of course, but American families had not yet proven their ability to survive there. Some earlier explorers described the land west of the Mississippi as the "Great American Desert," but later the government encouraged emigration to Oregon. Senator Thomas Hart Benton, of Missouri, was talking of "Manifest Destiny" (the idea of the United States reaching all the way to the Pacific Ocean). The Reverend Jason Lee claimed that the Willamette Valley was ideal for farming with rich soil and a mild climate--and the land was free. But it was still a huge risk to take.

There was a trail, of sorts, to Oregon, portions of it used by Indians for centuries. It was later refined and connected by mountain men who explored and trapped beaver throughout the West. Word was that a few wagons had made it all the way to the Willamette Valley in 1841 and '42. The next year a journey known as "The Great Migration" began at Independence, Missouri. Fifty wagons and three hundred men, women, and children headed west, with another three hundred people joining them in Kansas. When they reached the Willamette Valley, their numbers had doubled the population of Oregon. This was only the beginning, as over the next twenty years more than 300,000 people set out on the Oregon Trail. They were drawn by the promise of free land, and they had dreams and were willing to travel great distances to pursue them. Their ancestors had come west from Europe, then had gone further west across the Appalachian Mountains seeking a better life; moving west was in their blood. Henry David Thoreau captured their mood with the words, "Eastward I go only by force, but westward I go free....This is the prevailing tendency of my countryman. I must walk to Oregon." An anonymous old-timer put it another way when asked why he was headed for Oregon: "Just to get where I ain't."

By the time the Civil War broke out in 1861, Americans were firmly entrenched coast to coast, and America's "Manifest Destiny" had been achieved.

As we stopped for an ice-cold drink a few miles outside of town, thoughts of the Oregon Trail pioneers sobered us as we enjoyed the beauty of eastern Oregon on a warm day in June. I couldn't help but think about how much I love my kids, and how sad I would be if they headed off to a strange land far away, likely never to be seen again. This bike trip was the big adventure of our lives, but it paled in comparison to the experience of the people who had passed this way 150 years ago by wagon train.

It was the seventh day, and we were ready for a break. Six days of continuous riding was enough, and Cabbage Hill lay just ahead. Even though it had been a tough week for Roger, we were not physically tired. Neither was boredom a problem, as we had looked forward to getting on the bikes every morning. But a break was still a good idea, as much for mental as physical rest. It was a time to relax, have some privacy, and enjoy the sites.

Pendleton, Oregon, is a great place for a day off. Now famous for its world-class rodeo and woolen mills, Pendleton was once named the "Entertainment Capitol of the Northwest," thanks to its thirty-two saloons and eighteen bordellos. Its current attractions are a little tamer, but the tunnels under the downtown, called "The Underground," give you a flavor of those old days. That morning we toured those tunnels that once housed large numbers of Chinese workers and other Pendletonians. The Undergrounds were part of many western railroad towns. Most of the laborers that built the western railroads were Chinese, and although reliable and hard workers, they were not well accepted by the local citizens. They went underground--partly for their own security and partly because it was a common practice in China. The Chinese established laundries and other businesses in the Undergrounds during the railroad boom days. Later, the Chinese population in Pendleton declined, but other enterprises, the saloons and bordellos, took their place and kept the Underground humming. We all enjoyed and were educated by the tour.

Another part of Oregon's history is the wool industry. Sheep first came to Oregon in the 1840s with the wagon trains. Like their owners, they walked all the way from Missouri. The Pendleton Woolen Mills were founded in 1910 to later become Oregon's best known. They now have facilities in five states, with headquarters in Portland, the Pendleton Mill being the first. Though less colorful than the Underground, the mill was worth the stop as we viewed the process from fleece to finished fabric.

We missed the rodeo--probably a good thing for us, as the town swells from fifteen thousand to eighty thousand during the annual Pendleton Roundup in September. It has the largest rodeo purse in the country.

In Pendleton, we noticed some of our different travel patterns. Kirby has more flexible camping criteria than the rest of us. He was willing to put up with a little rain or a few mosquitoes if a campground was nearby. So while the threatening rain clouds and desire for soft beds and a hot tub drove the Wedels and Swinnertons indoors, Kirby chose to camp at a nearby RV park.

Kirby's Commandment No. 2 - "Camp whenever possible."

This commandment was budget-related to a large degree; Kirby planned to spend less money on the trip than the rest of us. We had not communicated well enough on this important issue in our planning, and it caused some stress for awhile. But we learned to compromise. If the rest of us wanted to stay in a motel and there was a campground nearby, we would go separate ways; if not, Kirby would stay in the motel with us.

Packing the van was another issue. Mary Anna and Lynn had very different packing philosophies. Mary Anna is a vertical packer, and she placed the camping gear in one column, personal gear in a second column, bike stuff in a third, etc. Lynn, on the other hand, believes in layering or horizontal packing. Each system has its merits. The problem was understanding which system or combination of systems was used on a given day. The packing was done by a committee of two well-meaning, but strong-willed, people with unpredictable results. We were having a heck of a time finding things. Mary Anna's system eventually prevailed when Lynn returned to California for a few weeks.

It was the eighth day, the 4th of June, and we could not put it off any longer--we had to attack Cabbage Hill. Our first flat tire occurred just outside Pendleton and delayed us briefly. My back tire was punctured by a piece of metal, probably from a steel-belted radial tire. Was that a bad omen? Not at all; the climb up Cabbage Hill, on old Highway 30, was not a problem (a 2,500-foot climb in seven miles), about like one of our training rides back home. Maybe the grade was not that steep; maybe it was the scenery (we could see ranch lands stretching over fifty miles to the Columbia River); maybe it was the lack of traffic (only two cars passed us during the two-hour climb). Even the weather cooperated, as it was cool with an occasional light shower. There were several switch backs and few trees, so there were ever-changing views in all directions. Sure, I got tired at times, but breaks were short so we could get going again and see what was around the next corner. Who knows exactly why, but climbing up that mountain was fun. We reconfirmed our hill-climbing confidence.

We traveled through the Umatilla Indian reservation on the way up Cabbage Hill. Cattle were grazing on the hillsides, and I couldn't help but let out a "moo" as we pedaled close to some. They spooked easily and scampered down the hill. Roger chastised me and pointed out how unhappy the Indian ranchers would be if they knew we were stampeding their cattle. Roger was right. That was my last "moo" of the trip.

Roger's Rule No. 5 - "Look, but don't yell at the cattle."

After reflecting on this incident, I couldn't help but think of the irony of it. There we were on Indian lands, disturbing their livelihood again. I felt stupid--how long would it take for some of us to understand

and respect others, especially when in their territory? Roger was right on this one in more ways than one.

The vegetation changed as we neared the pass: open grassland gave way first to some scattered brush and then to the majestic ponderosa pine. Ponderosa, or yellow pine, as it is known locally, is the predominant species east of the Cascade Mountains, growing in a less dense pattern than the Douglas fir. Yellow pine forests are often open enough to permit some grass and other low vegetation in the understory. In June, the grass was still bright green, while the yellow pine bark on the south sides of the trees was a rusty orange-brown color. The showers had moved on and patches of brilliant blue sky formed a backdrop. I wondered if the Oregon Trail emigrants enjoyed the scene as much as I did that morning.

The van caught up to us near Deadman Pass. Mary Anna and Lynn joined us for a picnic lunch, and then Lynn rode with us on the downhill run. Unfortunately, the ride was not so downhill, as there were another ten miles of rolling and uphill grades (still on old Highway 30) before we crossed the rest of this section of the Blue Mountains and started down toward La Grande. Lynn tired of my repetitive claims that "this ought to be the last hill." For the rest of the trip I was careful to avoid that phrase.

The downhill ride through the mature forest was worth the wait, except for my second flat tire. This one was an unusual compression puncture, caused by a protruding section of bridge surface. I hit it going about 35 mph and, bang! Two slits in my tube where it crunched against the rim. Fortunately there was no damage to the tire or rim. Kirby, Lynn, and Roger came down that same hill and crossed the bridge with no problem. They must have missed my spot.

We also learned how to ride across cattle guards that day. Cattle guards serve as extensions of fences across a road. Instead of a fence and a gate, ditches are cut across the road and covered with steel rails laid in parallel an inch or so apart and perpendicular to the direction of travel. Vehicles can cross over them, but animals will not. Until that afternoon, we men had been wary of cattle guards and always dismounted and walked across. Lynn would have none of that, and she rode right across the first one we came to at full speed. Kirby had just walked across and exclaimed in amazement, "She just rode right across." No doubt we engineer/scientists had over-analyzed the potential risk, and from then on we followed Lynn's lead (at least for crossing cattle guards).

Mary Anna found us a motel in La Grande, and Kirby received high praise for doing the laundry. We picnicked at a park across the street with grocery store deli food. Lynn got us started on deli picnics in Pendleton, a habit we would happily continue.

Early the next morning, we drove back and visited the Interpretive Center for the Blue Mountain Crossing of the Oregon Trail. Mary Anna had discovered the U.S. Forest Service facility the previous afternoon, checked it out, and enthusiastically recommended that we all see it. After parking the van, we walked through the trees and came upon what appeared to be remnants of the Oregon Trail. There, standing by a campfire, was a young woman dressed in nineteenth-century attire. A loaded covered wagon was behind her just off the trail, and she asked, "Have you seen my husband John?" Her daughter had been sick, she explained, and they decided to stop and wait while John walked back to the last settlement to find a doctor. Staying in character, she related that their wagon train had gone on and that her daughter had died and was buried nearby. She was hoping John would return soon so they could join with the next wagon train that came along. She responded to all of our questions in the context of her Oregon Trail experience, including what they were carrying in the wagon. The entire setting was realistic and her performance moving--a few federal dollars well spent and a new insight into life on the Oregon Trail.

It was interesting to reflect on the size and function of the Oregon Trail wagon compared to our van. The wagon was slightly larger but had to carry, for about the same number of people, a six-month supply of food and other items needed on the trip, as well as farm implements and household goods that would be needed after arrival. Somehow, our packing problem seemed pretty trivial.

After a picnic breakfast at the interpretive center, we drove back to La Grande, mounted the bikes and headed southeast toward Baker City. Mary Anna biked with us for the first ten miles, and Lynn drove the van that morning, stopping to shop a couple of miles from the motel. She told us later that she was surprised to see the motel owner as she got out of the van. He had been searching for our van in order to return a bag of our laundry we had left at the motel. Lynn accepted the bag in gratitude and amazement.

Ben Brown's Saloon

La Grande was named by its founders, in the early 1860s, for the beauty of the surrounding area. Ben Brown moved his family there in 1861, one of several Oregon Trail emigrants who returned to the Grande Rhonde Valley after completing their trek to western Oregon. They remembered the clear, dry air, lush meadows, and towering mountains and returned to stake their claims. Brown built his house/saloon right next to the trail, which by then was busy with freight wagons and stage coach traffic, as well as emigrant wagons. Others soon followed, and by 1863, they had a post office and needed a name for the town. Ben Brown proposed "Brown-something" but was outvoted by his neighbors; La Grande it was. The Grande Rhonde River flows through La Grande and thence northeast toward its confluence with the

Snake River. The city of twelve thousand lies at the foot of the Blue Mountains, with the dramatic Wallowa Range rising to the east across the valley. La Grande's economy is based on agriculture and forest products, and it is home to Eastern Oregon State College. The Nez Perce Indians and Chief Joseph also passed this way.

Chief Joseph and His Long March

For centuries, the Nez Perce roamed freely throughout central Idaho, southeast Washington, and northeast Oregon. The Wallowa Valley, just east of La Grande, was their most treasured land. For fifty years, the Nez Perce had lived peacefully with the white fur traders and settlers. Then a familiar pattern evolved. Gold was discovered on Nez Perce land, and they were asked to relocate to a reservation in Idaho. Chief Joseph and his tribe resisted the move and decided to escape to Canada. Their trek to Canada is considered by many historians as one of the most brilliant and courageous military actions in history. During the fifteen-week fighting retreat, 250 warriors, encumbered by 400 women, children, and elderly, traveled more than 1,500 miles over very rugged mountain terrain. They fought five standing battles against over 2,000 soldiers and almost made it to Canada. Chief Joseph surrendered near the Canadian border after over a third of his tribe was killed. His words of surrender are considered one of the saddest and most eloquent Indian statements ever recorded. It ended with the familiar words: "Hear me my chiefs, my heart is sick and sad. From where the sun now stands, I will fight no more forever."

Chief Joseph and his remaining tribe were eventually returned to the reservation in Idaho but never again saw their beloved Wallowa Valley.

We took the back road (SR203) out of La Grande, up the Grande Rhonde Valley, and rendezvoused with Lynn for B-2 in Union. The waitress offered Kirby their peanut-chocolate milkshake. He was willing to try anything that had "milkshake" at the end of the name, so he accepted their offer and smiled at the results. Kirby also noticed an unusual flowering tree as we were leaving Union, so he stopped to investigate. People are attracted to different things, and while I might stop and take a picture of a beautiful tree or animal, Kirby wants to identify it. He is very curious about all living things and at times would hear a bird singing and identify it, without seeing it. If he sees something he can't identify, he visits a library to find out. So it was always interesting to quiz him as we pedaled along. I never learned the name of that tree, but I'll bet Kirby did.

A mile or two further down the road, another unusual sight caught our attention. Some large draft animals were pulling a farm wagon and driver across a field, a quarter of a mile or so off the road. At first glance, they appeared to be horses, then cows. But that didn't make sense, so we stopped to take a closer look and realized that they were oxen. Some ranchers in the area have oxen, partly as work animals but primarily as show animals for the many events commemorating the Oregon Trail migration.

Mules versus Oxen

Mules and oxen were the options for draft animals on the Oregon Trail. Mules were faster, but oxen were cheaper, gentler, and stronger and, in an emergency, were better to eat than mules. But mules could eat shorter grass, allowing the wagon trains to get an earlier start in the spring. Also, mules were more desirable to the Indians and thus more apt to be stolen, or more valuable as a trading commodity. Arguments raged on regarding which was better. Both were used successfully.

We were tempted to ride down the ranch road and get a closer look at the oxen and talk to the rancher about them, but for some reason, the goal of getting to the top of the next hill and on to Baker City was paramount. So, we moved on and missed an opportunity to learn more about a unique local activity. Maybe the next time we came across something special we'd stop longer and ask more questions.

The railroad was with us again. It had crossed the Blue Mountains on a different route, but near La Grande it was back with us and would be for the next several days. There was a hill to climb between Union and Baker City, and a long Union Pacific freight train was moving slowly up that hill, only slightly faster than we were pedaling. It was within sight for nearly an hour, and as it rumbled past, a man in an open freight car toasted Roger with his can of beer and shouted, "This is an easier way to go!" We smiled warmly and pedaled on--our love affair with trains was growing. Roger counted every car, and Kirby and I discussed where it might have come from, where it might be going, and what it might be carrying.

When we reached the top of the hill, Lynn took her turn cycling for the downhill ride into Baker City. The view of the valley from the hilltop was well worth the climb. The snow-capped Blue Mountains were peaking through the clouds to the west, and ranches below were glistening from the recent showers, reducing the need for irrigation for awhile. It was easy to see why many of the Oregon Trail emigrants wanted to stop and homestead right there rather than continue on to the Willamette Valley.

Baker City and the "Stump Dodger"

Baker Valley was originally known as Lone Pine Valley for the single pine that stood beside the Powder River. It served as a landmark for the explorers and emigrants until its demise of an unknown cause. The valley was an oasis for travelers for decades but was not heavily settled until gold was discovered nearby in 1861 by Henry Griffin. Baker (as it was called until recently) was at the center of the gold fields and became known as the "Queen City of the Mines." Though a few miles off the main Oregon Trail, it soon became a popular detour. Some of the emigrants caught the gold fever and headed for the mines rather than the Willamette Valley. The city was named for Col. Edward D. Baker, who was at one time a law partner with Abraham Lincoln. Later he was the first senator from Oregon and the only U.S. congressman killed in the Civil War. The city of Baker also thrived as a transportation hub with freight wagons, stage coaches, the Pony Express, and eventually the railroad all passing this way.

Railroads made it possible to develop the area's timber resources, and a narrow-gauge locomotive, known as the Stump Dodger, *hauled millions of dollars worth of gold ore and timber from the Sumpter Valley to the main line in Baker. Today, the Sumpter Valley Railroad carries tourists from Baker City to the once thriving gold fields and ghost towns.*

Kirby was usually in the lead on long downhill runs and also the most likely of us three to stop and talk with local folks. Seeing a couple of fisherman walking across the road, he stopped to chat with them. We joined him and found that one of them was a transplanted San Franciscan who owned a bicycle store in La Grande. He'd wanted to escape the hubbub of the big city and the pressure his family put on him to become a lawyer and chose the solitude of eastern Oregon. He offered many suggestions about the route and restaurants along the way. Though interested in our trip, he showed little envy; somehow he seemed very content with his life.

We took another day off in Baker City, primarily to visit the National Historic Oregon Trail Interpretive Center. The center, managed by the Bureau of Land Management, is located a few miles east of town on Flagstaff Hill, where the emigrants first glimpsed the Baker Valley and Blue Mountains. Life-sized exhibits, audio-visual programs, artifacts, films, and nearby segments of the trail are used to effectively tell the migration story. We spent half a day there and would have enjoyed spending more. As much as we intended to smell all the roses we passed, it was still difficult to slow down.

Our home in Baker City was an RV park. Actually, the laundry building next to our tent site was our primary home as it rained on and off for the next two days. The laundry building had a couch and some comfortable chairs and tables, and it served us well as our gathering place. We must have been a sight: washing our colorful bike clothes, typing on a laptop computer, folding newsletters, and napping on the couch. None of the RV owners complained, for although their vehicles were different, they shared our adventuresome spirit. After two nights of waking up in the middle of the night on the hard ground, Lynn and Roger gave up on their leaky double-bed air mattress and bought two new bright pink single-bed mattresses at the local Payless drugstore. They slept much better after that, and within a few weeks the rest of us replaced our leaky air mattresses with the Wedels' "pink pad" variety--a colorful sight we were.

Mary Anna was just getting comfortable with the computer on that rainy day in Baker City. She had two main goals for our trip: one, get us all to Boston safely, and two, tell our family and friends about it through her weekly newsletters. She was diligent in both, keeping precise track of us on the trip and grilling us for interesting stories for the newsletter. She wrote the first edition on a portable typewriter but switched to Roger's laptop computer for the remaining editions. At that point, Roger and Mary Anna had to find a way to share computer time. Fortunately, Roger was more of a night owl and did his journal-writing in the evening, so before retiring, he would give the computer to Mary Anna. The routine was the same regardless of lodging. In primitive campgrounds, the computer ran on batteries, while in full-service campgrounds and motels it was plugged into an outlet. In campgrounds, Roger often worked in the dark, with the screen's illumination providing all the light he needed. He would slip the computer into our tent (or room) before retiring, and, often, the last sounds I remember at night and the first ones in the morning were the soft clickity-clack of the keys. Mary Anna could type several pages in the morning before her first cup of coffee.

We wisely followed the suggestions of our fishermen friends for two restaurants. The Haines Steak House was one of the featured attractions of Haines, "The Biggest Little Town in Oregon." The food and hospitality were great and very western. We were definitely in cowboy country and would be for the next month. Haines grew up around the railroad as a hub for the local ranchers. It is struggling a bit now, but the steak house and an impressive museum are enticements for tourists as well as locals to stop by and spend a few dollars. The Blue and White Café in Baker City, the recommended breakfast spot, is another winner. Their blueberry pancakes are world class and topped only by their customer policy:

COFFEE PRICES

1 cup	$0.50
1 hour	$1.20
Half the morning	$2.00
All morning	$3.00
All day	$4.50
All day with 1 hour lunch at home	$4.00
All week	ask about rates

Spoon knocking, cup waving,
whistling, and finger snapping variable, but we will charge.

The Blue and White's customers were like those in small town cafés across rural America, primarily older folks, some couples, but mostly small groups of men or women. The men wore baseball caps or cowboy hats and jeans or overalls. Discussions ranged from "the good old days" and the weather, to the current price for local crops. They grumbled some about politicians and big city lifestyles but in general were upbeat, laughed a lot, and seemed to thoroughly enjoy each other and themselves. They always knew the waitress by her first name and she knew theirs--what a great way to start the day. (I didn't ask how closely the café's proprietors insisted on adhering to the posted coffee policy.)

We left Baker City comfortable and confident despite a light but steady rain. The rain did not slow us down or depress our spirits. Wind was a more important factor, and it pushed us that morning. As it was mostly a downhill run, Kirby got out well ahead, lost concentration for a second, slipped off the pavement, and took a spill in the gravel. His injuries seemed minor and his bike was okay, so he continued at a slightly slower pace. His chest and shoulder injuries were more serious than we thought at the time, but they had little effect on his pedaling power.

Mid-morning found us at Durkee, Oregon, for coffee and drying out. A four-wheel-drive pickup truck was the only vehicle parked outside the Wagon Wheel Café. It was coated with mud, loaded with tools, and sporting a gun rack in the back window--didn't look like a tourist vehicle. There were two cowboys at the counter chatting with the waitress and another local resident, and they spoke to us in a friendly tone as soon as we walked inside. Maybe our wet, muddy rain gear and haggard appearance helped legitimize our presence and form some sort of a bond with them. We were curious about Durkee, and they confided that the town's population of 130 included dogs, cattle, sheep, and fleas, as well as people. The cowboys asked about our clothing as they had heard that bike pants were padded and wondered how they would work on horseback. Roger took their question very seriously and proceeded to strip off layers of rain gear and outerwear to demonstrate the inner workings of his padded pants. He didn't quite strip naked, but during the process, those cowboys were not quite sure. They loved Roger's demonstration and said, "Well, you're gettin' down in Durkee." Somehow, I doubt if they ever bought any bike pants.

The sun was breaking out when we wheeled into Huntington for lunch. This small town is located at the foot of a long hill, and there wasn't much there until the railroad came through in the 1880s. As the site of the last spike in the line connecting the Union Pacific main line at Granger, Wyoming, to the Pacific Northwest, it boomed during railroad construction. The Oregon Short Line came west from Wyoming, and the Oregon-Washington Railroad and Navigation Co. Line came through the Columbia Gorge and over the Blue Mountains. They met at Huntington, the very line we had been near for days. The last spike was driven on November 10, 1884, a great moment for the development of the Northwest. Travel from Boise, Idaho, to Portland, Oregon, that had taken weeks via stage coach or freight wagon would take only a couple of days on the train. This entire line is now part of the Union Pacific Railroad. Huntington is a pretty quiet town, but there is evidence of new life. An old hotel, restaurant, and bar were being refurbished when we came through, in the hopes of drawing more tourists off the nearby interstate highway to Snake River recreation sites. Mary Anna and Lynn caught up to us there for lunch, and afterward we enjoyed a leisurely stroll around town.

We discovered another reminder of the treatment of Chinese immigrants during railroad construction. On the side of an old building a sign, painted on the original brick, had just been disclosed as layers of stucco and whitewash were removed. It read, "White Help Only." I wondered if it will still be there when the building is fully restored. I doubted it, as the folks we met there seemed very tolerant. But on the other hand, with the proper explanation, it might have some redeeming value: a reminder that the "good old days" were not all that good for everyone.

A few miles south of Huntington, while coasting down a long hill, the Snake River came into view. We sped right by the entrance to Farewell Bend State Park, which was where the Oregon Trail heads inland away from the Snake River after following it for over four hundred miles. Fortunately, Lynn and Mary Anna stopped, took some pictures, and got the Farewell Bend story. The Snake River eventually feeds into the Columbia River not far from where we first encountered the trail near Umatilla, Oregon. So why didn't the pioneers just continue to follow the Snake? Hell's Canyon is in the way. It is deeper than and nearly as rugged as the Grand Canyon, and the early mountain men had discovered how to avoid it by developing the trail over the Blue Mountains, which later became a road and our bike route.

The afternoon's ride into Ontario, Oregon, was through irrigated orchards and farms, the healthiest we had seen since western Oregon. I snitched some fruit that was just "asking" to be picked as we took a maxi-butt-break next to a cherry orchard. This was our longest daily distance to date--eighty-five miles--yet it seemed like a routine day. The lack of head wind, traffic, and uphill grades helped, but also we were gaining confidence. We knew that, barring any serious mishaps, we could make it all the way.

Kirby had his first flat tire as he pulled into the motel, and Lynn made her first of many shopping trips to Wal-Mart. The evening was topped off in the motel's hot tub, quite a contrast to those evenings the emigrants spent nearby on the Oregon Trail. The next day we would cross the Snake River and enter the rich irrigated farm and ranch lands of southern Idaho.

5

THE RANCH

(Days 12-15)

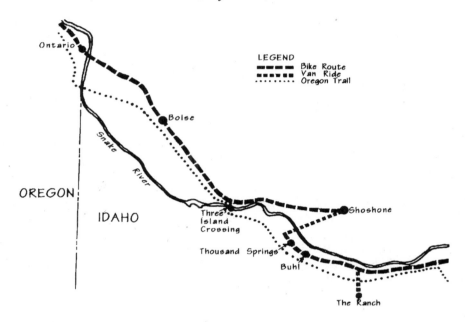

Kirby's shoulder and chest were pretty sore the next morning, but he had no intention of delaying our departure. We crossed the Snake River just west of Ontario and were welcomed to Idaho by the sign in the middle of the bridge. If our plan held, we would not see the Snake again for a week, until we reached the other side of the state near Idaho Falls. Our route would save a lot of miles by cutting across the lava flows and sagebrush on the northern edge of the Snake River plain. We knew this was pretty desolate country, but it was the most direct route. After all, our primary objective was to get across the country efficiently. This plan held for the first day, from Ontario to Boise, and for the last, from Idaho Falls to the Wyoming border, but in between it fell apart, much to our pleasure. The primary focus of the trip seemed to change as we crossed southern Idaho, from just getting there to the experience of getting there.

Boise was our first Idaho destination. I talked to my friend, Ray Miller, the night before about routes. Ray lives in Boise, and he agreed with our plan to take the back road through Emmett. Ray had just retired from the State of Idaho's Department of Lands. He was the stimulus behind much of the cooperative mapping between the Geological Survey and the State of Idaho and had become a good friend over the years. I always enjoyed visiting Ray's office--a log cabin in downtown Boise. It brought back memories of my days working on a Forest Service ranger station, and it reflected Ray's conservative, no-nonsense, get-the-job-done personality. Ray's uniqueness was reflected in the way he responded to the speakers at his retirement party: he had a gift for each of them. Knowing of our plan to retrace much of the Oregon Trail on our bike trip, he presented me with a copy of a publication titled, *The Emigrant Trails of Southern Idaho*. It was a great resource before, during, and after our trip and a reminder of our friendship.

The road to Emmett, like many, had its highs and lows. On the downside, it was our introduction to "kerplunk-kerplunk" road surfaces. Old roads sometimes develop cracks at systematic intervals across the roadway, and the surfaces on either side of the cracks are at different levels. It's like going over a small curb every forty to fifty feet. These may be barely noticeable in a car and only mildly disturbing on a fat-tired mountain bike, but for us they were bone-jarring. A few of them were tolerable, but "kerplunk-kerplunk" for several miles was a morale buster.

Fortunately, the scenic Payette River and farmlands compensated for the poor road surface. We followed the river for several miles and then climbed up on a bench (flat area) above the river and observed a variety of crops, including our first Idaho potatoes. Some of the fields were turning green, while others were still being plowed. A tractor in a distant field was moving toward the road, so I stopped to take a picture. It was a special photo opportunity as the tractor driver appeared to be no more than twelve years old. The rider beside him may have been seven or eight, and there was not an adult in sight. Their facial expressions said that this was serious business; they were not on a joyride. A field had to be plowed, and they were not at all distracted by a silly-looking cyclist taking their picture. As they plowed straight furrows across that field, they didn't slow down or even look my way as I took several shots. Maybe they were just anxious to get their work done in time for a ball game. I was impressed with the whole scene: the kids' skill, their parents trust in them, and the raw productivity of it all. My generation may be the last to have spent summers on a grandfather's farm. It's a shame that more kids cannot have that experience today.

The "kerplunk-kerplunk" took its toll on my camera. By the time we got to Emmett, the light meter was not working. Changing batteries didn't help, and for someone who loves to take outdoor pictures, this was a real bummer. Fortunately, the van came by, and Mary Anna took the camera into Boise to look for a fast and skillful repairman. She was successful, as was her custom, and the camera was ready to go the next day. Without the van, we may have been delayed a day or more, and I would have been a very frustrated photographer.

The van poked along with us up the hill between Emmett and Boise. The view back to the Payette Valley was striking: the valley's lush, irrigated fields in contrast with the sagebrush-covered hills. Lynn was taking pictures, so we had no break in our photo records.

On the long downhill run to Boise we passed a large, smelly, cattle feed lot. There was not a sign of vegetation as thousands of cattle were being fattened prior to shipping them off to slaughter houses. One might avoid or ignore this scene if driving, but from the seat of a bicycle it was an impressive experience, affecting several senses: sight, smell, and sound.

Lodging for the night was a KOA campground on the east side of town, but getting through Boise at rush hour turned out to be a chore. I knew there was a bike trail along the Boise River through parts of the city but did not know how to find it. As I had been to Boise several times, I took responsibility for navigation and did not bother to get detailed maps or find out about suggested bike routes through the city--a costly error we would not repeat. We wandered around in a busy industrial area before we finally asked for directions. Once we found the trail, it was great for as long as it lasted, but we were too soon back on busy streets with minimum shoulders. Without a map, finding the campground took some time, and we were disappointed when we got there. While the area was clean and neat, the campsites were small and close to an interstate highway and the airport. I found out later that the women had purchased a detailed city map as soon as they got to town and had no problem finding their way around, while my pride had added unnecessary time to our riding.

Boise's Roots

Pioneers bound for Oregon had been passing through Idaho for twenty years before many stopped off and settled there. By 1860, some Mormons had moved up from Utah into southeastern Idaho and had developed farming communities, but Boise was still only a stopover on the trail. Gold discoveries in the Boise River basin in 1862 changed all that. Almost overnight the town became a supply station for the mines. Eventually Boise became the territorial and state capitol and largest city in the state. While gold was the initial stimulus for Boise's growth, transportation, agribusiness, and other large corporations have kept it growing. It was on the Oregon Trail and later became a wagon-road hub between Salt Lake City, California, and the Pacific Northwest. Farmers began to settle in the region to supply the miners and the soldiers stationed at Fort Boise. With the completion of the railroad in the 1880s near those wagon routes, its leadership position in the territory was sealed.

Today, Boise is proud of its healthy economic climate and livability. It is home for Boise State University and many nationwide corporations, including a growing number of high-tech companies--as well as Ray Miller's log cabin.

Ray and his wife Bobbie came out to our campsite that evening for a visit and, among other things, discussed our planned route across Idaho. They were dubious of our route through the lava beds on Route 20. Their first recommendation was to swing further north through the Sawtooth Mountains and see some of Idaho's most spectacular scenery. Heading southeast to Glenns Ferry and the Three Island Crossing State Park, the state's premier park and where the Oregon Trail crossed the Snake River, was their second suggestion. At that point, we could still head back up through the lava beds or stay south along the Snake River. We were reluctant to take the extra time that the first route would have required but took their second suggestion--and will always be grateful that we did.

Interstate 84 was going our way again and, in fact, was the only road for portions of the route to Glenns Ferry. The next morning, just east of Boise, we got on it and rode for thirty miles. This time the interstate was great, with light traffic and good visibility. Although there were plenty of trucks, the wide shoulders provided an adequate buffer from their whiplash. We left I-84 near Mountain Home and took the old road the last thirty miles to Glenns Ferry. This was a three-star ride in Roger's journal, but it might have been four stars in mine. It was gently rolling country, mostly downhill toward the Snake River. There was no traffic (one of those places where the three of us could ride abreast safely for miles); the road surface had no "kerplunks"; the crops were greener, thanks to Snake River water; the air was clear and dry; and the wind was in our favor. We couldn't have asked for much more that afternoon, and Roger reported reaching 41 mph on one of the downhill runs. For awhile he just took off and tried to see how far ahead he could get, but approaching the Snake River at Hammett, he slowed down to look for a bargain soft drink. He was successful, so he and I followed,

Roger's Rule No. 6 - "Buy soft drinks in cups from self-service machines."

Again, Roger's rationale is purely economic. One gets a lot more for the money from the machines that have become widely used in convenience stores, compared to drinks in bottles or cans. Moreover, we could drink a large volume after riding for several hours on a warm day. The gas station/convenience store in Hammett had the best prices we ran across on the entire trip: seventy-two cents for a drink of forty-two ounces. Kirby did not care for soft drinks, so he missed out on the Hammett bargain.

Three Island Crossing State Park is located near the town of Glenns Ferry. Gus Glenn put in a ferry across the Snake River there in 1869, which eliminated the need for fording the river at the Three Islands. The park was as good as the Millers claimed, with large grassy campsites, and only half were occupied. Once camp was set up Roger broke out a bottle of red wine.

Roger's Rule No. 7 - "Drink red wine everyday for your health."

Roger cited the studies that have been published related to the health benefits of drinking red wine in moderation and only reluctantly admitted that he also likes red wine. He brought along an entire case for fear that some of the less civilized areas outside California would not have an adequate supply. It was a very pleasant way to relax before enjoying one of Lynn's delicious campground dinners.

One of the highlights of camping is walking around the campground to observe the various tents, trailers, and RV's and to talk to the campers. Most of them have considered the options and come up with the system that is best for them. It's fun to compare notes about their gear, as well as where they are from and their travels. Almost everyone is friendly and talkative in a campground--when the weather is good and the mosquitoes are somewhere else.

That evening we attended a living-history program at the park's outdoor amphitheater. A one-man show was put on by a history teacher dressed in Oregon Trail pioneer clothing. He had been the historian on the re-enacted wagon trip along the trail the year before, so he spoke with some firsthand knowledge. From our seats, we could see the trail coming down the sagebrush-covered hillside on the other side of the river and on toward the Three Island ford area. The scene looked placid from our vantage point a mile or so away. But 150 years ago it was very different down next to the river.

The Oregon Trail's Three Island Crossing

Water was always a problem on the Oregon Trail; there was either too much or not enough. Water for stock and people was in short supply, and to a large degree, the Oregon Trail was a series of trail segments connecting water sources. There was no shortage of water when the pioneers reached the Snake River. It was a raging torrent most of the year with several major rapids and waterfalls. The trail approached the river from the south, and a few wagon trains remained on the south side through Idaho and Oregon. The north side was far more desirable, however, as it was shorter, provided better access to water, and passed through the verdant Boise River Valley. The problem was getting across the Snake. The ford at what is now known as Three Island Crossing was the most heavily used. Two of the three islands were used as staging areas for crossing the next segment of the river. It was still a very dangerous task, and the women and children were usually ferried across separately in boats, often with the help of local Indians. Wagons were caulked, and the men, with the help of other emigrants or Indians, coaxed their draft animals into and across the water. They had crossed other rivers, and more lay ahead, but the crossing at Three Islands was the toughest.

John Charles Fremont, the famous western explorer and officer in the Army's Topographical Engineers passed this way on his second expedition in 1842. A howitzer was swept away, and several mules nearly drowned as his unit forded the Snake at the Three Island Crossing.

All five of us biked to breakfast the next morning. The day before, we had passed an interesting country club with a golf course carved out of a grape vineyard--or maybe it was the other way around. An attractive clubhouse/restaurant was located right in the middle of it. We were the first customers and got a choice table on the patio overlooking the golf course and vineyard. We could see the Snake River in the distance and watch the early morning golfers trying to avoid the grape vines. The sun was shining, the sky was blue, and the blueberry pancakes were superb.

After breakfast we had to decide which way to go. Would it be northeast through the lava fields or southeast along the Snake River? The lava fields won out largely because Mary Anna and Lynn wanted to visit Sun Valley (just north of the lava). It was still the most direct route, so the cyclists agreed, and we were off.

I was unusually "pumped" that morning and sprang to the lead. There are times in physical endeavors when you just feel like you can go forever or ride through a wall. That morning was one of those times for me, at least for the first hour or so. The road and riding conditions were perfect, and it was fun to leave the other guys in the dust for a change. It didn't last though, for after five or ten miles reality prevailed and they reeled me in. I took my rightful place in the rear as we climbed away from the Snake River.

Shortly before noon I felt a twinge in my crotch and thought I had just been pushing too hard and that it would be fine after a lunch break. Not so; the pain increased as we rolled through the high desert toward Shoshone, the day's destination. I had to ask Roger and Kirby to slow the pace a bit and suddenly had more empathy for Roger and his stomach ache and Kirby and his still aching shoulder. As the pain worsened, some negative thoughts crept in: Could it be a hernia or something else that could prevent me from completing the trip? The sissy inside was beginning to overcome that optimistic, daring personality that I like others to see. Fortunately, the last twenty miles were easy-going, and we pulled into Shoshone by mid-afternoon.

The van was parked on main street, and a bright pink note taped on the window gave us directions to the Governor's Mansion Bed and Breakfast, our lodging for the night. We didn't give much thought to the pink notes at the time, but they would prove to be an important communication device for the rest of our trip.

B&B's were not usually our lodging of choice (for economic reasons); campgrounds and one-star motels were the norm. There were not many overnight accommodations in Shoshone, however, and as we had camped two nights in a row, why not? By this time, we were comfortable with Mary Anna's and Lynn's lodging decisions. They knew our criteria, and besides, they were ready for a B&B themselves. The Governor's Mansion was a large Victorian house that had been restored by two transplanted Californians and had a large old claw-foot bathtub--just the thing for my aching crotch. That evening we noticed some late arrivals: a quiet couple who looked like locals in their jeans and boots. He tipped his black cowboy hat but didn't say much.

Mary Anna, Lynn, and Kirby headed up to Sun Valley that evening. They stopped by the Shoshone Ice Caves (formed by lava tubes and a source of ice for Indians) and returned via Carey, Idaho, which was to be our destination the next night. It was after dark when they returned. They were very enthusiastic about Sun Valley and the ice caves but less so about Carey and the route from Shoshone to Carey. There were no motels or campgrounds in Carey, and the road was desolate and narrow. We remained uncertain about our plans.

Roger and I had chosen to stay at the B&B that evening, do the laundry, watch the NBA playoffs, and, in my case, rest my aching body parts. Even though the ache persisted, Mary Anna eased my concern. She has a marvelous practical understanding of the body, and she concluded that my problem was a mildly strained muscle or ligament and suggested the following treatment: long hot baths, more padding on the bike seat, a slower pace, and aspirin. She was like a trainer for a football team, saying to a crying, hypochondriac player, "Put a bandage on it and get back in the game!" I wanted a little more sympathy but trusted her judgment. Although it took a few days to get back to normal, her remedies worked--and I still have that extra padding on my seat.

Breakfast the next morning was typical first-class B&B fare: pancakes, eggs--the works. The couple we had seen the night before joined us, and, after a brief awkward period, we warmed up to each other. They were taking a day off from ranching to celebrate their fifteenth wedding anniversary. There was a genuine quality to them that was infectious, and we soon felt very comfortable with them. I was a little surprised at their interest in our trip, for on the surface it seemed that our lives were very different and we might not have much in common. At that moment, Shoshone, Idaho, was our common experience, and we Californians had an interest in learning more about life in southern Idaho which Carol and Rodney Hopwood were happy to share with us.

They headed home to their ranch before we finished breakfast, and, over the last cup of coffee, we reflected on how we have met some of the nicest folks at B&B's. Ten minutes later, as we were about to get up, the front door opened and there stood the Hopwoods. We greeted them and assumed they had forgotten something. "No," they said, just standing there with small grins on their faces, "we'd like to invite you all to come by our ranch and spend a day or so with us." We, the cycling crew, all looked at each other, smiled back, and simultaneously said, "Yes!" There was no discussion, voting, or analysis of the impact such a diversion would have on our plans. We all knew the answer was a resounding "yes." Finally we could recognize a special opportunity and be ready to take advantage of it. It took them only a few minutes to give us directions to their ranch, and they were off again.

The ranch was south and east of Twin Falls, south of the Snake River, and a bit out of the way. It seemed prophetic that on a day when we were asking ourselves, "Which way should we go?" that strangers would come by and give us the answer. The Hopwoods recommended that we go back to Hagerman, on the Snake River, and take old Highway 30 through Twin Falls to Hansen and then south on the county road to the ranch. They would tie a red ribbon to their mailbox as a welcome sign. They also suggested that we see the Thousand Springs on the Snake River, one of the scenic highlights of the area. We decided to van to Hagerman, bike along the river to Hansen, then van the ten miles to the ranch and back to Hansen the next day to continue biking. Going back to Hagerman added about twenty miles to our trip, so we concluded that we would not be breaking our pledge to bike the entire way.

Lynn biked with us along the Snake River that morning. We pedaled across a bridge to the south side of the Snake. It took us only a minute, compared to the hours it took the Oregon Trail emigrants at Three Island Crossing. We soon saw the Thousand Springs--a dramatic sight. Rather than oozing out of the ground, water was gushing out of the basalt bluffs on the north side of the river. In parts of southern Idaho, some of the water draining south from the mountains percolates down through the lava until it hits the impervious basalt. It then forms underground streams and continues south until it breaks out at Thousand Springs and cascades down over one hundred feet to the river. There are reportedly fewer springs now than when the Oregon Trail emigrants passed this way, but they were still very impressive to us.

The springs area extends for several miles and includes a stretch of slack water where people were enjoying water sports from the docks of riverside summer resorts. Lynn and I were busy with our cameras. It was warming up as we approached a fairly stout hill that led away from the river. Lynn had done well along the river but was feeling a bit dehydrated by the time we reached Buhl, with lunch at the Train Station Deli. Fortunately, the deli was air-conditioned, so within a few minutes and lots of water she was fine.

The deli waitress was full of questions about our trip and felt it was worthy of an article in the local paper. She called the paper during lunch and urged them to send someone over to interview us and take pictures--to get the scoop of the week. She was not getting the response she wanted, so she put on her part-time reporter "hat" and interviewed us herself. Mary Anna gave her a copy of the one-page write-up/press release she had prepared for just such an occasion. Though no reporter arrived, apparently the paper's editor promised to send a photographer to meet us a few blocks away at Smith's Dairy, which the waitress recommended as a must-stop for milkshakes. The shakes were great; Kirby even sampled their potato milkshake. But there was no sign of a photographer. As we were about to pedal away, the waitress arrived and took pictures herself. She was determined to not let this story get away. What a great example of the friendliness and resourcefulness of people in small-town America.

I was in some pain again that afternoon and decided to stop ten miles short of Hansen. Roger assured me that as we had added twenty miles to our trip by backtracking to Hagerman, I still had ten miles "in the bank" and would theoretically be riding the entire distance. Our code of ethics for the trip was again interpreted in a new light. Mary Anna and Lynn soon came to my rescue with the van, and we caught up to Roger and Kirby at Hansen.

The Hopwoods, including their four kids, were away when we arrived, so they had arranged for friends to be at the house to greet us. We learned that Rodney and Carol had just purchased a ranch a few miles away and were there with their calves. This ranch where we waited was their home only for the summer while the owners were away. We were anxious to see the Hopwoods but happy to have time to relax and enjoy the scene before they arrived. The house and ranch buildings were about a half mile off the road--down a tree-lined gravel lane, through a grain field, across a creek, and at the foot of a hill, just like a movie set. Irrigation sprinklers were giving the fields a drink, while the surrounding hills were thirsty and brown. What a beautiful setting--a great place to be a kid, or for kids of all ages to experience life in its most basic form.

There was a swimming hole nearby, so Kirby chose to take a dip while the rest of us took baths. Carol soon arrived with Maggie (thirteen), Wes (eleven), and Caleb (six). She welcomed us then got the barbecue started for dinner. The kids had chores to do, so we tagged along to get our first lesson in ranch life. Maggie and Wes had steers they were raising as 4-H projects. They explained the life-cycles of beef cattle: what they eat, where they pasture, the illnesses to which they are vulnerable, what it costs to raise them, and so on. They were not boastful; they just knew a great deal about the natural world and how their family makes a living in it. Wes even discussed grazing on federal versus private land, something I was a little familiar with from my days with the U.S. Forest Service. Wes looked and acted a lot like his dad: he moved and talked slowly, with authority and warmth. Tamzy, a priceless two-year-old, soon arrived with her dad and joined us.

Maggie moved on to feed the other animals and then returned to the house to help her mom and Mary Anna prepare dinner. Wes paired up with Kirby, shot baskets for awhile, then gave him a roping lesson. Tamzy took a shine to Lynn and became her shadow. Caleb tugged on my arm and asked if I would like to take a walk down to the creek.

Caleb was something else. He had the lean, confident look of his dad and Wes, but he liked to talk a whole lot more. That walk was a moving lecture. Caleb described the flora, fauna, and geology in his own way. He asked if I knew what this grass was or that tree or rock. When I showed my ignorance, he had an answer or a story. My favorite was an explanation of how Indians can travel a long time in dry country without water by sucking on a certain type of rock. He searched around, found one, and gave it to me, explaining how only this particular type of rock would work. When we reached the creek, Caleb walked along the edge, carefully searching for something. He asked if I knew where salamanders live and proceeded to show me by turning over just the right rock. It was getting close to dinner time so I suggested that we ought to head back to the house. "No," Caleb uttered, rubbing his chin in a thoughtful way, "We have time to go see the swimming hole." Who was I to argue? There were a few active irrigation sprinklers between us and the swimming hole, but Caleb knew just the right route and pace to run and avoid the water. The hole was just that, a pond about twenty feet across and deep enough to swim in. We had to repeat the water-dodging exercise on the way back and almost made it unscathed. I may never know how much of Caleb's knowledge and tales were the whole truth, but totally truthful or not, he was an awesome performer and an entertaining host.

After a delicious ranch dinner of hamburgers and all the fixings, Roger, Lynn, and Kirby accompanied Maggie, Wes, and Caleb to the swimming hole. Maggie jogged, Lynn walked, and the others rode a variety of ranch bicycles. In Roger's words, "It looked like a scene from the movie *ET*." The crowd, with various modes of transportation, had a little more trouble dodging the sprinkler water. I wish I had been there with a video camera to record that exercise.

The air and water were cool, so the adults stood by as the kids took a very fast dip. Caleb forgot his bathing suit but went skinny dipping anyway--and was caught in the act by Lynn and her camera.

That evening, we eagerly learned more about Rodney's and Carol's lives. They had each grown up around ranching, as had their parents, but could see the chain breaking with their kids. It was tougher to make a living, and they wanted their kids to have opportunities to do other things. The kids loved life on the ranch, but they knew about the limitations. So they were open to different futures, like kids everywhere. Rodney talked about the frustrations of having to rely on federal land for grazing cattle. Private lands in the area were limited, so federal grazing permits were needed in order to maintain an economically viable beef herd. Grazing policies and fees at the national level are changing because the government wants to reduce cattle and sheep grazing on the national forests to return them to a natural state. They are doing so by dramatically raising grazing fees. Local federal officials have a lot of authority as well, and their actions are hard to predict. Rodney and Carol loved working cattle in the high country (usually national forest land), but it just wasn't worth it any more. They had to find a new way to make a living and had just begun to do so: raising young dairy calves. We learned that the calves must be fed early in the morning, and we were invited to help out. No discussion was needed; we were all eager to try it.

At some point that evening the conversation turned to how Rodney and Carol decided to invite us to the ranch that morning after such a brief encounter. It was certainly not the kind of thing we were used to in the Bay Area, inviting strangers to spend the night in our home after a few minutes of conversation. Two things had motivated them: first, they were naturally hospitable people, and second, they had spent some time with strangers a few years earlier, liked it, and were ready to try it again. Trust and hospitality were the norms among the southern Idaho ranchers.

The ranch to which we had been invited was owned by friends of the Hopwoods who were away for the summer. Rodney, Carol, and their family were house-sitting before moving to their new place. So they had invited us to stay with them at someone else's home, trusting that the owner would approve. What seemed unusual to us was just a natural instinct for them: if you trust people, you can invite them home for supper and a night's lodging.

The strangers who had passed this way earlier were Peter and Barbara Jenkins. They were walking across America and wrote books about their experiences. They had sought some legitimate Idaho cowboys or cowgirls and were led to Rodney and Carol. That was fifteen years earlier, when the Hopwoods were newlyweds living in a mountain cow camp. Meeting us at the B&B in Shoshone brought back some pleasant memories; we were the "second coming" of the Jenkinses. The coincidence went even deeper, as we had a copy of the their book, *The Road Unseen*, in our van. The Hopwoods are highlighted in that book, as well as *The Walk West*. We slept well that night, feeling that we were meant to be there.

The next morning we were up at 5:45 a.m. and ready to feed calves (though we were not yet sure what that meant). Wes and Rodney came along with us as working supervisors after Carol got us started with a light breakfast. The other kids got to sleep in, as we were the labor that morning. We were welcomed to the barn by the wails of fifty hungry calves, ranging in age from a day to a few weeks. They were all dairy cattle. Rodney explained that dairy farming is a growing industry in southern Idaho. Dairy farmers like to sell their calves right away to get the mothers back to producing milk, so people like the Hopwoods buy the calves and feed them for a few months. Females and the best bulls are then sold back to dairy farmers, and the other bulls are sold for beef. Hopefully a profit can be made by those who buy and sell the calves, as well as the dairy farmers.

After that brief explanation we went to work. Rodney handed us each a half-gallon bottle of milk with a large nipple and pointed us toward the younger calves. Wes demonstrated how to put some milk on a finger and stick it in the calf's mouth as a way to jump-start the process, if they were reluctant to take the bottle. My first calf was more interested in mooing and jumping around than drinking, so Kirby had to help hold her still while I got the nipple in her mouth. The older calves were easy to feed, as they drank from pans. We also learned to use the finger method to wean the young ones from the bottle to the pan. Between feedings we mixed up formula and washed bottles and pans.

As we neared the end, one calf got loose. Wes saw me standing in its path to the door and asked me to stop him. Like a good defensive tackle, I grabbed him low and picked him up. (From watching football, I learned that if his legs are not on the ground, he can't go anywhere.) The problem was what to do next. I could barely hold him up and couldn't walk a step without falling down. Wes finally came to my rescue after everyone enjoyed the scene for awhile. As we were washing some of the last pans, someone asked how to be sure the calves have had enough to eat. Rodney responded with a smile, "Just listen." It was deadly silent compared to the boisterous mooing that greeted us earlier.

Carol had a huge breakfast ready for us when we got back to the house and patiently listened as we recounted our morning labors. During the last cup of coffee, Carol invited us to come to church with them (it was Sunday morning) and stay another day. They mentioned that they were searching for a new pastor and had a substitute preacher that morning, but we were welcome to come. Mary Anna had been involved with pastor search committees in California and asked about their process. Rodney and Carol were both on their search committee, so that led to a whole new conversation.

Caleb approached me as we were getting up from the table. He had something in his hand that looked like a piece of parchment paper, gray with ragged edges. "I have a piece of wasp's nest for you," he said. "Thank you, Caleb. That's terrific," I said, wondering what I would do with it. But then I looked closer and nearly cried. Carefully penned on the fragile material were the words, "I hope you have a good trip - Caleb." That piece of wasp's nest is carefully protected among my most special treasures and will always bring back warm memories of Caleb and the ranch.

It was time to move on, or it somehow seemed so as we were still concerned about our schedule. After a few more pictures, many thanks, some hugs, and promises to write, we piled in the van and headed back to Hansen. It was a solemn ride; later we all agreed that we should have stayed longer.

6

SNAKE RIVER COUNTRY

(Days 16-20)

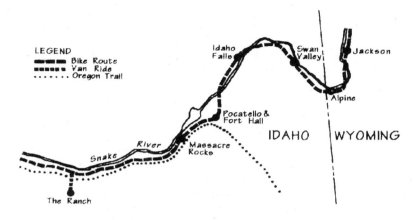

We headed east from Hansen on Highway 30, across the lush Snake River Plain. Potatoes were abundant, along with sugar beets, corn, peas, herds of sheep, and beef and dairy cattle. Water was also part of the landscape, moving through canals and sprinkler systems to the thirsty crops. We didn't talk a lot that morning, nor do I remember much about it; we were probably still thinking about the previous day with the Hopwoods. After a few miles, we took the continuous green-carpeted landscape for granted. Had we passed this way on a wagon train before the Civil War, then returned in 1994, we would have been shocked and wondered where all the sagebrush had gone.

The "Greening" of the Sagebrush Plain

Near the continental divide in Yellowstone National Park, Wyoming, the Snake River begins its one-thousand-mile journey to its confluence with the Columbia River near Pasco, Washington. It drops over seven thousand feet in elevation from Yellowstone Lake to the Columbia and drains an area larger than the entire state of Idaho. In its natural state it is a raging torrent over most of its length. It includes many cascades and waterfalls, the largest of which, Shoshone Falls, near Twin Falls, is 212 feet high, higher than Niagara Falls. The Snake pours out of the mountains near Idaho Falls to begin a westward trek across southern Idaho. This is dry country with very little summer rainfall. The Shoshone-Bannock Indians referred to the Snake as the "The River of the Sagebrush Plain." If one looks at a relief map of the western U.S., the Snake River plain stands out like the great California valleys, as a large, flat feature in a mostly mountainous landscape. The open, U-shaped plain, over four hundred miles long and forty to fifty miles wide, was a logical route across the intermountain west.

Early explorers tried in vain to float down the Snake. Emigrants with wagons never tried floating it. Instead, they stayed on the trails south of the river until they reached Three Island Crossing. Though relatively flat and much easier to cross than the mountains to the north or south, the plain still had its problems. The little summer rainfall made water scarce. The river was nearby but often difficult to get to with basalt cliffs on either side. Old lava flows had to be crossed that were rough on wagon wheels, animals, and people. But cross it they did on their way to Oregon farmlands and California gold fields.

Though hundreds of thousands of emigrants crossed southern Idaho in the 1840s and '50s, hardly any of them stayed and settled there. The dry climate and lack of good transportation were reasons enough to move on. It was a long, slow wagon ride to any sizable markets; the railroad had not yet crossed the Mississippi. So for the early emigrants on the Oregon trail, the Snake River Plain was a way to get there but not a place to stay.

Idaho's first permanent white settlers were Mormons migrating north from Salt Lake City in the 1850s. They diverted water from small streams to irrigate their crops, and the "greening" of the plain began--but just barely. Only a tiny fraction of the land could be irrigated by diverting small streams. The Homestead Act of 1862 was designed to lure Americans westward by offering 160 acres of free land, if the recipients could demonstrate that they could make a living on the land. Although 160 acres was adequate for a family farm in the East or in Oregon's Willamette Valley where rainfall is adequate, in the arid west it was not nearly enough unless irrigation water was available. The Desert Land Claims Act of 1877 extended the allowable homestead acreage to 640 acres but required that the land be under irrigation within three years. It was usually not practical for individual farmers to build water storage and distribution systems for that size of a farm, so settlement was still very slow.

Transportation improved in 1884 when railroads crisscrossed the plain and provided links to the transcontinental lines in Wyoming and Utah. The east-west route followed the Snake River, while the north-south line connected Salt Lake City and the Montana mine fields via Pocatello and Idaho Falls. Completing the railroad brought about a revolution in transportation and communication. The two-thousand-mile trip from Missouri to Oregon, which took Lewis and Clark eighteen months and the Oregon Trail pioneers four to six months, was reduced to a week via the railroad.

Water was plentiful in the river, but there was not yet a practical way to get it to distant farms. In the late 1890s and early 1900s, a group of federal and state officials and private venture capitalists combined their visions and developed a way to water the plain. The Carey Act of 1894 provided a mechanism to transfer large blocks of federal land to the states, if they agreed to reclaim it (provide water to it). One of the early successful applications of the Carey Act was near Twin Falls, Idaho. A plot of 270,000 acres was deeded to the state and then sold to a private development company, which in turn built Milner Dam, pumping stations, and miles of canals to distribute water from the Snake. The development company then sold the land with water rights to individual farmers. Twin Falls became an agricultural boomtown, and all 270,000 acres were soon green with crops.

Other privately-funded projects were less successful. By 1900, the government recognized that if the plain's full agricultural potential was to be realized, a larger, more reliable source of funds was needed. The National Reclamation Act was passed in 1902, establishing the Federal Bureau of Reclamation. The bureau built additional dams and major distribution canals and became a partner with state and local officials, private water companies, and farmers in turning the sagebrush plain into some of the most productive farmland in the country. More recently, sub-surface water has been tapped and distributed through sprinkler systems of all shapes and sizes to complete the "greening" of the plain.

It was Sunday afternoon and we were on I-84 again on our way to American Falls, Idaho. Interstate highways look the same everywhere; if you don't look carefully, the landscape does too. But this was much different than I-84 through the Columbia Gorge--little traffic and wide open spaces. We took a maxi-butt-break at the interchange of I-84 and I-86, where there was not a tree or bush in sight, much less a gas station or rest stop. But, when you've got to go.... So Roger took care of all of his necessities right there in front of the whole world. No problem, there was not a vehicle in sight. I have a picture of that scene, and I am saving it for just the right opportunity.

We'd had a late start and the wind was wearing on us, so we flagged down the van and asked them to meet us at the Raft River exit. Sixty-five miles was enough for that Sunday. Mary Anna and Lynn drove us to the campground near American Falls and would return us to the same spot on the interstate the next morning. We appreciated seeing that van everyday. How much tougher the trip would have been without it and those wonderful women driving it.

We left the cook stove and some utensils on the table that night and forgot to cover them with a tarp. Sometime after midnight the wind must have awakened us, and I heard someone moving around outside of the tent. It was Lynn unfolding a tarp to put over the table; she was the most conscientious tarper of our group and had crawled out of her perfectly comfortable sleeping bag to do it again. I had considered doing it for an instant before hearing her, but instead I rolled over, gave Mary Anna a hug, and decided that a little more water would not seriously damage anything. Lynn was moving cautiously as she took a circuitous route back to her tent. I heard her whisper to Roger, "I think it's a skunk." Thanks to Lynn's stealth, she managed to get back in the tent without stimulating any response from the curious skunk, and all was quiet for the rest of the night.

I noticed the exit sign for Massacre Rocks State Park when we drove back to our starting point the next morning. As there was no suitable camping space, we had not stopped there the night before. We were ready to get going, so we went right on by again. Later I learned the story of Massacre Rocks, the Oregon Trail pioneers, and Paiute-Bannock Indians that had passed this way.

Hazards Along the Oregon Trail

Contact between the Oregon Trail emigrants and Indians was infrequent and conflict rare. Most of the recorded conflicts were along the Snake River with the Bannocks, a band of the Paiute Tribe. Like the Yakima tribe, the Bannocks had guns when the first Oregon Trail emigrants approached the Snake River, and they also had Spanish bridles for their horses. (Mexican territory was just south of the Snake River at that time.) The most notable Indian-emigrant conflict was at Massacre Rocks on August 9, 1862. Seven emigrants were killed in an ambush at the rocks and in a later skirmish. Such attacks were rare. The more common conflicts occurred when Indians or emigrants were isolated from their groups. Communication was usually poor, and sometimes loners would be shot on sight. But most contacts were friendly, even along the Snake, especially in the early years. Indians served as trail guides, assisted in river crossings, and led wagon trains to grass and water. Sometimes they also stole horses from those they had just helped. There were more frequent conflicts after 1850 when on some days three hundred emigrant wagons with thousands of cattle and horses would pass a given spot. By then, the white emigrants were having a severe impact on scarce grazing lands. Conflict was inevitable.

Indians were only one of the problems facing the emigrants, a minor one compared to the others. From 1840 to 1860, less than four hundred emigrants were killed by Indians while about seven hundred Indians were killed by the emigrants. About 20,000 emigrants died on the trail of the 300,000 or so who began the journey, the major killer being cholera. Accidents were also a far more frequent killer than Indians: emigrants were drowned, run over by wagons, struck by lightning, kicked by horses, bitten by snakes, and shot accidentally by another. Most of the victims were buried along the trail; there were about ten graves for every mile.

The ride to Pocatello on I-86 was fast (tail wind) and smooth (good shoulder). Roger and I were bent low on our profile bars nearly all morning and felt like we were flying. Kirby was still riding tall in the saddle, but he had no trouble staying in the lead most of the time. His chest and shoulder were still bothering him, but his legs were like pistons. We had been climbing gradually since Three Island Crossing from 2,000 to 4,400 feet elevation but hardly noticed it that morning.

Kirby arranged for us to have lunch in Pocatello with an old friend. Although he hadn't seen her since elementary school, the two had kept in touch through their families in Texas. Sarah Bowman had recently completed her Ph.D. and was teaching at Idaho State University. She was a lively and interesting lunch companion, and she filled us in on some Pocatello highlights. The city had been a crossroads for fur traders and Oregon trail emigrants, then a railroad center, and, finally, a college town. A replica of Fort Hall, the old trading and military post, was nearby.

Fur, Fort Hall, and Beaver Hats

Fur was considered the most valuable natural resource in North America for more than two hundred years. While the sea otter trapped on the west coast was prized by the Chinese, beaver and other furs found inland were highly valued in Europe. The French pioneer fur men moved into the Great Lakes and Upper Mississippi Valley in the early 1600s. When the British conquered Canada in 1763, they took over the fur enterprise and managed it through two companies: the Hudson's Bay Company in the East, and the Northwest Company in the West. The companies later merged into a greater Hudson's Bay Company. By the early 1800s, the British fur traders were well established across Canada and in much of the Oregon Country. Americans had been blocked from the most valued fur regions by the French, the British, and their Indian allies. Moreover, Americans were more interested in building a nation and developing agriculture and industry.

The Louisiana Purchase changed the equation by opening up the central part of the continent for Americans. The Oregon Country was also open by then, and the Astorians were the first American fur men to find an efficient route to the west coast and establish a foothold there. Jim Bridger, Jedediah Smith, and other trailblazers followed and improved the trails. In 1832, L. E. Bonneville and Nathaniel Wyeth used those trails to get to the Oregon Country with the goal of setting up permanent American fur trading *posts. Although these Americans were not successful businessmen, all of them contributed to the growing "Oregon fever" back east. Wyeth left a landmark on the Snake River: Fort Hall. Though it was sold to the British after Wyeth's financial collapse, Fort Hall remained an important supply point for the Oregon-bound pioneers until it was closed in 1854.*

Americans had lost the Oregon Country fur trade competition to the British by the 1830s, but that loss turned out to be of little importance, for at about that same time the international fur market dramatically declined. Silk replaced beaver fur as the material of choice for hats, forever reducing the importance of beaver as a trading commodity. Americans lost the "fur battle" but won the "Oregon war" by using the fur trade infrastructure to move people west.

We left the route of the Oregon Trail that afternoon and headed north toward Blackfoot. We had been near the trail for eight hundred miles and had developed some attachment to it. But we would reunite in central Wyoming, so it was not a final good-bye.

Having had good luck on the back roads for most of our trip, we decided to take Highway 91 rather than I-15 to Blackfoot. This time it was a mistake. Traffic was heavy, shoulders were nearly non-existent, and thanks to the potholes and cracks, we experienced a new level of "kerplunk-kerplunk." We wanted to get back to the freeway in the worst way, but there was only one interchange, and it was too far away to make the change worthwhile. Mary Anna and Lynn came back and told us how to find our motel for the night, then went on to visit the Potato Emporium Museum and learn more about growing, storing, and processing potatoes. They didn't dispute Blackfoot's claim to be the potato capitol of the world. We cyclists bumped along for a few more miles, and by the time we rolled into Blackfoot, I felt a bit like scrambled eggs.

What a change a day makes. One of our first acts each morning was looking for signs of wind direction and speed: a blowing flag or leaning trees or grass. That morning the signs indicated a four-star wind day, at least for our first leg to Idaho Falls. It was blowing about 20 mph right on our backs, and we could hardly wait to get started. Highway 91 was just a bad memory. We were back on the interstate highway, I-15, with wide, silky-smooth shoulders. With a great road and strong tail wind, we covered the thirty miles to Idaho Falls in a little over an hour. There are many different pleasurable experiences in biking: seeing a beautiful landscape, watching marine traffic from a high bridge, smelling freshly cut hay, or talking with kids on bikes in small towns. But, it's also great to just go fast on a smooth surface with a minimum of effort. In that case it doesn't matter where you are, you just get down low on your handlebars and fly. You forget that conditions are so favorable. You have the illusion that it's all your own superhuman effort that is carrying you along, that you could win the Tour de France bike race that day if given the chance. Well, the dream was nice, but reality soon hit and we were back on an average road, with the wind cutting across our bow instead of on our back. But as we approached the Rockies and the Wyoming border, we reflected on this eastern edge of the Snake River Plain and wondered about the origin of Idaho Falls.

Flathead Crossing and Idaho Falls

Rebecca Mitchell stepped off the train in Eagle Rock, Idaho Territory, in 1882. A Baptist missionary from Chicago, Rebecca would soon organize Idaho's second public school district on that sandy plain next to the cascading Snake River. She brought some of the first elements of culture to the frontier town that would be Idaho Falls.

Decades earlier, Shoshone Indians and fur traders had passed this way at a nearby ford called Flathead Crossing, and by the early 1860s, the area was named for the Eagle Rock Ferry that crossed the river at the same spot. Gold was discovered about that time in Montana, and a bridge was needed to handle the increasing traffic to the gold fields. Taylor's Toll Bridge, the first bridge across the Snake River, was completed eight miles downstream from the ferry. A town formed, for awhile calling itself Taylor's Bridge. In 1872, the townsfolk became disenchanted with Taylor and renamed the town for the prominent Eagle Rock nearby. The railroad came through town in 1878 and created a short-term growth spurt. The construction of irrigation canals brought another boom in 1891, this time in farming. Some land speculators came to town and encouraged the townsfolk to come up with a more enticing name, and Idaho Falls it became.

Idaho Falls is now the home of fifty thousand people, much agri-businesses, and the Department of Energy's Idaho National Engineering Laboratory.

Leaving I-15, we headed up Highway 26 along the Snake River, eastward and upward into the foothills of the Rocky Mountains. It was time for more rigorous pedaling--but not before lunch. Ririe was the last town we would see for the next thirty-five miles, and it had a friendly-looking café on the edge of town. Like so many small-town cafés, the food was fine, the price was right, and the conversation was educational and fun. Agricultural economics and transportation were the subjects for a farmer and a trucker who were having lunch in the next booth. The farmer talked about the trade-off of storing his grain and waiting for the best price before selling versus selling immediately after harvest and saving storage costs. The trucker was proud of his role in moving the farmers' crops to market and stated with confidence that "if it don't have eighteen wheels, it ain't a truck."

It was a slow, steady climb out of the plain and into a different landscape of natural grassland and scattered trees. We stopped at a highway rest stop and enjoyed the view overlooking the river and the now distant plain. No more flatlands for awhile. Roger fixed his first flat tire, and Kirby and I welcomed the extra break. He had picked up a piece of steel, probably from the remnants of a steel-belted tire. We took another break later at the top of a hill, and Kirby and I nearly fell asleep. It had been cool and windy riding, but it was warm and comfortable stretched out on the grass under that crisp, blue sky. Roger was anxious to get going, though, so he cut our naps short. He was putting up with more frequent breaks than he preferred, but he could not tolerate naps. Roger liked to smell the roses along the way as much as we did, but not so much near the end of the day's ride. So we learned,

Roger's Rule No. 8 - "No midday naps on bike trips."

Kirby and I yawned and reluctantly got rolling again. We were all a bit curious about our destination, Swan Valley. We had climbed to about six thousand feet and began to see some high, rugged mountains. Then a warning sign caught our attention, indicating two miles of steep downhill grade ahead. Downhill runs are great while they last, but we knew that there was a steady climb into Jackson Hole, so every downhill meant that much more climbing later. This was a bittersweet downhill. Swan Valley and its mountain backdrop were in full view, but I could not fully appreciate it; I had to keep my eyes on the road and hands on the brakes all the way down. The cross winds kept me off balance at high speeds, especially when a truck passed. Kirby was having better luck as he was going fast enough to cut through the wind and stay ahead of the trucks. Roger was struggling with the wind also and took it easy with me until we neared the valley floor.

And what a valley floor it was. Split-rail fences paralleled the roadway, cattle grazed in the tall grass, and rustic fishing cabins and ranch buildings were tucked away in aspen groves along the river. Wildflowers bloomed and beautiful mountains surrounded it all--truly inspiring scenes in all directions. We didn't know yet what our lodgings would be that night but hoped it would be nearby. Sure enough, just ahead we could see the van with Lynn waving us down. They had found vacancies at the South Fork Lodge fishing resort, and Lynn had negotiated a special volume discount. Lynn loved a bargain as much as Roger did and was becoming our designated negotiator.

This was no backwoods, primitive lodge. The individual cabins were rustic in appearance but were clean, fairly new, and had all the conveniences--for $40 each. Roger exclaimed that the view from the front porch could have been from the film *A River Runs Through It*. The air quickly chilled; snow flurries were predicted later that night, so even Kirby was glad to be indoors. But it was not snowing yet, and the clouds added another dimension to photo opportunities, so Lynn and I got busy with our cameras. Our morale lifted even higher that afternoon in Swan Valley. It was a beautiful change in landscape and another milestone. We were in the Rockies and feeling great.

There was no sign of snow the next morning but plenty of wind-- in the wrong direction. Lynn decided to ride with us. The first four miles were tolerable, but after B-2 at a roadside café, we headed directly into the wind. Kirby the Wind Slayer took the lead and plowed a small hole in the wind that Roger could draft behind. "Drafting" is a term used by auto racers as well as bicyclists. The lead auto or bicycle creates a vacuum behind it a few feet long of which others can take advantage if they stay in close. If they fall too far behind, that advantage is lost. I was having difficulty keeping pace and Lynn even more so, so I hung back and let her draft me for awhile.

Snow and rain remained only a threat that day, but the wind never quit. It was only thirty-four miles to Alpine, Wyoming, but, thanks to the wind and hills around Palisades Reservoir, thirty-four miles was enough. Roger later dropped back to stay with Lynn, so we got pretty strung out. We were breaking our "stay in sight" policy, but we were not worried. There was only one road to Alpine and the area was not that isolated, so we just fought through the wind at our own pace.

Kirby was back in his tent that night as Mary Anna had found a motel with an adjoining campground. Alpine had once served nearby gold mines. It now happily accepts the gold credit cards of tourists on their way to and from the Grand Teton and Yellowstone National Parks. The Bakery Café across the highway was recommended by some local folks, and it served us well for dinner as well as breakfast the next morning.

Our feelings were a little mixed as we mounted our bikes the next morning: good about being in a new state, Wyoming, and completing our first thousand miles, but concerned about some accounts we had heard of cyclists being harassed nearby. On the other hand, we were happily anticipating Jackson Hole and the national parks which lay just forty-one miles to the north. Kirby, Mary Anna, and I had been there and knew what a treat lay ahead. Roger and Lynn were just as anxious to get there; in fact, Roger was the one who had urged us to leave the Oregon Trail for awhile and come this way.

Cycling conditions were reportedly poor for the next twenty-three miles with a narrow road, lots of traffic, and usually a head wind; therefore, we got an early start. All those things were true, so again it was difficult to fully appreciate the scenery. The Snake River passes through a narrow canyon there, and it is a popular spot for whitewater rafters. A colorful raft swept by as we took a break at a roadside viewing area called Lunch Time Rapids.

A short time later, I was drafting too close to Roger and nearly ran into him when he slowed down. I had let my mind wander and became oblivious of my surroundings. That's the danger in drafting at too high of a speed. This near collision was a warning.

It was good to see the sky again as we left the deep, narrow canyon and approached Hoback Junction. The General Store had everything we needed for lunch, and then some. The proprietor was very friendly and told us about a group of two hundred cyclists that had come through the previous weekend. It had been a busy one-hour layover as some shopped for food and all lined up to use his single unisex rest room. His septic tank was probably still trying to recover, but he was good-natured about it. We hoped he was typical of others we would meet in Wyoming.

The final eighteen miles to the city of Jackson was through a wide valley. We saw no sign of the dramatic Teton Mountains yet, but it was beautiful ranch land and a much wider and smoother road. As we entered Jackson about 1:00 p.m., the van pulled up and we discussed lodging options and plans for the afternoon. The van went ahead, but in just a few blocks we saw it again at a gas station, with Mary Anna waving at us to stop. The heavy load had taken its toll on the van. Both rear tires and the rear shock absorbers needed to be replaced. Wouldn't you know it--the nearly new van broke down before the old bicycles and much older cyclists did. Not wanting to take time to shop around, we had the repairs made at the gas station and moved on.

Lynn had done her negotiating again and found us a bargain motel in mostly upscale Jackson, while Kirby chose to stay at the youth hostel. Jackson still had the western motif that I remembered from my first visit in 1953, including the elk antler arches in the town square. It was different though; there was money in the air. Prices in most motels and restaurants were quite high, like those in California. There were more high-priced cars than old pickups, and fine clothing stores and art galleries were abundant. It was all very tasteful, but somehow for me it had lost some of its authentic western charm. Maybe I was just entering my "old fuddy-duddy" period of life, wanting some things to stop changing.

Mary Anna wanted to get the second newsletter printed, so we took her computer disk to Bliss Advertising, which was equipped to meet her needs. The PowerBook computer was working great and would be used for all subsequent newsletters.

Later, Kirby, Lynn, and Roger drove out to the nearby wildlife refuge to look for elk. They got their first glimpse of the Tetons, but, unfortunately, the elk were away for the summer in the higher mountains. That evening we went separate ways--a recommended action for any group that is in close quarters for an extended period of time. Roger and Lynn celebrated their anniversary by going to see a performance of *Oklahoma* at a local theater. Kirby toured the area on his bike, while Mary Anna and I walked around town and shopped for a hat.

I like to wear hats both for shade and to keep my thinning hair from blowing around; however, so far on the trip I had a problem keeping track of them. The first hat was left hanging on a chair in an Astoria restaurant, and the second one made it to somewhere in Idaho. I wanted the third one to fit in with the western styles we would see for a few more weeks and also have some type of security device. Mary Anna threatened to pin it on me, like she used to pin school notes on the kids' clothes. We found the perfect hat: an Australian "outback" model with a leather thong that came under my chin. When not wearing it, I could let the hat hang on my back, as effective as a pin and much more stylish.

Night life was active with lots of loud music pouring out of the bars and clubs, but Mary Anna and I are morning people and we'd had a long day, so we turned in early.

7

JACKSON HOLE AND THE ROCKIES

(Days 21-24)

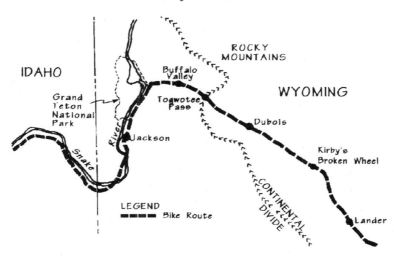

There was frost on the windshields on June 17th in Jackson; we wondered how cold it gets in January. Despite the morning chill, it looked like it would be a gorgeous day. After a minimal breakfast from ingredients in the ice chest, we were off to see the Tetons.

The road to the national park goes by the National Elk Refuge that Roger, Lynn, and Kirby visited the day before.

Save the Elk

In the late 1800s, elk were hunted to near extinction in western Wyoming. Their normal winter range had been the lowland plains north and southwest of present-day Jackson. The elk's winter forage proved to be excellent hay for livestock. Settlement of those plains did not prevent the elk from seeking winter refuge near Jackson. They became pests, living off the haystacks that ranchers meant for their cattle, thus were still vigorously hunted. The local folks wanted to save the elk, so from 1911 to 1913, a special partnership was developed as follows: local ranchers donated hay; the state government appropriated funds for more food; the federal government purchased land and established the National Elk Refuge; and the Isaak Walton League donated additional land to the refuge.

Though we didn't see the elk, it was nice to know that a herd of fifteen thousand was still in the area and could be seen up close in the winter when they come to the National Wildlife Refuge for food.

It was still cool when we reached the top of the hill north of town and first saw the magnificent Grand Teton mountains--a breathtaking sight, just as it is each time I am there. There are no foothills in Jackson Hole; the mountains rise abruptly from the valley floor. Trees carpet the base but soon give way to bare rock and finally to ice and snow. The Teton's crest looks more like the teeth of a giant cross-cut saw than a woman's breasts, for which they were named. For those of us who love the mountains, the Tetons have a supernatural attraction. We cannot explain it; we are just in awe of the whole thing: the shapes, colors, textures, and the pleasure they bring to our minds and souls.

B-2 that morning was in paradise. Looking for a hot meal, we turned into the visitor center complex at Moose Junction. Some teepees and outdoor tables looked promising. Getting closer, we could smell bacon and pancakes cooking--this was definitely the place. It was a semi-outdoor restaurant, with the cook stoves and some limited seating under large teepees. Additional seating was available outside, overlooking our old friend the Snake River and those spectacular Teton Mountains. Needless to say we vied for outdoor seating, and I broke one of Roger's rules to have orange juice with my coffee, sausage, and blueberry pancakes. I can't remember a more peaceful setting or a more enjoyable meal. Even Roger was willing to linger awhile. We toasted each other and exclaimed, "Yes! This is why we made this trip!" And I again whispered a prayer of thanks, just for being alive in that place, on that day.

This was one of those rare times when we were reluctant to get back on the bikes, but get on them we did, for there was a lot more park to see. The van caught us near the Chapel of the Transfiguration, a rustic little Episcopal church with a picture window facing the mountains. It was a highly spiritual place and offered many photo opportunities. Our cameras clicked busily. At the other end of the parking lot, a path led to an old log cabin, originally the home of William D. Menor who homesteaded there in 1894. Menor owned a small ranch, a blacksmith shop, and a general store, but he is best known for the ferry he built across the Snake River. Until then the river could only be forded during low water periods. The ferry remained in operation until 1927, when a bridge was built nearby.

Flat land, spectacular scenery, and nice weather were enough to entice Lynn to join the cyclists for the rest of the day. Signs to Jenny Lake caught our attention. Having been there before, I remembered Jenny Lake as one of the gems of the park. We noticed a single motor launch on the lake, ferrying hikers to trailheads on the other side. Kirby remembered taking his family on the ferry a few years earlier, and we promised to return and do it another day. A one-way road around Jenny Lake was ideal for cycling that day. The one-way rule only applies to the half of the road that is reserved for cars, while the other half is a bike lane. It was a very slow ride, probably the slowest of our trip, as new spectacular vistas awaited around every turn and over every hill. Lodgepole pines frame the lake, mountains, and glaciers in subtly changing ways. And the sky--how could it be so blue? We stopped often to take it all in and to capture it on film.

After a brief rest stop at Jenny Lake Lodge, we pedaled north again at a more normal pace. Jackson Lake, the park's largest, soon dominated the landscape, and we pulled into the Signal Mountain Lodge area to just look and take more pictures. Back on the main road traffic was still moderate and slow-paced, a good thing for us as it was difficult to keep our eyes on the road or the cyclist ahead. Roger commented that it had been "the most perfect one-day bike ride" he had ever had. None of us disagreed.

Lodging that night was to be at a KOA campground east of Moran Junction, and Mary Anna went ahead to make reservations. Mosquitoes were pretty thick when we stopped for a break just below the Jackson Lake Dam. We wondered if the mosquitoes knew about the campground. Mary Anna soon came by and verified that they did. The campground, located along a swampy, meandering stretch of the Snake, was a major mosquito hangout. By this time, Mary Anna could read our minds and knew we would prefer something else. So on the way back to find us, she followed a rickety sign that pointed up Buffalo Valley Road and read, "Food, Phone, and Lodging." She found the Atkinson Motel next to the Heart 6 Dude Ranch. The motel consisted of two house trailers that had been converted into four motel units. As usual, she knew exactly where we would be and quickly brought us the news. Kirby was willing to try camping anyway, but we out-voted him and asked Mary Anna to make reservations at the motel.

Before she left, Mary Anna had to tell us about her moose-sighting. Before checking out the KOA, she had driven north to revisit Colter Bay, where we had camped with our family seventeen years earlier, and Leeks Lodge, where she and I had stayed shortly after our wedding. That was fun, but seeing a moose up close was more fun. Rounding a curve, she saw cars parked on both sides of the road. A baby moose was between the road and the fence, and its mother was on the other side of the fence. The baby was getting frantic. The mother calmly found a hole in the fence, came through it, and led the baby across the road in front of the cars and off into the trees.

As soon as we started up Buffalo Valley Road toward the motel, we knew we were in for a treat. The road climbed gradually away from the valley floor and along the edge of a large meadow with fifty or more horses grazing. A stream meandered through the meadow, and as we neared the motel, we looked back and could see the full range of the Tetons. For me, it was the most stimulating scene of the day.

The pure, natural settings inside the national park are wonderful, and I hope they will always remain so for future generations to enjoy. But when the works of man can be gently overlaid, the picture has so many more stories to tell. The motel unit was on a slight rise overlooking a barn, a corral, and Buffalo Valley, as well as the horses, the road, and the Tetons. While unpacking, I continually turned back to take in the whole scene and again wondered who else had passed this way.

Jackson's Hole

The valley east of the Teton Range was named for David E. Jackson, one of a group of American fur trappers that explored the area in 1824. A few other American and European explorers had been through the area since 1807 but had not lingered. The valley was very remote, and the only river access was up the Snake and through the narrow canyon through which we had cycled. It was virtually impassable then, so most of the early explorers came over the mountain passes that were only open briefly in the summer.

The Shoshones and other Indians had been coming to the valley for as long as a thousand years--but only in the summer to hunt. It was too cold and inaccessible to support year-round habitation.

Jackson preferred to trap there and apparently fell in love with the place. His partner, William Sublette, named it for him in 1829. Fur trapping and trading with the Indians continued on a seasonal basis for the next ten years until worldwide demand for beaver fur nearly disappeared due to silk's growing popularity.

It was quiet in Jackson Hole for the next fifty years. There were some failed attempts to find gold in the surrounding hills, rumors that outlaws hid out there, and a few straggling fur trappers but few permanent settlers.

Ranchers and a Town Come to Jackson Hole

Word got out that a couple of ranchers were having success growing hay in Jackson Hole, and in 1889 a caravan of six wagons with families came over Teton Pass from Idaho to homestead. It had to be a rigorous trip. Wagons were uniquely rigged: both of the larger rear wheels were put on the downhill side to avoid tipping over. On the way down, the rear wheels were locked by placing a log through their spokes, and other logs were dragged behind to provide additional braking. Somehow they made it, increasing the population of Jackson Hole to sixty-four.

The town of Jackson was laid out in 1897 by Charlie Hedrick, and soon stores, saloons, a theater, a post office, schools, and churches were built. Originally the town was supporting the area's cattle ranches, but in 1910 the first easterners came to the area, and the ranchers and townspeople found ways to entertain them. A new industry was born.

And women came to town. In 1920, Jackson gained national attention by electing a female mayor and an all-female city council. There were many precedents in Wyoming for women in politics. In 1869, it became America's first state or territory to allow women to vote and to hold public office. In 1870, Esther Morris became the country's first female judge, and in 1924, Nellie Tayloe Ross became its first female governor. Wyoming is more than just a cowboy state.

A National Park

A group of local citizens met with the superintendent of Yellowstone National Park in 1923 to discuss their concerns over growing tourism and commercialization. They welcomed the tourists but wanted to preserve the area's natural qualities. By 1929 the original Grand Teton National Park was established in the mountainous section of the current park. John D. Rockefeller, Jr., had seen the area in 1926 and became interested in preserving the valley. Thanks largely to his donation of 32,000 acres in 1950, the national park was expanded to its current boundaries.

Cattle and dude ranching continue to thrive in the area in harmony with the natural setting, just as those caring citizens in 1923 had hoped. People first came to Jackson Hole because of its spectacular beauty and wildlife--and they still do.

While enjoying a delicious buffalo burger dinner at the café next door to our motel, we watched ranch hands deliver a load of hay to horses in the meadow and a couple of cowgirls working with horses in the corral. It was like a dinner theater with a very large stage. After dinner, we walked up the road. A bald eagle soared overhead, a horse-drawn buggy came by with a load of "dudes," and the sky was full of colors as the sun set over the Tetons. This may sound like a western novel, but it is true. The only hitch was that mosquitoes had found us again. I think Kirby was glad to be inside that night. Despite the slight tilt to the motel's floor and our beds, we slept well and looked forward to having the next day off.

Kirby, Roger, and Lynn headed north in the van to Yellowstone National Park. On the way, they stopped by the Moran Junction Post Office for Kirby to pick up a package that was sent from his home via Idaho Falls. It had not arrived yet when we went through Idaho Falls, so Kirby called the post office there and had it forwarded to Moran Junction. Unfortunately, the Moran Junction Post Office was not open on that Saturday morning at 8:30 a.m., or at 9:00 p.m. when they returned. The "adventures of the package" were unfolding.

They loved Yellowstone's geysers, lakes, and wildlife. Once, Lynn feared she was too close to a buffalo while taking a picture, so she ran behind the van to take refuge. Apparently, the buffalo was just posing for a close-up and sauntered harmlessly away. I could just hear it muttering to itself, "Oh, these tourists!" Damage from the forest fire that recently devastated one third of the park was still evident. Some vegetation was returning, but it would take many years for the forests to mature again. They had a delicious trout dinner at a remote lodge on the way home and vowed to return someday for a longer visit.

Mary Anna and I had a relaxing day observing the scenery and dude ranch activities. It was like being on a movie set, watching the people and horses come and go with the mountains and bright blue sky as a backdrop. A short bike ride up Buffalo Valley filled out our day. Along the way we saw only one pick-up truck. Jackson Hole and the Tetons have been special places for us for many years, and it seemed like we had them all to ourselves that day.

Blueberry pancakes at Hatchet, Wyoming, got us started the next morning. Hatchet was our last fueling stop on the road to Togwotee Pass and the continental divide. I had a full stack, preparing for the nearly three-thousand-foot climb to the pass. The waiter and waitress were modern vagabonds: a brother and sister who run that café in the summer and another in Florida in the winter. They were friendly and served great pancakes but did not know much about the road condition ahead. They just kept the tourists fed--probably had never been up to the pass. This was quite a contrast to the help and advice we had received from local folks in cafés along most of our route.

The climb was steady but not too steep. I was dragging behind Roger and Kirby most of the way but thoroughly enjoyed the morning. Traffic was light, and the scenery was gorgeous. It was exciting to think about seeing water on the other side of the divide flowing toward the Mississippi River and the Gulf of Mexico, rather than the Pacific Ocean. We stopped and chatted with another touring cyclist who had just come over the pass from the eastern side. His description of our remaining climb was comforting: a flatter grade, with just a couple of miles to go. As we neared the top, I saw Roger speaking to Kirby. He was suggesting they slow down and let me catch up so we could go over the pass together, a gesture I warmly appreciated. We were three independent souls and happy to be so for much of the trip, but it was nice to be a team for special occasions.

The women reached the top just before we did and were ready with cameras in hand. What a great feeling. Togwotee Pass, at 9658 feet, was lower than many other passes along the continental divide, but it was just right for us. We found a lake nearby with picnic tables and celebrated our milestone event with sandwiches and some of the homemade beer my son Mike had given us in Astoria.

Mike had brewed a special batch, complete with custom computer-drawn labels commemorating our trip. The label had an image of a bicycle and these words: "Michael John's Brewery, Happy Trails, May the sun shine on your helmets and the wind be at your back." With my somewhat puritanical background, I had some uncomfortable feelings when Mike first started brewing beer in our house while he was in college. Love, time, and great-tasting beer changed my attitude, and thanks to Mike I have come to enjoy good beer. Needless to say, I was thrilled with his gift and proud to share it with the others. Over our little celebration, Roger reminded us that it would be all downhill from here to the Mississippi.

Though our spirits were high, the temperature was not. There were patches of snow on the north side of the lake. The few scattered trees were stubby and wind-blown. Wildflowers were just budding; it was early spring on the 19th of June at Togwotee Pass. We understood why settlers were late in coming to Jackson Hole.

Lynn joined us for the thirty-mile, mostly downhill, run to Dubois (pronounced like "two boys," with the emphasis on the "two"). The downhill disappeared too soon, and we were back to reality: a gravel roller-coaster of a road, which was under construction for the last few miles. But it didn't spoil the elation of cresting the divide. That remained one of the high points of our trip.

Mary Anna found a teepee for us to sleep in that night. Entering town, we saw the van parked by the Circle-Up Campground and RV Park. The large Indian-style teepees were available for $15 per night, with no limit on the number of guests per teepee. All five of us easily fit in one teepee, and it could have accommodated several more. We were hardly roughing it as there were showers, a nice indoor swimming pool, a store, and a telephone. For the tightwads we all were, these were deluxe accommodations at a bargain price.

Dubois has long been a wintering area for bighorn sheep. Like elk, the bighorn sheep spend their summers in the high mountains, thus were nowhere to be seen. But their story was well told at Dubois' National Bighorn Sheep Museum. After visiting the museum we had dinner at the Ramshorn Inn. While reviewing the menu, Kirby asked the waitress about one of the items listed: bull fries. She was patient with us as we were the only patrons not wearing jeans and cowboy hats; we were obviously tourists. "They are bulls' balls," she said quietly. Kirby couldn't believe what he thought he'd heard and asked again. She repeated her answer, a little louder the second time, and explained that they were deep-fried and sliced and very good. She had sold six orders earlier that day and had no complaints. We were all intrigued but still decided to order something else. On that occasion, we failed to follow to the ultimate degree,

Roger's Rule No. 9 - "Always eat food that is popular in the local area."

We had beef that night, so we did not technically break this rule, but hindsight says we missed an opportunity to follow it more precisely. After dinner we drove up a steep gravel road to a plateau to watch the sunset. The rocky hills around Dubois are colorful during the day but spectacular at sunset. Lynn and I were busy with our cameras. Lynn was much more patient, using her tripod and searching for a unique shot. One of her Dubois sunset shots was my favorite of the trip: the top of the van, with Mary Anna's bicycle mounted on the roof rack, fills the foreground and is silhouetted against the colorful sky. Many who have seen that photo have encouraged Lynn to submit it for publication.

While waiting in line to use the phone back at the RV park, Mary Anna talked to a couple from North Carolina (her home state) about their travels. They had retired from teaching school and had been on the road for over a year in their RV. The woman mentioned that her mother kept asking if they were tired of traveling and if they would be home soon. They were having the time of their lives and not all that anxious to go home, but she was having difficulty explaining that to her mother. They were also seeing the country slowly: they moved fast on the road but spent quality time in each area they visited.

Cowboys woke us up early the next morning. They were unloading horses from trailers and leading them up the road next to our teepee. It was the right sound for Dubois, Wyoming, but the wrong time for us--5:30 a.m. We needed to get an early start but not that early. "Oh well," we groaned, "we may as well get rolling."

The next seventy-five miles to Lander was through some pretty remote country, so we fueled up on pancakes before leaving Dubois. The first twenty miles or so was very colorful, along the Wind River and through red rock country--like a miniature version of Arizona's Painted Desert. I was further back than normal in my traditional "tail gunner" position because of the many photo opportunities. The red rocks, cascading river, blue sky, sagebrush, and patches of irrigated hay fields were very photogenic. Roger and Kirby patiently slowed their pace, and with the mostly downhill grade, I could stay reasonably close to them. By mid-morning we were in the Wind River Indian reservation and had climbed away from the river. The landscape became monotonous: rolling sagebrush and less colorful rocks. Then a cross-wind came up, clouds rolled in, and we had several miles of rough surface where the road was being repaved. So every day and every mile were not perfect.

Things got even worse for Kirby. He was drafting Roger down a long gentle hill. They were a hundred yards or so ahead of me and, at that distance, appeared close enough to be on a tandem bicycle. Suddenly Kirby took a tumble and was down in the middle of the road. His front wheel had collided slightly with Roger's rear wheel, and at that speed it was enough of a jolt to damage his front wheel and cause the fall. Fortunately, Kirby's injuries were limited to abrasions, and Roger's body and bike were unscathed. Kirby's front wheel was history, though, and we could barely pull it off of his bike. While just beginning to consider our next move, Mary Anna and Lynn came to our rescue. The front wheel from Mary Anna's bike was installed on Kirby's bike, and within minutes we were on our way again, thankful for Mary Anna and Lynn and their perfect timing. The story does not end there, as within a mile we came to a rest stop with shade and running water where Kirby could wash and treat his wounds. This was the only such facility for over thirty miles in either direction. And there's more: when we arrived in Lander, Mary Anna had a new wheel for Kirby, identical to the damaged one. The bike store carried the same model of bicycle as Kirby's, so the owner had simply removed the front wheel and sold it to her--at a discount. He could reorder another front wheel and was happy to be of service to graying, cross-country cyclists.

Getting back to our afternoon ride through the Wind River Indian reservation, we stopped at a roadside marker referencing Sacagawea's nearby grave site. It seemed out of place, a long way from where she had assisted Lewis and Clark on their expedition.

Sacagawea Helps the Americans Across the Rocky Mountains

Lewis and Clark spent the first winter of their expedition with the friendly Mandan Indians at the mouth of the Knife River in North Dakota. During the layover, they recruited two additional crew members: Toussaint Charbonneau, a French-Canadian, and his pregnant teenage Shoshone wife, Sacagawea. Charbonneau was of little use, but Sacagawea became famous and dearly loved as a guide and interpreter. She gave birth that winter in the Mandan camp and carried her baby on the entire trip. She was invaluable in negotiating the purchase of horses from the Shoshone Indians that were needed for crossing the Bitterroot Mountains (a range of the Rockies). They crossed the Bitterroots the next fall, and, quite by coincidence, Sacagawea met her brother near a Shoshone village. They had been separated since her kidnapping by another tribe years before.

Sacagawea, Charbonneau, and their son, Jean Baptiste, returned with the voyagers as far as their home in North Dakota. Sacagawea's later life is not well known, but the common belief is that she eventually reunited with her Shoshone tribe on the Wind River reservation, where she died.

Charbonneau remained in the upper Missouri country and continued to live an undistinguished life.

The Wedels' sons, Scott and Mark, drove up from Scott's home in Steamboat Springs, Colorado, to visit for the next day and a half. Scott brought his bicycle so he could ride with us. Mark delivered a set of profile bars that Roger had ordered for me before we left and a new case of red wine (per Roger's order). It was nice to see the boys and all the goodies, and they arrived just in time for one of Lynn's superb spaghetti dinners. We celebrated a belated Father's Day with fresh wine, family, and gifts of decorated T-shirts for the dads--a nice touch of home.

Mary Anna raved about the bike store on the east edge of town, so I went back to shop for a replacement for my old, thread-bare utility bag. It was a first-class store, friendly and competent service with a good selection of merchandise. A group of teenage touring bicyclists was out front having a picnic supper, another indication of a service-oriented store. I bought a great bag and a gel cover for my saddle. Mary Anna was convinced that extra padding would help my aching crotch, so I added the quarter-inch-thick gel pad to the quarter-inch strip of foam, all held in place by her thick sheepskin seat cover (borrowed from her bike). It was like sitting in a comfortable, old easy chair. It was not something that serious cyclists would normally use but just right for me.

Lander has another small-town rarity: ATM machines. These were the first we had seen for awhile.

8

WIDE-OPEN WYOMING

(Days 25-27)

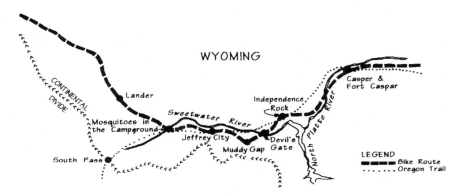

High mountains, trees, and colorful rocks were behind us; miles and miles of sagebrush lay ahead. And there was some work to do first thing the next morning: a gradual thousand-foot climb up to a rolling, wide-open plateau. We were leaving the Wind River, which had turned north, and were heading toward the Sweetwater and Platte Rivers and the route of the Oregon Trail. It was barren country--even the sage brush was struggling to survive. U.S. Highway 287 stretched out for miles ahead without a car or truck in sight. There were lots of touring cyclists, though, heading to and from Yellowstone and Grand Teton National Parks and following the Oregon Trail.

Riding with us for a day was hardly a challenge for Scott Wedel. He is a computer scientist who works out of his home in the Colorado mountains and does not own a car--only bicycles. At one point we saw him riding in the opposite direction talking with another cyclist, and we had to look twice to make sure it was Scott. He had cycled far ahead of us, saw a group of cyclists coming, and decided to ride back toward us with them. He rode on past us for a mile or so before turning around again and catching back up to us, and he was not even breathing hard. I felt like an old bear trying to keep up with a jackrabbit. One of the touring cyclists Scott talked with was a seventy-four-year-old woman who was keeping up pretty well. It would have been fun to listen in on that conversation. After that episode, Scott settled into a more moderate pace for him but still brisk for us. Roger loved it all. He was proud of his son and rose to the challenge of trying to keep pace with him.

While taking a break at a roadside rest area, Lynn and Mark (in Mark's car) joined us, and a few minutes later Mary Anna pulled in with a young man and his bike. He was with four other friends, riding from Oregon to Virginia, and was having a series of flat tires. His group had passed us earlier and continued on. He had run out of patches and extra tubes and was happy to accept a ride. We found the trouble: the rough end of a spoke kept piercing his tube. We trimmed it off, and Roger traded him a new tube for his multi-punctured one. He and Scott then took off on their bikes to catch his group after Scott agreed to meet us at the River Campground on the Sweetwater River.

I wondered what that guy would have done if Mary Anna had not come by and helped. He described how these five friends were traveling across the country by rotating the van driving among them. Most of them had not trained for the ride, and he admitted that the first couple of weeks were pretty rough. They had a different way of keeping in touch: if someone didn't show up at the end of the day, they would go out looking for them. It was a far cry from our rule of staying in visual sight. Ah, the optimism of youth.

In less than an hour later I had a related experience. Roger was well ahead, Kirby was behind him, and I was guarding the rear when my rear tire went flat. I yelled to Kirby, but he was too far away to hear and soon disappeared over the top of a hill. It took about twenty minutes to put in a new tube and another half an hour to reach the top of the hill. There was no sign of Kirby or Roger or anyone else for that time. I was frustrated and a little angry as we had agreed to stay within sight of each other, especially in remote areas. It was each rider's responsibility to keep track of the rider behind. Just before I reached the crest, Roger came back over the hill. He apologized and explained that he didn't know I was missing until he stopped for a break and asked Kirby where I was. As Kirby didn't know either, they turned back to look for me. We agreed to only modify the "stay in sight" rule when we got further east into more populated areas, but in the middle of central Wyoming, it remained a darn good rule.

Kirby had gone on again before I had a chance to talk with him. I vented my frustration with Roger but never did with Kirby, and it festered for awhile. In hindsight we all recognized that tensions will usually develop between even the best of friends when they are in close quarters for a long period of time. We should have had a mechanism to debrief and discuss concerns that any of us had. We seldom would have needed to do that, but it would have helped that day.

We reached the River Campground about noon. It was only another twenty-five miles to Jeffrey City, but, according to our publications and advice from local people, there was no lodging there, not even a campground. It was sixty-five miles beyond Jeffrey City to the next possible lodging, so it looked like the River Campground would be it. The only problem was that hordes of mosquitoes had already occupied the campground, and they love to eat cyclists. Based on our Buffalo

Valley experience, we learned that lodging guide books are often incomplete for small towns and remote areas, and local folks don't always know either. You have to go look for yourself. This time Mark and Lynn volunteered to scout out Jeffrey City while the rest of us shared our lunch with the mosquitoes.

Reaching the Sweetwater River put us back along the route of the Oregon Trail. In the summer of 1850, 55,000 emigrants passed this way, and at this point they were within fifty miles of crossing the continental divide at South Pass.

South Pass: Doorway to Oregon, California, and Utah

Early explorers and mountain men had found many routes across the Rocky Mountains, most of them quite rigorous and impassable by wagons, until they found South Pass. They reached it by following the North Platte River across present-day Nebraska to eastern Wyoming, then up the Sweetwater River to the pass. The route had ample grass and water for the livestock as well as the most tolerable terrain. Crossing the divide at South Pass was a major milestone for every emigrant. Since leaving Missouri they were in the Louisiana Territory and had already seen land, animals, and weather that defied their imaginations. When they reached South Pass they were in Oregon Country. Though less than halfway to the Willamette Valley, they were on the Pacific side of the continent and were confident they could make it.

In the early 1840s most of the wagon trains coming through South Pass were headed for present-day Oregon. The discovery of gold in California and persecution of the Mormons in the Midwest changed all that. Of the 55,000 that came through in 1850, the largest number were headed for California, and nearly as many were Mormons on their way to the Salt Lake area of present-day Utah.

South Pass was one of the most strategically important geographic features in the West for nearly thirty years, until the transcontinental railroad crossed the divide at another pass further south. Important it was, but scenic it was not. South Pass is a thirty-mile-wide grassy valley that slopes gently to the east and west. So wagons didn't tarry there; they didn't even know they had crossed it until they were clearly headed downhill. But at the first sign of water the celebrations began.

Lynn and Mark returned with good news: there was a motel in Jeffrey City, reasonably priced, and our reservations were made. We were back on our bikes and on our way in minutes. At the time, we were not thinking of the historic significance of South Pass; we just wanted to escape from those hungry mosquitoes.

Just as we were leaving the campground, an old bus pulled in covered with bike racks on top. It was the support vehicle for twenty-two cycling students from Hoover Junior High in San Jose, California, very near our home. We encountered the cyclists a few miles down the road. They had taken the train to Rawlins, Wyoming, then a bus to Casper, and were biking along the Oregon Trail. They would be camping at "mosquitoville" that night and riding over South Pass the next day. They got a good dose of life on the trail that night: first the mosquitoes, then a steady rain.

It was clouding up when we reached Jeffrey City. The darkening sky added to the town's eerie look. Many buildings were boarded up. Our motel was not fancy but dry and mosquito-proof. Roger and Kirby wanted to ride a few more miles and then van back to the motel. There was still some daylight, and they wanted to get through central Wyoming as quickly as possible. I was feeling a little fatigued, though, and talked them out of it. Maybe I was also still bristling over being left in the desert with a flat tire, needing some space as well as a hot shower.

During dinner, at one of the two bar/restaurants in town, we learned that Jeffrey City had been a uranium boomtown in the 1970s. With declining production of nuclear energy and weapons and less expensive uranium imported from other countries, the city was struggling to survive. Enrollment in the high school dropped from six hundred to forty after the uranium mines closed in the 1980s. Now, the Jeffrey City Longhorns are the only coed high school basketball team in Wyoming; there are not enough boys for the team. But, fortunately for us, there is still a motel in town. Visiting Jeffrey City was not an upbeat experience, but it was educational to see a place that was so seriously affected by worldwide economic, political, and environmental conditions.

Lynn, Mark, and Scott Wedel left that evening for Steamboat Springs. Lynn was flying back to California for a month before rejoining us in Michigan. Lynn and Roger are not ones to show much emotion publicly, but we sensed it was hard for them to part. At least I sensed those feelings, as I loved having Mary Anna on this trip and would not have been happy if she were leaving.

It was raining lightly and overcast, so after a cold breakfast, we donned our rain gear for the twenty-three-mile leg to Muddy Gap. Two major highways intersected there; surely there would be cafés and hot breakfasts, right? Wrong! A gas station was the only building in sight. They didn't even have coffee and told us the closest place for a hot meal was Jeffrey City. The other option was Casper, which was on our route but eighty miles away. That news hit us like a wet blanket. We had water and plenty of trail mix (nuts, raisins, and other bits of dried fruit), so we were not really suffering, but they were of little solace after thinking about hot coffee and food for the past hour. After no more than ten minutes of feeling sorry for ourselves, the van appeared on the horizon, probably ten miles away on that treeless, rolling landscape. Just seeing it was a morale booster. Knowing that Mary Anna was driving and would come up with something to fuel and comfort us was even more reassuring, and she did. "Well, let's see," she said. "I'll go on to the Devils Gate rest area and heat up something on the camp stove. I'm not sure what it will be, but I'll figure out something." After she reached the rest area, she used her binoculars to spot us a mile or two away and then cranked up the camp stove. When we arrived, water was boiling and something was heating in a large pot. B-2 that morning was hot chocolate and warmed-over spaghetti, and a welcomed meal it was.

Devils Gate is a notch cut by the Sweetwater River through a large rock formation. Oregon Trail emigrants passed nearby and could see the gate from miles away. We saw what we thought were antelope grazing down by the river. Mary Anna mentioned that one of them had run along beside her at about the same speed as the van as she was approaching Devils Gate. The animals were actually pronghorns, known locally as pronghorn antelope or just antelope (though they are not in the antelope family). They live in the deserts and grasslands of central North America. Most of the U.S. herd is in central Wyoming. Pronghorns have been clocked as fast as 60 mph for short distances, so the one Mary Anna encountered was just running at its normal speed. We found out later that three-fourths of all the pronghorns in the U.S. are within 150 miles of Casper.

The rain stopped, but head winds were with us again when we left Devils Gate. Leftover spaghetti had lifted our spirits, but the head wind, rough road, cloudy skies, and monotonous landscape made this leg a downer. Our next stop was Independence Rock, a state historic site.

Independence Rock by the Fourth of July

"It looks like a half-buried egg in a flat spot next to the Sweetwater River. You can't miss it." Those were the words of fur traders, Oregon Trail emigrants, stage coach drivers, and Pony Express riders who followed this route west. William Sublette gave the 135-foot-high rock its name when he celebrated the Fourth of July there in 1829. It was also the goal of wagon trains on their way to Oregon or California to reach the rock by the Fourth of July, in order to get over the mountains before snowfall. William Sublette carved his name in the rock, as did thousands of others who followed. Many of those names are still legible.

Mary Anna had gone ahead to Alcova to check out lodging possibilities. Finding none, she returned, recommending that we ride to Alcova and then van into Casper. We easily agreed; sixty-five miles of head winds, rough road, and warmed-over spaghetti would be enough for that day. It was at Alcova, where the Sweetwater and North Platte Rivers meet, that the Oregon Trail leaves the North Platte to follow the Sweetwater to South Pass. That confluence is now under the Pathfinder Reservoir, which provides irrigation water to local ranchers.

We began to see less sagebrush and more green pasture land and hayfields as we approached Alcova. Some of the ranches are huge. We passed the Pathfinder Ranch with its elaborate gateway and signs indicating that its boundaries are posted for five miles along the highway. This was clearly cattle country.

Cattle Come to Wyoming

Like Idaho's Snake River country, Wyoming was a thoroughfare for people moving west but not a place to stay, until the late 1860s. There was plenty of grassland, ideal for cattle, but poor transportation to markets. The growing season was too short for most farming, and Indians and buffalo were still competing for the best land. The first transcontinental railroad, completed in 1869, crossed southern Wyoming. By then, most Indians were confined to reservations and the buffalo had been nearly annihilated by white hunters. Wyoming's grasslands were perceived by the white man to be available for other uses.

Cattle were first brought to Wyoming overland from Texas, where grass was becoming scarce. Early cattlemen had free rein, often getting there before the government surveyors did. Over the next twenty years, cattlemen faced increased competition with each other and from sheepmen and farmers. There was still only limited law enforcement in place, so many conflicts were settled with guns. Wars between cattlemen, sheepmen, and farmers continued into the early 1900s. Though the land was well-suited for raising cattle, the 160 acres per family allowed under the Homestead Act were not nearly enough for a viable ranch in most of Wyoming. The acreage was later raised to 1120, but that was still not enough. Law and order finally prevailed, and the cattlemen found ways to acquire larger tracts of private land, making ranching more efficient. Wyoming's ranches now range in size from a few thousand to over 100,000 acres, and additional grazing land is leased from the federal government.

Raising sheep also became profitable in Wyoming; conversely, farming has always been limited because of the cold weather and short growing season. Of the three, cattle ranching won out as the predominant form of agriculture, and today the University of Wyoming's football players are known as the Cowboys.

This was Mary Anna's first day alone in the van. She was superb at Muddy Gap and Devils Gate, and continued her good work by negotiating a discount rate for two nights at the Royal Inn Motel in Casper. Lynn's negotiating skills had rubbed off.

We vanned back to Alcova the next morning for a terrific thirty-four-mile ride to Casper. Skies were clear, the road was smooth and downhill, and, best of all, the wind was our friend. As the country was colorful again, I wanted to stop often to take pictures. We decided to split up since we were in built-up country again. Roger and Kirby took off and made it to the motel in a little over two hours, while I took a more leisurely pace and was unusually content that morning. Good riding conditions, freedom, and photo opportunities were part of it, but then I realized I just felt better physically than I had in weeks--the crotch pain was totally gone.

<u>Notes to the reader:</u> This will be the last mention of illness or physical problems on this trip. Kirby's injury from his fall in Oregon continued to hamper his lifting ability, and I still rode a little slower, but none of us had any more illness or injuries that affected our riding. So no more medical reports.

Future travelers passing through Muddy Gap may now be able to get refreshment there. By the summer of 1997, a visitor center will be completed to remember Mormon pioneers who passed this way in 1856. As part of the opening of the center, a group of 3,600 people will re-enact a portion of the pioneer trek, pulling handcarts similar to those of the emigrants. On their way to Salt Lake City, fifty-six emigrants died in a snowstorm a few miles to the west of Muddy Gap.

9

PRAIRIES, FORTS, AND CRAZY HORSE

(Days 28-30)

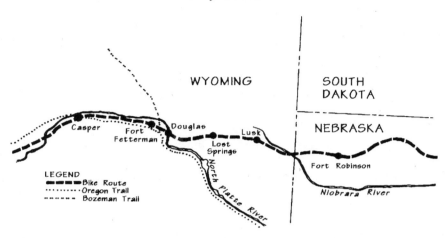

We had a full afternoon in Casper visiting Fort Caspar, where we found a nice museum and living-history demonstration. The restored fort was originally built in the 1860s near a toll bridge across the North Platte River. It protected a nearby telegraph station and travelers on the Oregon Trail (known here as the Oregon-California-Mormon Trail). It was named for Lieutenant Caspar Collins, who was killed nearby by Indians while trying to protect an Army supply train. His father already had a town--Fort Collins, Colorado--named after him; thus Caspar Collins' first name was used in naming the fort. Thanks to Director Richard Young of the Fort Caspar Museum, we learned that the spelling of the town of Casper was due to a clerical error in some military records.

While there we printed and mailed out forty copies of newsletter #3. We were already getting some positive feedback on the newsletter, so Mary Anna was inspired to keep at it.

We window-shopped downtown and bought hats together. The hat shopping took awhile. Kirby wanted protection for his face and neck, with an absorbent headband inside. As it turned out, he was less concerned with style (at least in our opinion). He researched all the options in several stores and eventually came back with suntan lotion but no hat. Roger, Mary Anna, and I had not intended to buy hats, but while waiting for Kirby, we learned in a bike store about the Casper Classic professional bike race. The store had three remaining baseball caps with the Casper Classic logo, so we each bought one and continued to wait for

Kirby. Finally, we suggested to Mary Anna that she help Kirby find a hat. In another twenty minutes or so, they were back with one that met his criteria but looked a little weird. It had an oversized bill and a flap that covered his neck. Roger commented that it looked like something one might buy at Disneyland as a souvenir. Kirby took our kidding in stride, though, and faithfully wore that hat, in public, for the rest of the trip.

On our way out to Fort Caspar, we drove by a large oil refinery that appeared to be largely inactive.

Wyoming's Oil

Oil was discovered near Casper in 1889, and though extraction was slow for a few years, World War I brought on an oil boom that continued for decades. Much of the oil was federally owned, and the fields were leased to private oil companies through competitive bidding. In 1924, Casper came into the national limelight when the nearby Teapot Dome oil field was leased without competition to an oil company. The Secretary of the Interior was removed from office and jailed after being found guilty of receiving bribes from the company. Oil production declined in the late 1970s when the fields neared depletion and the price of foreign oil became more competitive.

A concert in the park with the Casper Municipal Band rounded out the day. It was a touch of Americana: children were running and dancing to the show tunes, and families were lying on blankets or sitting in folding lawn chairs. The sun set colorfully behind the band shell as we all stood for "The Star-Spangled Banner."

And there was one more thing: dessert at Granny's Diner, a 1950s-style café complete with a working juke box. Kirby had discovered Granny's that afternoon while looking for a malt. Granny herself came out to greet us, and her homemade pie was delicious. Granny's pancakes were incentive enough for us to skip our cold breakfasts and return there the next morning. We highly recommend Granny's Diner on East 2nd Street as a must-stop for anyone visiting Casper.

The wind was still in our direction when we headed for Douglas. Mary Anna's timing was perfect again; she caught us in Glenrock having coffee (a morning malt for Kirby). Glenrock was suffering from reduced oil production in the area. An old refinery outside of town was abandoned, and some of the commercial buildings in town were boarded up. I reflected on the people affected by the loss of the major industry in town. I always had a job and lived in places where jobs were plentiful. Glenrock and Jeffrey City were reminders that economic conditions are very dynamic in many parts of the country; some people have to move on to other locations and other vocations just to survive. Changing economic conditions, and how they touch people, became a little more real that morning in Glenrock.

State Highway 20 merged with I-25 east of Glenrock, so we were back on a freeway again. Ranches looked healthy as the North Platte River flowed nearby and irrigation sprinklers were at work in the fields. The temperature was in the mid-eighties, traffic was light, and the shoulder was smooth and as wide as most roads. Again, when a long way from metropolitan areas, the interstate highway proved to be ideal for biking.

Just ahead was a sign to Fort Fetterman. The fort was north of the highway and down near the North Platte River. It was built in 1867 as a military post to protect the wagon trains heading west and as a supply station for the Army's campaigns against the Sioux in Wyoming's Powder River country.

Captain Fetterman's Boast

By the summer of 1866, the tribes of the Sioux nation had been pushed back to the western Dakotas and eastern Wyoming and Montana. They particularly prized the Black Hills of South Dakota and Wyoming's Powder River basin, north of Fort Caspar. The Cheyennes were friendly with the Sioux and inhabited the same area. They each had been in conflict with the white settlers and U.S. Army since the 1850s and gradually were forced to pull back from the Great Plains that they once roamed freely. Gold had been discovered in Montana and northern Idaho. Thousands of emigrants were poised to travel to the gold fields via the Bozeman Trail, which started on the Oregon Trail near present-day Douglas and went north, right through the Powder River country. Some tribes were willing to sign a treaty allowing whites access to the trail. Chief Red Cloud, of the Teton Sioux, and many other tribes were not. They felt they had lost too much land already and decided to resist any white intrusion up the Bozeman Trail.

A column of troops, led by General Henry B. Carrington, marched into the Powder River basin in the summer of 1866 and began construction of Fort Phil Kearny. Red Cloud and thousands of his followers gathered in the hills nearby, harassed the soldiers, and interfered with the fort's construction-- the beginning of a siege that would last two years.

On December 21st, Captain William J. Fetterman led a column out of the fort to relieve some soldiers who had come under attack while cutting firewood. Fetterman had been given strict orders to simply help the woodcutters return to the fort and to not pursue the Indians into the wooded hills. Fetterman was a professional soldier with a brilliant Civil War record and was anxious to make his mark in the Indian wars. He blatantly disobeyed his orders and pursued a small band of Indians over a ridge and out of sight of the fort. where hundreds of Sioux and Cheyenne warriors lay in ambush. Crazy Horse, who was twenty-four and already a respected leader, was reported to be among them. Fetterman and all of his forty-seven troops were killed.

Concerned for the safety of his remaining detachment, General Carrington asked for volunteers to ride the 236 miles to Fort Laramie for help. John "Portugee" Phillips, a trapper and scout, made the ride in sub-zero weather in two days, one of the most heroic rides in American history. Reinforcement arrived in time to avoid further disaster. General Carrington was the scapegoat for Fetterman's defeat, while Fetterman was glorified and a new fort named for him.

In 1868, Red Cloud signed a treaty that ceded all of the Powder River country and the Black Hills to the Indians. Fort Phil Kearny was abandoned and the Bozeman Trail closed to travel by whites. Red Cloud and Crazy Horse had won, for the time being.

Fort Fetterman was closed as a military post in 1882 after the Plains Indian Wars were over.

It was quiet along the North Platte River as we approached Douglas. We cruised along the freeway at 15-20 mph, very fast compared to the pioneer wagons that plodded along the trail at 2-3 mph.

The Jackalope KOA was home for the afternoon and night. Douglas calls itself the home of the "jackalope," a local taxidermist creation that has a jackrabbit body and antelope (pronghorn) horns. They inhabit souvenir shops all over Wyoming. Douglas has a ten-foot statue of a jackalope in its town square to commemorate the beast; that weekend they were preparing to celebrate "Jackalope Days." We had a leisurely afternoon at the KOA, swimming and reading, while Mary Anna scouted out the town.

Mary Anna's maiden name is Pritchett, so her initials are MAPS. She takes those initials seriously, saying she was destined to marry a cartographer. She also is a natural navigator; it's in her blood. With a map, a car, the yellow pages, and a little time, she will quickly find out where everything of interest is in a town and know the best route to get to each of them. So she was much more than a freight hauler, referee, morale booster, purchase agent, and scribe for our crew. She fully reconnoitered Douglas and offered a plan for the evening. The Plains Restaurant, her suggestion for dinner, was located in a rustic complex of buildings that combined recycled and new materials to produce a unique look of the Old West. Stairs from a local grade school, doors from the county court house, and windows from a demolished old house were all incorporated. The ceiling was made of doors from a Casper hotel, and the candy counter was acquired from a truck stop in the Midwest. Somehow it all fit together and felt like an authentic Old West eatery. And the food was fine, especially the salad bar. (As we all like abundant salad makings, this was a special treat.)

After dinner, Mary Anna showed us the town, ending up at the fairgrounds where the State High School Rodeo Championship was underway. We stood out like sore thumbs with our Bermuda shorts, sandals, and T-shirts in that sea of jeans and cowboy hats, but we went in anyway and loved it. There were families all around us cheering for their brothers, sisters, and kids, just like at a football game. While cheering for the calf ropers and bull riders, we learned that rodeo is a varsity sport in Wyoming high schools and western universities, so those kids were competing for athletic scholarships as well as ribbons. I took a break after an hour or so and walked around the grounds where the horses fed and contestants warmed up. One young man was roping a set of steer horns that were lashed to a saw horse. Some cowgirls sat on the ground nearby, admiring his skills. He smiled, tipped his hat, and tried just a little harder when I took his (and their) picture.

As we left Douglas the next morning, we also left the Oregon Trail for the last time. It continues southeast along the North Platte River and across southern Nebraska, while we headed east across northern Nebraska on Highway 20, the more direct route to Boston. Being on or near the Oregon Trail for three weeks had made lasting impressions on us and left memories we would probably share for the rest of our lives.

The Oregon Trail: Some Closing Thoughts

Migration on the Oregon Trail from the 1840s through the 1860s meant many things to many people. It was economic opportunity for Americans seeking land and a better life. It was nation-building for visionary politicians. It was another step toward a ravaged culture for Indians that had lived there for thousands of years. For an Army lieutenant on the frontier, it was a chance to hone his skills for conflicts to come, and for an unemployed fur trader, a chance to stay out west by providing services to the emigrants. For a "forty-niner," it was a way to chase his dream to California's gold, and for Mormons, a route to religious freedom in Utah. It was a time for great leaders--of the nation, of families, of businesses, of Army regiments--and churches struggling to loosen the ties of a European-oriented nation to grow their own America, out west. It was a time for great Indian leaders to struggle for survival, balancing their visceral tendency to fight with their recognition that continued warfare could mean extinction. By the end of the Oregon Trail migration, the United States of America, the great experiment in democracy, had reached the Pacific Ocean. The land would soon have railroads and telegraph lines tying its people together coast to coast. It was on its way to greatness of a new kind. As Oregon had attracted midwesterners, America was becoming a magnet to the unfulfilled people of the world.

Several hundred miles of rolling landscape lay ahead of us with small (some, *very* small) towns scattered thirty to forty miles apart. There was not a tree in sight, so we were prepared for days of monotony. Wrong again--new and wonderful experiences lay ahead.

Back on Highway 20 there was a hill to deal with, as there always is when going from one river basin to another. It was a long but gradual climb to the plateau separating the North Platte and Niobrara Rivers, and we rode close together. One nice thing about climbing hills is that as I go much slower, I tend to notice more of my surroundings, and, if we stay close together, we can talk to each other.

I was suddenly aware of a change in the predominant vegetation. Previously, the landscape had been changing gradually, but now it was dramatically different than the vegetation only fifty miles behind us. I asked Kirby and Roger if they were aware of a change (not using the word "vegetation"). They were not. The answer was grass instead of sagebrush. We had been in and around sagebrush for three weeks; now we were in rolling grasslands, or prairies. It was different. It looked and even smelled different. Sagebrush had been fine, but the change was stimulating. It signaled another milestone.

At the top of the hill the van was parked by a gas station/post office/café, the only building in town. A sign announced, "Shawnee, Population 2." Mary Anna had been visiting with the gas station attendant/post mistress/waitress and learned that we were on a popular cycling route between the Black Hills and Yellowstone National Park. The proprietor told of an athletic, tanned, petite cyclist who stopped by one day. Dressed in shorts and a halter and with a scarf around her hair, she looked from the back to be youthful. What a surprise when she turned to expose a tanned and wrinkled face. She was eighty-two, had a post office box in Phoenix, and was bicycling through all fifty states alone. Her grown children were concerned, but she was having the time of her life. We took time for a cold drink, and, as we were leaving, the owner suggested that we go on another five miles to Lost Springs for our picnic lunch, as they had a nice city park.

"Lost Springs, Population 4," the sign read. They had a city park? Indeed they did, and a complete one at that: covered picnic tables, a lawn, a playground, and a rest room with running water. The town citizens built the park as an attraction to local ranchers and passersby like us. The mayor is paid $3 per year to oversee maintenance of the park and city street. She also keeps the town hall spiffy for weddings and other special events. Two people live above the bar across the street from the park, and the other two live behind the antique shop. After lunch, Kirby stopped by the antique shop and found out a little more about the town. Lost Springs had been a busy railhead for cattle for many years, but now the ranchers transport their livestock directly to market by truck, so most of the jobs are gone. We were impressed by the spirit of those Lost Springs residents and felt that their town would be around a long time--if they keep the park as well maintained as it was for us.

A long coal train was just cresting a hill ahead of us as we got back on Highway 20. The Chicago and North Western tracks had been near us most of the day. Several trains passed us heading east, each with one hundred or more fully loaded coal cars; others heading west were empty. We could see the entire train in that rolling, treeless country, a friendly sight as it rambled by.

Coal for the Midwest

Coal lies under forty percent of Wyoming's surface and has been a factor in the state's economy for over one hundred years. It influenced the location of the transcontinental railroad. Coal was plentiful along the rail line, and the railroad company owned much of it. Alternating square miles of land (and mineral rights) for several miles on either side of the rail line were given to the railroads by the federal government as a subsidy. So the railroads had their own fuel supply as well as a source of revenue.

Much of the coal now being mined lies in the Powder River basin north of Casper and is transported by train to the Midwest to fuel power-generating plants, thus the coal train that was bearing down on us near Lost Springs.

Most of Wyoming's coal is still in the ground. During the energy crises in the 1970s, many planners and forecasters thought that coal production would increase faster than it has. Various economic and environmental factors have limited that growth. Who knows how many coal trains will pass through Lost Springs twenty years from now?

Home for our last night in Wyoming was BJ's Campground in Lusk, an immaculate private RV park and campground in the middle of a residential area. There were showers, electrical hookups, and a carefully manicured lawn--the best camping we'd had since Three Island Crossing. When Kirby rode into town to mail a letter, he met a young man cycling alone from Durango, Colorado, to Philadelphia. He had been riding north into a head wind all day and planned to continue north to the Black Hills the next day. After hearing of our plans, he considered changing his route and riding with us for awhile. But when we awoke the next morning, he was gone on his way, unhampered by slower riders and their itineraries.

This was beef country. Mary Anna had prime rib for dinner, and Roger was tempted but had fish instead. He failed to follow his own Rule No. 9 (to eat the local food). Mary Anna raved about the prime rib, and Roger moped, ever more confident that he should always follow his own rules.

Lusk has always been a transportation hub. The Texas Trail, just east of town, was used to drive cattle overland from Texas to Wyoming and Montana. The Cheyenne-Deadwood (South Dakota) Stage Line ran right through town. Gold was discovered in the Black Hills in 1874, and the miners rushed in, despite the treaty with the Indians that promised to keep the whites out. Millions of dollars worth of gold was hauled through Lusk on stage coaches like the one in Lusk's Stagecoach Museum. Lusk is also the county seat of Niobrara County, which forms the headwaters of the Niobrara River. Months later I mentioned to a friend, from Nebraska, that I had never heard of the Niobrara River before taking this trip. "What?" he said in jestful disgust. "Why it's one of the three major rivers that traverse Nebraska from west to east, and it's mentioned in Lewis and Clark's journals!" He was right; I should have known of the Niobrara. I soon would, as we were always near it on our trek across northern Nebraska.

We packed a lunch the next day, as towns were pretty scarce. Node, population 2, and Van Tassell, population 12, each had a post office but little else. Van Tassell also had an American Legion Post that it claims was the first one chartered in the United States. Patriotism runs deep in the small western towns--we often noticed that the American Legion Post was the most prominent building in town.

Mary Anna caught up to us at lunch time and we picnicked next to the "Welcome to Nebraska" sign. It was just a wide spot in the road and very quiet; only two cars came by in half an hour. She was then on her way again to find the night's lodging. We pedaled on through the windy grasslands that reached to the horizon in all directions.

It was easy to tell the wind direction, and to some degree its velocity, by just watching the grass. In the distance, acres of grass leaned with the wind and appeared to move like ocean waves. Sometimes the gusts varied within short distances, so the grass adjoining the road was a better indicator for us. Cross winds, like we had that day, were very tricky. If slightly in our face, they were a pain; if slightly on our tail, a blessing. It was a southeast wind that day, about 20 mph and in our face-- not a pleasant welcome to Nebraska.

Northwest Nebraska probably has not changed much over the past hundred years. The nearby railroad track was there in 1886 but had been abandoned by 1994. Those coal trains we had seen near Lost Springs, Wyoming, must have taken another route. Highway 20 was paved and probably a little straighter than it used to be, but people were still pretty scarce. Towns were at least forty miles apart and ranch houses not much closer. It is a place for independent people who cherish privacy and self-reliance.

By late afternoon there were hills ahead with trees along the ridge tops, a nice change after miles of prairie. And then we headed downhill for eight miles, through a pine forest and out of the wind. It was one of those perfect cycling hills: we could coast at about 35 mph without braking and were smiling the whole way. I stopped once to take a few pictures and also to stretch out the experience. I thought of it like a good dessert, no need to rush.

Mary Anna met us at the bottom of the hill with a big smile on her face and said, "We are staying in the officers' quarters at Fort Robinson State Park. You're going to love this place." Kirby had done our planning for Nebraska and had suggested Fort Robinson as a place to spend the night. The lady at Shawnee, Wyoming, recommended it also, but we restrained any anticipation until we could see it. This time they were both right. The park is in the White River Valley, down out of the wind. Like that part of Nebraska, it is large and uncrowded. The park is primarily the restored elements of the fort. A campground has been added, but otherwise it has the feel of the nineteenth-century cavalry fort it once was. Home for the night for all four of us was one of the restored officers' quarters facing the parade ground: two bedrooms with a kitchen and bath for $45. Mary Anna and I stretched out on the beds to rest for a few minutes. It was warm and quiet, and we could smell the grass outside. I knew this was going to be a very special experience. "You did good," I whispered and then dozed off for a few minutes.

For the first week or two of the trip, we had debated about lodging and eating choices. At first we men liked to be part of the decision process, so Mary Anna and Lynn would usually check with us before making reservations. Gradually we came to understand each other's desires and limits, and the women began picking the places without checking with us. This process continued when Mary Anna was alone, and we developed full confidence in her judgment. A couple of times at first I had questioned her choice and rationale, and Roger had chastised me. "Don't waste your time debating with Mary Anna," he said. "You should know she is always right." Fort Robinson and the officers' quarters were further evidence of her good judgment.

While walking around Fort Robinson's grounds before dinner, we more fully understood Mary Anna's enthusiasm for the place. Highway 20 bisects the park which, beyond the fort's buildings, is grassland and scattered old trees. There are several large brick homes (the newer officers' quarters), restored barracks used for an inn, museum, playhouse, restaurant, and extensive stables (with horses for rent).

The fort was established as Camp Robinson in 1874 as one of many military outposts on the western plains. It was a base of operations for fighting the Sioux Indians in the 1870s and later for their re-settlement onto reservations in South Dakota. It was designated a permanent fort in 1878 with a mission of keeping watch on the Sioux. Its mission changed in later years, but it remained an active Army post. The Army tested high-wheeled bikes (unsuccessfully) for field use at Fort Robinson--the dawning of the mechanized army. Horses and mules were housed and trained there until after World War II. The K-9 corps--dogs that served as guards and messengers--also trained there. And German prisoners of war were housed there during the war. The Army abandoned Fort Robinson in 1948, and in 1972 all lands and remaining facilities were transferred to the state of Nebraska to become the treasures they are today.

Dinner entailed a chuck wagon cookout with buffalo stew and cornbread. We rode out to the picnic site in old hay wagons pulled by jeeps. The majority of our group of fifty or so were part of a family reunion. They each had T-shirts with their family tree on the back and were having a grand time. A songfest around the campfire rounded out the evening.

On the way back to the main compound, I noticed a sign designating the site of the Red Cloud Indian Agency.

White Men and Indians Clash on the Plains

Until the early nineteenth century, America's Great Plains were the exclusive domain of Indians. White Europeans and Americans had been exploring the area between the Mississippi River and Rocky Mountains for nearly three hundred years with only occasional conflicts with the Indians. When the United States took possession of the land via the Louisiana Purchase in 1803, it was used primarily as a thoroughfare to areas further west. The Indian Integration Act of 1834 documented that intent: Indians agreed to allow passage through what they considered their lands, and Americans agreed not to settle there.

Both sides honored the agreement for the next twenty years, the period of the great migrations to Oregon, California, and Utah. But the flood gate opened for more westward expansion, and in 1854 the Kansas-Nebraska Act was passed by Congress, establishing the Nebraska Territory and opening the plains to white settlement. Gold was discovered on Pikes Peak, Colorado, in 1858, and miners and others moved there, along with Army units to protect them. Conflict was coming.

Migration slowed during the Civil War, but the Pony Express and the telegraph improved communication coast-to-coast. The Homestead Act passed in 1862, and the first transcontinental railroad (Union Pacific) crossed the Mississippi in 1865. The laws and infrastructure were in place to entice more Americans westward. After the Powder River War was over in 1868, the Indians agreed to pull back north of Nebraska's Platte River. The Red Cloud Agency, near Fort Robinson, was one of those established by the Department of the Interior to provide food and other services to the Indians.

By the early 1870s, most of the fifty million buffalo that once roamed the plains had been killed by hunters, depriving the Indians of their main source of food, shelter, and clothing. Cattle from Texas was moved north in great herds to take advantage of the grasslands that were no longer needed by the buffalo. The second transcontinental railroad (Northern Pacific) reached the Dakotas and pressured the government for permission to build westward across Indian lands. General George A. Custer and his troops accompanied them, providing protection for the surveyors and construction crews. The noose was tightening around the Sioux and other Plains Indian tribes.

In 1874, gold was confirmed in the Black Hills by an expedition led by General Custer. Within a year thousands of miners swarmed over the hills. The Black Hills were some of the Sioux's most cherished lands. Crazy Horse and his followers would not back away; they harassed and killed many of the miners. The United States government and its Army would not back away either.

Crazy Horse and Custer Meet: The Last War on the Plains

President Grant ordered the Sioux to move to a reservation east of the Black Hills in the spring of 1876. Most of them refused, and thousands went to Sitting Bull's encampment in southeast Montana, near the Little Bighorn River. Thousands of others from the Cheyenne tribe joined them. The gathering of up to ten thousand Indians was one of the largest in American history.

General Custer moved out with nearly a thousand troops, part of a larger Army campaign to force the northern tribes to move back to the agency. He was confident that despite the numbers he would easily prevail and enhance his lagging career. The battle at the Little Bighorn was short and decisive. Custer had divided his command and was overwhelmed, losing 265 soldiers and civilians. This conflict ended in the American Indians' greatest military victory in history over the white man.

Following the battle, Sitting Bull could no longer keep the tribes intact, and he and some of his followers took refuge in Canada. He returned to the U.S. in 1881 and was sent to the Dakota reservation. Crazy Horse fought a running battle throughout the winter, but by spring his group of about one thousand men, women, and children was near starvation and out of *ammunition. They'd had enough; they agreed to return to the Red Cloud Agency. They would no longer fight nor hunt, just survive.*

Crazy Horse spent an uncertain summer adjusting to agency life. Fearing that he was planning to escape and foment more violence, the Army, with the help of friendly Indians, arrested and planned to exile him. Upon realizing he would be locked in a cell, he resisted and was killed by a soldier.

His body was returned to his family, lashed to a travois, and taken back to the Dakotas to its final resting place. He has since gained recognition and honor among all Americans. Captain John G. Bourk, an officer who fought against him said, "Crazy Horse was one of the great soldiers of his day.... As the grave of Custer marked the high water mark of Sioux supremacy...so the grave of Crazy Horse marked the ebb." There would be more skirmishes, but the war on the plains was over.

We didn't have time to visit the museum the first day, so we agreed to start late and do it the next morning. I always enjoy seeing fine museums in large cities, but there is nothing like visiting one that is part of the story that is told. Seeing the parade grounds and horse barns from the second story window made the museum's exhibits come alive. Transferring the old headquarters building to the Nebraska Historical Society for a museum was the first step in forming the great state park that it is today.

Kirby and Roger had shared a room the night before, and Kirby had snored quite a bit. Roger woke up several times and asked him to quit. Finally he spoke in desperation, "Kirby, roll over." That did it--but not until the sun was about to rise. However, it would take more than a poor night's sleep to slow Roger down. He quickly went through his (and our) normal routine: checked the grass and trees for wind direction, filled his water bottles, checked his tires, replenished his supply of trail mix, applied sun screen, and "saddled up." Kirby seemed to have slept fine, so we were on our way.

10

SAND HILLS AND CIRCULAR IRRIGATION

(Days 31-35)

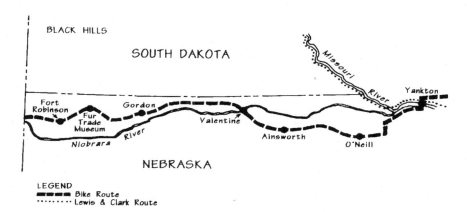

As we did for most of the trip, we spread out enough that morning to make conversation difficult, so there was a lot of time for reflection. I was thinking about my first trip driving across the country after graduating from high school in Silver Spring, Maryland. Three of us bummed a ride with a vacationing teacher to our summer jobs with the U.S. Forest Service in northern Idaho. I remember how different the country looked when we got to Nebraska. The vegetation was different, no more eastern hardwood trees. There were some odd rock formations in the distance, and farms were larger; some entry gates announced a ranch rather than a farm. It felt like we were out west. That was a great adventure for a mostly city-bred eastern teenager, just like this bike trip.

Mary Anna timed it right again and caught up to us for lunch in Chadron, home of Chadron State College and county seat of Dawes County. Many of the small, railroad towns in the Midwest and plains area lost population as farms required less labor and farm products were transported to markets over highways, rather than railroads. Many of the towns that have thrived serve as county seats, have a college, or both, as does Chadron. Mary Anna found a laundromat after lunch. As there was an electrical outlet available and no one there to say she couldn't, she plugged in the computer and worked on the newsletter while the clothes were washing--never an idle moment for her.

Beyond Chadron the road was new and smooth and heading southeast, directly with the wind. It was a time to fly again, but only for three miles. A large historic sign and quaint old building beckoned us to the Museum of the Fur Trade. It didn't look like much at first. Probably another of those little one-room local museums that many of the small towns proudly maintain, I thought as we got off our bikes. But we enjoyed the historic signs and felt the museum might be worth a quick look, which it surely was. Though a Nebraska-based institution, the museum is international in scope, covering two hundred years of fur trade activity in North America.

There are exhibits of furs, weapons, and trade goods, a library, maps, and a restored trading post. The old log trading post with a sod roof was originally occupied by James Bordeaux in 1833 as a "wintering house" and was a subsidiary of the major trading post at Fort Laramie. Such field offices of the fur trade were established near the Indians' winter camps. The animal's fur is in prime condition in winter, so that was the ideal time for hunting and trading. The beaver trade was in decline in the 1830s, but the demand for buffalo robes and deerskins was increasing. The Bordeaux Trading Post changed hands in 1849 but remained active until 1876 when the Army closed it, mainly because members of the fort were trading weapons to hostile Indians. Unfortunately for her, Mary Anna drove by the Museum of the Fur Trade without noticing it, a disadvantage of moving faster than 15 mph.

Shortly beyond the museum, Highway 20 stretches through a beautiful pine forest, seemingly out of place in those grasslands. We thought that stretch deserved to be designated a "scenic highway," as it rivals the beauty of others we had seen. Then came the grasshoppers. They nearly covered the road for a few miles and even jumped into our spokes. We managed to pedal on through them, though, and were reminded that there is occasionally an advantage to riding in a car.

Soon enough we were back in open grasslands and hayfields. Windmills dotted the landscape, providing the power to pump water into stock-watering tanks. Harnessing wind power is nothing new to Nebraska's farmers and ranchers. A tractor emerged in the distance pulling a large machine, so we stopped to watch. Every few minutes a huge, round hay bale rolled out of the rear of the machine. The hay had been cut and raked into rows, and now it was being baled. The round bales were about six feet in diameter and, we later learned, weighed 1400 pounds. Kirby climbed a wire fence, walked over to a bale and tried to roll it. No luck, it wouldn't budge. I was reminded of summers on my Granddad McCully's farm in Ohio. At that time all the hay bales were about eighteen inches square and four feet long, small enough for one man to carry. I couldn't carry one at ten years old and could barely manage one at sixteen. Those small bales were the standard when I had last driven across the country in the 1970s. There are still a few small square bales around, but the big round ones are now the standard.

Rushville was our home for the night. We'd gotten a late start and had a lengthy layover at the museum but still covered fifty-five miles easily. Our expectations regarding daily distances were changing. Originally, we planned to go no more than fifty to seventy miles per day, but by the time we reached mid-Nebraska, barring fierce head winds, that distance seemed easy.

The Antler Motel was not fancy, but reasonable, clean, and had TV's and phones in the rooms. As much as we enjoyed the privacy and remoteness of that wide-open country, it was good to get caught up on the outside world. The World Cup soccer matches were underway. Roger had coached and refereed soccer for years and was glued to the TV while we enjoyed our daily glass of his red wine.

I walked down a few blocks to the main business street and took some pictures of the store fronts. The architecture was like most of the small towns in that area, vintage 1890s and early 1900s (so imprinted on the most prominent building in town). By that time, the railroads had come through, Indians had been moved to reservations, and most of the prime agricultural land was settled. That was the boom period, when the towns were built and labor needs were high on the farms and ranches. Mechanization has since taken its toll in many of the towns, but Rushville seems to be doing fine. I stopped into the five and dime store to pick up a few things and chatted with the proprietor, who appeared to be in his eighties. He had owned that five and dime store for decades; he loved his shop and hoped it would always be a five and dime store. And, yes, there were still a few five- and ten-cent items for sale.

There was little sign of growth in Rushville, but neither was there deterioration. A new golf course was under construction, and the town was neat and clean, appearing to be economically solid. As the seat of Sheridan County, Rushville has one of the ingredients for small-town success. Over dinner at Schroeder's Family Dining & Bowling, the waitress told us about another economic ingredient. The Pine Ridge and Rosebud Indian reservations were just over the South Dakota line, thirty miles north of town, and Rushville welcomed the Indian trade. Apparently that hospitality has paid off, as many of the Indian people shop there.

That night Kirby suggested Roger leave the air conditioner on so he would not hear Kirby's snoring. It must have worked as we heard no complaints from Roger the next morning.

Gordon was only fifteen miles down the road, just the right distance before B-2. As it was warm and sunny, with a gentle northerly wind and light traffic, we made it in an hour and found a café across the highway from the Gordon Golf and Country Club. The customers were like so many we had seen having coffee in small farming and ranching towns: mostly guys in their sixties and seventies wearing overalls, with baseball caps that advertise the local granary or farm equipment dealer. They appeared to have been friends with each other and with the waitress for a long time, like a family get-together.

Gordon is the home of Mari Sandoz, distinguished author and daughter of one of northwestern Nebraska's early settlers. Her writings capture the spirit of the local Indians as well as early settlers of the region. Her most famous work, *Old Jules,* is the story of her father arriving in Nebraska and of her childhood on a nearby homestead. Some of the incidents reported in her book reflect the kind of intelligence, strength, combativeness, and entrepreneurial spirit that was common among those early Nebraska pioneers.

"Old Jules" Passed This Way

In 1884, Jules Ami Sandoz, age twenty-five, was heading west with all of his belongings, having left his parent's comfortable home in Switzerland two years earlier to seek land and a new independent life. He took the railroad to its western terminus in Valentine, Nebraska, and spent a few days there at the land office, studying the survey maps and learning of areas still open to homesteading. At that time even recent emigrants could acquire 160 acres of free land if they could subsist on it for three years.

Northwestern Nebraska was still raw country in 1884. The well-traveled Oregon Trail and first transcontinental railroad were far to the south. The Sioux Indians had been moved onto reservations in South Dakota. Many questioned if the land and climate could support farming. It was good grazing land, had been for centuries for the buffalo. But by the time Jules arrived the buffalo had been hunted to near extinction, and cattlemen from Texas were moving their herds north for better grass. Some had stayed, built ranches, and grazed their cattle on the federal land that had not yet been homesteaded. They could acquire deed to only 160 acres of federal land per family, but as in Wyoming, they needed thousands of acres for a viable cattle operation. There was very little government oversight of the open range, so in a way they considered it their own to use.

Neither was there much law and order. One evening while Jules was in a bar in Valentine, a man was shot as he bragged about standing up to the local vigilantes. There was little commotion over the shooting. The man's body was just hauled away, and life went on as if nothing had happened. From then on Jules always kept his rifle and ammunition nearby.

He drove an open wagon 150 miles west of Valentine before selecting his first homestead along the Niobrara River. The soil looked good, there was water and wildlife nearby, and the railroad would be coming through within a couple of years. (Ironically, this was the same railroad line that was no longer being used when we pedaled through in 1994.) A small band of Indians was camped across the river. Jules befriended them immediately, knowing that their local knowledge could be helpful to him.

He was an excellent marksman and impressed the Indians by shooting an eagle in flight and giving them its highly treasured feathers.

Jules built a small sod house and returned to Valentine to record his land claim and recruit others to join him. They gradually came, mostly emigrants from Europe and Scandinavia. By 1900, half of the population of Nebraska had been born in another country, but somehow they learned to communicate, survive, and eventually thrive there.

As the farming settlement grew, so did conflicts with the cattle ranchers. The settlers put up fences to protect their crops from wandering cattle, occasionally shooting one that got through. Cattlemen would retaliate, first by threats, then by destroying property, and, ultimately, murder. Very few incidents were dealt with by law enforcement authorities, who were too few and far away. Gradually the cattlemen pulled back from the homesteaded land but fenced off the remaining public land for their own use. Though the settlers were primarily farmers, they realized there was profit in cattle. So they acquired some of their own and grazed them on the same public land used by the cattlemen. Conflicts intensified, and one of the victims, Jules' brother Emile Sandoz, was shot in cold blood in front of many witnesses. His killer was brought to trial and found guilty of manslaughter, the first cattleman found guilty of a crime against a settler in the Niobrara country.

And there were other hazards. While climbing out of a newly dug well, Jules fell sixty feet to the bottom and severely broke his leg and ankle. His neighbors left him to seek help in Valentine. After several days of waiting, he crawled out to a nearby military road and was picked up by a cavalry unit and taken to Fort Robinson. As the Army surgeon was preparing to amputate his leg, Jules objected and threatened to kill the doctor if he proceeded. A few months later he limped back home, crippled but with two legs.

The early homesteaders were bachelors who spent much of their free time trying to figure out how to get women to join them. The women eventually came, through family contacts in the old country or through newspaper advertisements, without first seeing their future husbands or their future home. It was a shock to come from civilized life in Europe or an American city to a cold, leaky sod house in Nebraska. Many did not adjust: some divorced and returned home, some committed suicide, and some were admitted to mental institutions. Jules was married and divorced three times before finding a life partner in Mary. He spent his time encouraging others to come to his area, combating the cattlemen, hunting, and corresponding with the government and agricultural research stations. He was a manager, scientist, carpenter, surveyor, and community leader. He expected his wife to do physical work on the farm as well as in the house. When she refused he physically abused her.

Somehow Mary survived the abuse and bore and raised six children, none with the aid of a doctor. Jules treated his children in the same authoritarian and violent manner. Mari always feared him and took a great risk when she left home to continue her education beyond the eighth grade.

The Kinkaid Act of 1904 allowed homesteaders to acquire an additional 640 acres of land. Jules grabbed the opportunity and claimed his new land, this time in the Sand Hills to the south and east of his original property. The Sand Hills had never been occupied by human beings. Indians hunted there but never stayed. Cattlemen grazed on the fringes but were reluctant to penetrate the rolling sand dunes that were considered remote and unproductive. The Kinkaid Act was incentive enough for both cattlemen and farmers to give the Sand Hills a try. Most of the hills were suitable only for cattle and are today some of the most productive cattle lands in the country, but some areas were also good farmlands. Jules found these areas. He experimented with different strains of corn, wheat, and fruit trees until he found successful ones. He even ordered wheat from Russia, and Mary and the kids planted, watered, cultivated, and harvested, developing a thriving farm.

Old Jules mellowed a little in his old age, finally learning to respect his daughter Mari's accomplishments. Thanks to her we have a record of his vision and leadership in opening a new land, as well as the harsh reality of life on the homesteads.

Railroads, Beef, and Cities

Route 20 and the railroad follow the same general route across northern Nebraska that Old Jules took with horse and buggy between his homestead and Valentine. The Chicago and North Western Railroad line was completed only as far west as Valentine when Jules arrived in 1884, but it reached across the state a few years later and was the region's transportation backbone for nearly one hundred years. When we passed this way in 1994 the tracks were overgrown with weeds, replaced by trucks and an improved Route 20.

The railroads also played an important role in the development of cities. When the Chicago and North Western line reached western Nebraska, beef cattle were shipped to Chicago for processing. Nebraska's politicians, who had pressed the federal government to ease Am rica's export laws in order to benefit their beef industry, suddenly turned projectionist. They passed a state law requiring that all beef grown in Nebraska had to be processed in Nebraska, thus assuring Omaha's growth as a major beef processing center.

Shortly after leaving Gordon we realized why this country is called the Sand Hills. The dunes cover nearly twenty thousand square miles (about one fourth of Nebraska), and some say that from a high point you can look further and see less than at any other place in America. Route 20 is a roller-coaster ride through the grass-covered dunes. The underlying sand shows up occasionally where the road slices through the grass.

People are scarce, but cattle are numerous. We took one of our maxi-butt-breaks near a herd that was watching us with apparent curiosity. Kirby reached out to feed a cow some grass, and Roger and I reached for our cameras--but too late. There was something about us they didn't like, our brightly colored shirts, the bikes, our cameras, who knows? But as soon as we were ready to take a close-up picture, they were off. They ran just a short distance away, still curious but not cooperative. That was not the first time we encountered such behavior from ranging cattle and would not be the last. Often they would follow us along the fence for a mile or so, but as soon as we stopped and tried to get close, they took off again. I guess they figured that people were supposed to be on horses, in pickup trucks, or on tractors, and we hardly fit that mold.

Despite the rolling hills and fairly rough road we were making good time and covered the forty-five miles to Merriman, population 91, by 11:00 a.m. Mary Anna arrived at about the same time, so we had an early lunch. Coffee was free, and large milkshakes and malts were ninety cents. We would always remember the bargains in mid-America.

The day's destination was still up in the air. Cody, twenty-four miles ahead, had a campground, and there was probably nowhere else to stay between there and Valentine, another 38 miles. Kirby pushed for the free campground at Cody. Roger and I voted to go that far and then decide; we could always van into Valentine if need be.

During lunch, an elderly, but sprightly, man came over to our table and asked where we were headed. He wore overalls and a baseball cap and had the tough, suntanned skin of the local farmers and was anxious to chat. He had passed us on the highway and was full of curiosity. He seemed genuinely interested in our story and wished us well. He also hoped we would return to further explore the Sand Hills someday. When we asked him about the round hay bales that had become so common, his eyes lit up with pride as he explained how the round bailing machines had been developed ten to twelve years earlier and changed the entire haying process. One man could now cut, rake, and bale the hay. With a front-end loading fork on a tractor, he could load the hay on a truck and take it to another field to be distributed to cattle with still another machine. One man could feed five hundred cattle in an hour--no more lifting hay bales by hand or tossing it to hungry cattle with a pitchfork. He seemed to have no bitterness about the dramatic changes that technology had wrought, that fewer farmers were needed as one man could now do what used to take a dozen or more. Farmers are economists as well as gardeners. He knew that those bailing machines helped the Nebraska farmers compete in a world market, making it possible for at least some of them to stay on their farms.

After lunch Mary Anna visited the Arthur Bowring Sand Hills Ranch State Park, just north of Merriman.

Arthur and Eva Bowring Passed This Way

Arthur Bowring's father homesteaded near Gordon in 1886, two years after Jules Sandoz filed his claim on the Niobrara. Arthur left home at age twenty-one and filed his own claim near Merriman. He worked and lived on the Bar 99 Ranch for the next fifty years, expanding the original 160 acres to 12,000. He believed in the future of ranching in the Sand Hills and acquired land from farmers and other cattle ranchers who gave up and sold out, as well as homesteading more land through the Kinkaid Act. As a cattleman, Bowring was on the other side of the farmer-rancher hostilities from Sandoz. Like Sandoz, though, he stuck it out and accumulated land that was ideally suited to his vocational interest, in his case for raising cattle.

There is a saying in Nebraska, "People afraid of coyotes, work, and loneliness had better let ranching alone." Bowring dealt with the loneliness by marrying Anna Holbrook, a local school teacher, in 1908. She was not a strong woman, though, and died with her baby in childbirth the next year. Arthur was alone for the next twenty years, and then Eva Forester came to town. Eva was a traveling saleswoman, whose territory included Merriman. She had four children from a previous marriage and knew nothing about ranching at the time of her marriage to Bowring in 1928. But she learned, and the Bar 99 thrived under their joint care and for another forty-one years after Arthur's death in 1941.

Like Arthur, Eve (as she preferred to be called by her friends) was dedicated to public service and eventually served in the U.S. Senate as the first woman from Nebraska to enter Congress. Eve outlived all of her sons and arranged to have the ranch donated to the state of Nebraska at the time of her death, to serve as a living history museum dedicated to Sand Hills ranching.

Leaving Merriman on Highway 20, we bisected some of Arthur and Eve Bowring's old ranch. Cattle were grazing on both sides of the road, probably just the way they were fifty years ago. The wind and road conditions were favorable that afternoon, and we covered the twenty-three miles to Cody in a little over an hour. Kirby wanted to camp there, but Roger and I voted to keep going. Our motivation was based on several reasons: it was still early in the afternoon, Mary Anna reported that the road was smooth for several miles ahead, we were all feeling strong, there was a great tail wind, there was not much to do in Cody (population 177), and, most importantly, there were mosquitoes in the Cody campground. It was thirty-nine miles to Valentine, and if we made it we would have cycled 107 miles, our longest day of the trip and of our lives. We decided to go for it. Conditions remained favorable, and no doubt our adrenaline was pumping more than usual as we completed one hundred miles. Seeing Valentine in the distance was a bit like seeing the top of Cabbage Hill; we felt the excitement of accomplishing something special.

We pulled into Valentine at 6:30 p.m., having lost an hour as we crossed into the central time zone. Camping was still a possibility, but even Kirby agreed that a soft bed would feel good after our first "century" ride. Mary Anna found us reasonable lodging at the Valentine Motel that would be our home for the next two nights. We had cycled 620 miles since leaving Jackson Hole, ten days earlier, and were ready for a day off.

Valentine was named for E.K. Valentine, an early Nebraska congressman, and celebrates its name by offering to send out cards to a sweetheart, with its postmark, on Valentines' Day. With a population of 2,900, Valentine is the big city of the Sand Hills. It was the western terminus of the railroad for awhile in the 1880s, before the line was extended westward, and it hosted the government land office that was used by Jules Sandoz and Arthur Bowring to claim their homesteads, as well as Fort Niobrara, a cavalry outpost in the 1880s and 1890s. Today, Valentine seems to be thriving as a county seat, a commercial center for Sand Hill farms and ranches, and a transportation and recreation hub. Roger discovered a store named Valentines that featured high quality Indian arts and crafts. He bought Lynn some birthday presents after learning about the mythical significance of several items.

We slept late the next morning, read, and watched the World Cup soccer matches for awhile, but we found it hard to totally relax. We wanted to see the town and surrounding area. Mary Anna and I rode our bikes around town while Roger and Kirby tuned their bikes, washed the car, drove around the area, and shopped. And Kirby's well-traveled package was waiting at the post office, having been in transit for a month since leaving his California home.

By the next morning we were restless and ready to hit the road again. It was Thursday, June 30th, and the landscape was changing again; the rolling grass-covered Sand Hills gave way to flat croplands. Our Nebraska road map had color tints for the state's topographic regions. We had been in the "yellow" Sand Hills region for the past couple of days. We were now in the "purple" plains region, and the map was right. The natural grasslands were gone, replaced by healthy-looking grain and cornfields. No doubt this land was already settled when Jules Sandoz passed this way seeking his homestead.

The early morning ride was tough, with strong head winds and a rough road. Two hours later we finally finished the eighteen miles to Wood Lake where we stopped for B-2. This was "Cornhusker" country, the nickname for the University of Nebraska's football team. Their colors are red, and there was lots of red in that café, including some bandannas for sale that predicted that the "Cornhuskers" would be rated number one in the country in the forthcoming season. Though seemingly a little arrogant at the time, it turned out to be a correct prediction. I'm sorry I didn't buy one of those collector's items.

How quickly conditions change on the plains. By the time we finished our blueberry pancakes, the wind was coming out of the west and the road was heading more easterly. What was a struggle earlier became easy.

Leaving the Sand Hills also meant a little more population; towns were still small but were now ten to twenty rather than thirty to forty miles apart. They were still enough of a novelty, though, that we usually pedaled around each town and stopped for a butt-break. Johnstown, population 48, was one of these. There were only a few old buildings on the one street that was just off the highway, but they were in fine repair. And there was a well-manicured city park with a monument noting the location of a buried time capsule. The capsule was buried in 1983, Johnstown's centennial year. The inscription read, "To be opened in 2033 and 2083." We rode on through the cornfields, again amazed at the pride and imagination of folks in small-town America.

Mary Anna found us in Ainsworth with her usual precise timing and tracking ability and was excited to tell us of her morning's newsletter printing adventure. She had finished typing newsletter #4 in Valentine but could not find a place that could read and print from her disk. She was advised to try the County Education Computer Center in Ainsworth. They didn't have the right software either, so they sent her to the local computer specialist. His company was in the back of a bank building. He was able to print out a hard copy and advised Mary Anna where to run off her forty copies most economically. He also noted that with additional software in the computer, she would have a lot more options in printing out future editions. He installed the software free of charge, asking only to receive future copies of the newsletter, which Mary Anna happily agreed to do. Our encounters with friendly and helpful people in small-town America continued to impress us.

The story of how this computer specialist came to Ainsworth is worth repeating. His career was thriving as vice-president of a software firm in the Southwest, but things turned sour when he and his wife returned home one day to find their home ransacked by an intruder. They decided they'd had enough of big city life and moved to Ainsworth, his wife's childhood home. He now has software development and maintenance contracts with several nationwide firms and seldom has to leave Ainsworth. His business is no doubt typical of the Information Age.

Bassett and the county fairgrounds' campground was our planned destination, but mosquitoes again chased us away. They were thick at the fairgrounds, there was no shade, and it was only mid-afternoon, so we wanted to keep going. However, accommodations ahead were uncertain. Our literature indicated no camping or motels until we reached O'Neill, another 48 miles east on Highway 20. Once again Mary Anna and the van came to our rescue. We pedaled another twenty miles to Stuart, where we met Mary Anna and vanned the last 28 miles to O'Neill. Much of the road to O'Neill was being resurfaced and nearly impassable by bicycle, and there were no alternative secondary roads in the area, leaving us with a dilemma for the next day.

At population 3,800, O'Neill is larger than most of the towns we had been through for several weeks, and it had a hotel. Mary Anna chose the historic Golden Hotel from the other accommodations available--a good choice. Opened in 1913, the Golden was a favorite stop for businessmen traveling on the Chicago and North Western Railroad. The train no longer comes through town, but apparently enough motorists and cyclists do to keep the hotel thriving. It was recently restored and is now listed on the National Register of Historic Places. With single rooms going for $20 per night and with only double beds in the rooms, Kirby and Roger decided to get private rooms. (Kirby could snore to his heart's content.) O'Neill was settled by Irish immigrants and maintains its Irish heritage by painting shamrocks on the street corners and holding a major celebration on St. Patrick's Day. It also has a nice Mexican restaurant, Tia Zia, where we fueled up for the next day.

We planned to leave U.S. Route 20 at O'Neill and continue directly east on State Route 59, in order to bypass Sioux City, Iowa. This was to be our first experience with a Nebraska secondary road, so after dinner Mary Anna and I drove over the first few miles of the route. The road was just okay, but the irrigation systems were spectacular. We had seen a variety of systems since entering the arid country of eastern Washington, but none compared to those we saw, heard, and felt outside O'Neill that evening. To avoid excessive evaporation, the heaviest watering time is the cool evening and early morning hours. Water was shooting out of sprinklers as far as we could see on both sides of the road, and I stopped the car to take some pictures of a system that was operating next to the road. It was beautiful to see the water spray across the reddening sky, but it was more than beauty. The irrigation structures were about ten ten feet off the ground and the water was being thrown more than one hundred feet to either side of the main pipe. Corn next to the fence was getting a good soaking, but hardly a drop of spray was wasted on the road. We could hear and even feel the water surging through those pipes. These were center-pivot systems that pump water from a well and distribute it in a circular pattern through aluminum pipes mounted on rubber tires. We were at the end of a line that originated well beyond our sight in the darkness. Many of the center-pivot lines are a quarter of a mile long and irrigate 160-acre fields, truly an engineering and agricultural marvel. It was appropriate to see them up close, near O'Neill, as they were first developed there. Those circular fields are a curious sight from a jet airplane at 35,000 feet, but standing next to them on a summer evening is an awesome experience.

The next morning an article in the newspaper caught our attention. Mixed in with stories on the recent tornado and a planned new soccer field, a headline in the *Holt County Independent* announced, "Rails-to-Trails Announces Plans for Cowboy Line." The "Cowboy Line" was the local name for the Chicago and North Western line we had been following across Nebraska. The Rails-to-Trails Conservancy is a non-profit organization which facilitates the conversion of abandoned rail lines to recreation trails. They work with the railroad company and various private and government entities to arrange financing and management plans. A few hurdles still loomed ahead, but they were optimistic that within a few years the entire trail would be operational and that many more cyclists and hikers would be drawn to northern Nebraska.

Back to our dilemma about how to cover the twenty-eight miles west of O'Neill. Most of the fourteen miles furthest west was under construction and a nuisance to drive, much less pedal through. One of us came up with a proposal that stretched our "ride the whole way" policy a bit. The proposal was this: cover the twenty-eight miles by starting from O'Neill, riding fourteen miles west, then turning around and returning to O'Neill. We would travel a total of twenty-eight miles, avoid interfering with the construction, and save Mary Anna fifty-six miles of driving. Our argument may have been a little flimsy, but we considered it adequate. With a brisk, southeasterly tail wind the western trek was a piece of cake. However, the fourteen-mile return to O'Neill and most of the day was back into the wind and real work.

By afternoon, the flat land gave way to sharply rolling, glaciated terrain, and the easterly winds increased. We actually had to pedal downhill and then agonized climbing uphill. The sky darkened. There had been tornadoes in the area recently. That afternoon was my toughest of the trip so far. Somehow the wind is far more demoralizing than mountains, as you can't see it and you wonder if it ever ends. Climbing Cabbage Hill and the continental divide were fond memories compared to fighting the wind over the glacial moraines of eastern Nebraska.

The agony finally ended. During an afternoon break at the intersection of State Routes 14 and 59, Mary Anna met us and announced there were no overnight accommodations at Creighton or other nearby towns. She had made reservations at a motel in Niobrara, a Missouri River town, twenty miles directly north via Route 14. I was leaning toward quitting for the day and vanning into Niobrara but finally agreed to continue riding. The sky was clearing, and the ninety-degree turn made such a difference. That southeasterly wind became our friend, and the last twenty miles of the day was a pleasure. The rich rolling farmlands that were a blur when fighting the wind were now a scenic wonderland. We stopped again in Verdigre (a Czech-settled town) and sampled their *kolaches* (flat, circular sweet-dough pastries with fruit filling). Lynn Wedel's ancestors were Czech, and, having visited Czechoslovakia with her, Roger was familiar with kolaches and gave these a high rating. Then Roger and Kirby rode far ahead of me the last ten miles. Roger was always anxious to finish the day's ride, and Kirby loved to fly when conditions were right, so they soon disappeared. I lolled along, soaking up the scenery and stopping often to take pictures of farms, wildflowers, mailboxes, and the nearby Niobrara River--a great ending to a tough eighty-two-mile day.

Those dark clouds returned and opened up just as I pulled into the motel. The thunderstorm lasted for only a few minutes but long enough for us to fully appreciate being under a roof.

At dinner a friendly young man came by to chat. He had seen us on the road earlier and wondered where we were headed. A long-time resident of Niobrara, he taught high school computer science on the nearby Santee Indian reservation and had just returned from an educational conference in Boston. He was proud to live in the area and happily filled us in on its history. The town of Niobrara was founded in the late 1800s, destroyed by an Indian raid, rebuilt, flooded out by the Missouri River, and then moved to higher ground. It was moved again in 1975 when the Gavin Point Dam was built downriver on the Missouri. The flood plain along the river is now their golf course and city park. The golf course was built through local fundraising. Annual fees for unlimited play is $156, very reasonable by any golfer's standards.

After dinner the sky cleared and we all drove over to the Niobrara State Park, located at the intersection of the Niobrara and Missouri Rivers. Lewis and Clark passed this way as they headed up the Missouri and noted the Niobrara River as being "150 yards wide and no more than four feet deep." It looked about that size to us as we crossed it to get into the state park. The sun was setting and the air was fresh after the shower, nice conditions to see most anything. But that park was truly beautiful. The land rose gradually from the water, allowing spectacular views up and down both rivers. Picnic areas and campgrounds were clean and widely separated, cabins and horses were available for rent, the visitor center had informative displays, and lush, knee-high grass carpeted the entire park. Had the weather been nicer, we surely would have camped there.

It was nearly dark when we returned to the motel. An auto dealership across the street was just closing. It was misnamed for it should have been called a truck dealership as there were hardly any cars in the lot. That was a common sight in the western and prairie states. A car is a luxury to farmers and ranchers who need to travel off-road, as well as on miles of unpaved secondary roads. Most towns have trucks for sale; only the larger towns sell an occasional car.

Mary Anna and I were usually the earliest risers of our group. The next morning we found a nice café within walking distance of the motel and enjoyed an early hot breakfast and conversation with a lady that was attending the Niobrara High School alumni celebration. All alumni are invited back every year. She lives in Colorado Springs but still tries to make them all. There is something very special about the loyalty people in small towns feel for each other.

We were slow getting started after breakfast. The Wimbledon matches were underway in Great Britain and we had TV's in our rooms, so Kirby was reluctant to leave. He is as fanatical about tennis as Roger is about soccer matches. Roger and I were eager to go as we were headed for Yankton, South Dakota, and would be crossing the Missouri and completing the first half of our trip (Roger loved those milestones). But a key Wimbledon match was just getting started, so Kirby urged us to go ahead and promised he would catch up. Roger and I were concerned for multiple reasons: this was contrary to our "stay together" policy, the day's route and lodging were not yet confirmed, and Kirby had a tendency to occasionally take a wrong turn. But we finally agreed and took off.

Kirby's Commandment No. 3 - "Tennis is better than biking."

After a pleasant, cool ride along the banks of the Missouri River, we headed inland, upward, and back into the wind as we entered the Santee Indian reservation, another reminder that it is not all downhill after you cross the continental divide. The only sign of life for twenty miles was what appeared to be a funeral procession going in the opposite direction. I kept looking back for Kirby, but he didn't catch us until we stopped for lunch in Crofton. We didn't talk a lot about Kirby's absence, but we were glad to see him. We were supportive of each other's health and well-being and determined to finish our adventure together.

Mary Anna soon arrived with lodging news. It was July 2nd, beginning the Fourth of July weekend, and there were no vacancies in any motel or campground in the Yankton area. Lewis and Clark Lake on the Missouri River was a major drawing card, and Mary Anna had to use her best negotiating skills to find us a place to stay in an old RV park on the Nebraska side of the river. They had an open area large enough for our tents, with an electrical hookup and water, but no rest rooms or showers. And the adjoining Lazy D Saloon was already rocking. But the price was right (free), and the proprietor even arranged for us to use the rest room in the convenience store across the highway. We had become pretty flexible by that time; there was hardly a complaint about having to cross the four-lane highway to visit the rest room. It was probably the worst place we stayed on the entire trip, but Mary Anna received kudos for her commitment to cost-containment.

After setting up camp we drove across the river, toured Yankton, and picked up some supplies at a Wal-Mart store (my first Wal-Mart experience). I don't like to shop but had to admit that the store was impressive. At twelve thousand, Yankton was a big town for us, with a classy restored old downtown and neat suburbs. We drove a few miles upriver to see the Gavins Point Dam and Lewis and Clark Lake. Kirby chose to take a swim while Roger, Mary Anna, and I drove across the earth-fill dam, which is one and a half miles wide, to the visitor center on Calumet Bluff. The center was closed, but we still peeked through the windows and could see displays of what appeared to be Lewis and Clark meeting with the Indians.

Lewis and Clark and the Yankton Sioux

When Lewis and Clark started their voyage in the spring of 1804, they were concerned about encountering the Sioux, who controlled transportation and commerce on the upper Missouri River. They'd had friendly councils with members of the Kickapoo, Missouri, and Oto tribes earlier. In late August they approached Sioux country, near present-day Yankton. Fish, elk, buffalo, deer, and small game were plentiful, and the Missouri River was an important trade route, so it was easy to understand why the Sioux were so protective of their area. One of Lewis and Clark's goals was to explain to the Indians that the United States had purchased "Louisiana" and the Indians new "great white father" was in Washington, D.C. The Sioux's only contact with white men until then had been French and British fur traders. Their reaction to these Americans was totally unpredictable.

As Lewis and Clark's flotilla approached a camp of Yankton Sioux on the north side of the river (near the Gavins Point Dam site), one of their boats hit a snag and was damaged. They crossed to the south side to make repairs, set up camp under what would later be called Calumet Bluffs, and waited to receive the Indians. After some preliminary negotiations a group of sixty Indians crossed the river on August 29, 1804, to meet the Americans. They greeted each other under the stars and stripes which fluttered from a flag pole nearby. All went well. Meetings, weapons demonstrations, and exchange of gifts continued for three days. Finally, the pipe of peace (calumet) was smoked, and on September 1st the Americans continued upriver.

Future encounters with the Sioux and other Indian tribes would be more tenuous, but through Lewis' patience, skillful negotiations, and, perhaps, some luck, there was only one violent conflict on the entire trip: when returning through Montana, the Americans killed two Indians as they attempted to steal guns and horses. Only one voyager died on the trip, apparently from appendicitis. He is buried on a bluff near Sioux City, Iowa.

Kirby was hungry after his swim, so we found an all-you-can-eat chicken and ribs restaurant near the lake and fueled up for the next day's ride. Despite the highway traffic and the roaring music from the Lazy D Saloon, we slept just fine. Apparently, some fresh air and exercise, a good meal, and lack of mental stress easily overcame the background noise.

11

BLUE ROADS, CORN, AND THE FOURTH OF JULY

(Days 36-44)

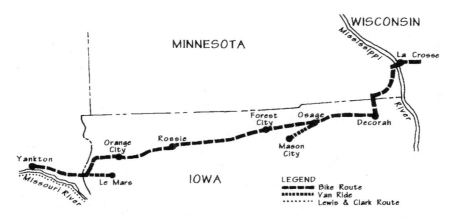

It was sixty-eight degrees and threatening rain when we left camp on July 3rd to bike across the Missouri River, carrying rain gear for the fourth day in a row. The old drawbridge was double-decked, with one deck for each direction of traffic. There were no shoulders or sidewalks, so we had to hustle to avoid holding up traffic. On the other side we stopped to take pictures of the bridge and river, after which we looked for a place to have a hot breakfast. Surely there would be something open-- wrong again. On Sunday morning in the Midwest everything is closed, so we headed east, low on caffeine and carbohydrates.

The original plan was to angle northeast to Beresford, South Dakota, then east to Orange City, Iowa. Because of the holiday weekend, there were no vacancies in Orange City, and the only one Mary Anna could find was in Le Mars, Iowa. So Le Mars it was. We were on a county road which ran parallel to State Route 50. Kirby was looking forward to visiting the town of Violin that was only slightly out of our way (music is one of Kirby's passions). Mary Anna was waiting for us where we expected to turn north for Violin. She reported that Violin was very small, nothing was open, and that Route 50, to the south, had an excellent shoulder and light traffic and would more likely have an open restaurant. Kirby was still determined to see Violin, but we outvoted him and headed for Route 50. As we approached Route 50, there was a sign pointing north to *Volin*. I checked the map again, and, sure enough, we had earlier misread the spelling. There never was a Violin, so harmony settled among us again.

We moved right along on Route 50 despite a light, but constant, head wind. Roger and I were bent low over our profile bars while Kirby the Wind Slayer led the way. I had a strange thought while drafting behind Roger. So far Kirby'd had accidents in alternating states--Oregon and Wyoming. He'd made it through Washington, Idaho, and Nebraska unscathed. Did that mean he was due for trouble again in South Dakota? At that point I looked up, and I was about to collide with Roger. It was too late to avoid hitting him as I was going nearly 20 mph and he was stopping to fix a flat tire. The noise sounded like a severe accident as my bike and body crunched into his, part of it being my panicked yell. My bike went one direction and my body another, but somehow Roger was still upright, just as he had remained after Kirby rear-ended him in Wyoming. Thanks to the protection of my rain gear, I was not injured, and somehow Roger was not either. While getting back on my feet I looked over to survey the damage to our bikes, remembering the sight of Kirby's bent front wheel in Wyoming. Miraculously, Roger's bike was unscathed, and mine only had a broken arm pad (part of the profile bar). I calmed down as Roger fixed his flat tire, but only after ripping the visor off my helmet and tossing it into the ditch. Mary Anna had rigged a visor system by cutting off a visor from a baseball cap and attaching it to the helmet with Velcro. It was nice to have when facing the morning sun, but it cut down on visibility, especially when bent over profile bars. I had barely missed colliding with Roger in Wyoming under similar circumstances. The visor had to go, or at least that was one way to reduce my feelings of guilt and stupidity.

Dick's Dictate No. 3 - "Visors and profile bars don't mix."

Mary Anna met us near Vermillion and directed us to a restaurant next to the University of South Dakota campus. It had rained hard after our mishap, so it was good to dry out as well as have a hot brunch. Vermillion is also home to the Shrine to Music Museum, with over six thousand rare antique musical instruments. Knowing Kirby's love of music and especially after missing "Violin," we agreed to visit the museum after lunch. Unfortunately it was not open because of the holiday so we pedaled on to Richland, the Big Sioux River, and Iowa. I guess it was just not meant to be Kirby's day for music.

Storm Clouds gathered as we approached the Big Sioux, so we loaded up the bikes in a hurry and barely got under cover before the rain started. Anxious to celebrate the Fourth in a small town, we made reservations for two nights at the Amber Inn Motel.

The Fourth could not have been better scripted. Le Mars was celebrating its quasquicentennial (QQC, 125-year) anniversary, as well as Independence Day, and there were wall-to-wall activities planned. By mid-morning the skies were blue, so Mary Anna and I biked around town. The Le Mars Sentinel (first published in 1871) had a special insert on the QQC events, which ran from June 30th through the Fourth of

July. We had missed the previous day's fun: Fly-in Breakfast at the airport, Open Trap Shoot at the Sportsmen's Club, Antique Tractor Exhibit at Dave Hawkins' farm, Talent Show, Ice Cream Social featuring Blue Bunny ice cream at the Methodist Church, Coon Creek Model Railroad Open House, and the Free Watermelon Feed. But we didn't miss much on the Fourth. The Rumbles were in concert at Westmar University playing music from the last three decades. (Westmar was associated with the United Evangelical Church of the Midwest for many years but was then being purchased by the city of Le Mars.) We stopped and listened for awhile. It was a little loud for our middle-aged tastes, but the youthful crowd loved it. The whole town was like a Norman Rockwell painting: families walking to the concert with their kids, dogs, lawn chairs, and picnic baskets; four little girls with a lemonade stand; clapboard houses on tree-lined streets; and American flags flying from nearly every house and store. We wondered if this was a new section of Disneyland or a real place. It turned out to be very real.

Kirby took his own tour of Le Mars in the morning while Roger cleaned up his bike and watched the World Cup soccer matches. We got back together for dinner and were happy to find the Country Kitchen restaurant. This one was our first since leaving the west coast that was totally non-smoking, with a menu that included grilled as well as fried food, a welcome change.

After dinner we walked over to Foster Park where the Le Mars Community Chorus and Municipal Band were giving concerts. The bandstand in the center of the park was draped with flags, and the grassy areas were covered with lawn chairs and blankets as people of all ages enjoyed the music. As I drifted around the crowd taking pictures I noticed a group of girls in their early teens that seemed to be following me. One finally came up and asked what I was doing. "Oh, just taking some pictures and doing a story for *The New York Times* on the Le Mars QQC celebrations," I said, with a half-serious twinkle in my eye. That got their attention. "Would you take our pictures?" they asked, trying to be innocent and glamorous at the same time. "Sure," I answered, and there went another half of a roll of film. But I did finally tell them the truth. They frowned at first but then giggled and ran off.

An information booth was set up in the park, so I picked up some background material on Le Mars.

Settlers, a Railroad, and a Name

The first settlers--Captain B.F. Betsworth, his wife, ten sons, and four daughters--came to the area in 1866 and squatted on land owned by the

Illinois Central Railroad. By 1869, the railroad selected the site for town development. It was common practice for the railroads to develop towns in Iowa every ten to twelve miles along the railway near water sources. The railroads sold the land, which had been given to them by the government as a subsidy, as a way of recouping some of their construction costs. A spacing of ten to twelve miles was about the right distance considering the use of horse-drawn wagons for farm-to-market transportation.

The name Le Mars is neither Indian nor French and has a unique origin. When the town was platted in 1870 and lots were offered for sale, a group of railroad executives, their associates, and their wives came to the site to celebrate. The wives were asked to propose a name for the new town. Their first names were Lucy, Elizabeth, Mary, Anna, Rebecca and Sarah; thus the town name was derived by using the first letters of the ladies' first names.

And Captain Betsworth eventually owned his property legally, buying it from the town, to whom it had been deeded by the railroad.

The English are Coming

Some wealthy English families bought land in and around Le Mars in the 1870s and sent over their second sons to learn how to farm and raise stock. They brought culture and high living to Le Mars but were more interested in playing polo, hosting parties, and visiting the pubs than working. At one point, Le Mars had a famous polo team, but the English enterprise eventually failed and the young Englishman returned home. Serious farming would be left to the German, Dutch, Irish, and Scandinavian immigrants that came before and after the English invasion.

The Kiwanis Club was selling fifty-cent Blue Bunny ice cream bars and was doing a brisk business in the warm, humid evening. (Blue Bunny ice cream is made in Le Mars, and the town has been designated by the Iowa Legislature as "The Ice Cream Capital of the World.") As the crowd was leaving after the concert, one of the ice cream vendors was trying to get rid of the last few bars, so Kirby surprised us all by aggressively negotiating a price for the final four. He returned with a smile, proudly announcing that he got all four for a dollar (half of the asking price), giving Lynn credit for enhancing his bargaining skills.

After the band's final encore the crowd dissipated, and most walked, as we did, the half-mile to the Plymouth County Fairgrounds for the 10:00 p.m. fireworks display. Cicadas were chirping and lighting bugs brightened our way as we strolled along the sidewalks. These were new sights and sounds for Roger, our native Californian. Kirby and Mary Anna reminisced about their youth, especially about capturing lightning bugs and putting them in a jar in hopes they would produce enough light to read by (apparently it never works, but all kids try it).

It seemed like all of Le Mars' 8,276 people came to the fireworks display (funded by receipts from voluntary collection of aluminum cans). It was an awesome show; Roger commented that it was the most impressive fireworks display he had ever seen. Seven hundred rockets were fired over a thirty-minute period, beautifully choreographed to recorded music. Fire and safety regulations were more relaxed than we were used to, as the support crew were dressed in sandals and shorts rather than fire-resistant suits, and the crowd was right up close to the action. A John Philip Souza march accompanied the finale, a forty-eight-inch rocket that left a mighty red glare in the sky. As the crowd dispersed, it was a quiet walk back to the motel, each of us reflecting in our own way about how lucky we were to be in Le Mars, Iowa, on the Fourth of July, 1994.

Mosquitoes were thick at the Big Sioux River bridge on the morning of July 5th, so we unloaded the bikes and got going in a hurry. Remembering our problems of finding breakfast in South Dakota, we stopped at the first source of pancakes we saw. Akron was just six miles down the road, and good smells were drifting out of the café. Someone commented to Roger before the trip that pancakes increase in size as you travel inland and then decrease after crossing the Mississippi. So far we agreed with that observation, and the Akron Café continued the trend. Their pancakes may not have been the thickest, but each one covered an entire dinner plate. We were well fueled for the day's ride to Orange City.

Pedaling eastward, away from the Big Sioux River, we climbed a little in elevation and soon could see cornfields stretching to the horizon in all directions. There was hardly a sound, almost no traffic, and very little sign of activity--not a town or tractor in sight, just corn. Every mile or two a gravel road crossed at right angles, and a farm house was visible well back from the road. It was a little eerie. How did all this corn get here? I wondered. Who is taking care of it and where are they? And there was no sign of irrigation. Mother nature was supplying the water to Iowa's cornfields without any help from man. Seeing that deep, black soil between the rows of corn, I could understand why Iowa is almost synonymous with farming. I'd heard it was the nation's top producer of corn, and that July day I had no doubt it was true.

We saw few trees in Iowa except where man intended for them to be, in towns and around farm houses. After rolling over miles of gentle hills and still seeing oceans of corn, we were thrilled to finally see some trees and a water tower in the distance. In much of the West and Midwest, trees and water towers, as well as grain elevators, are the sure signs of a town. The bright orange water tower on the edge of town was like a large sign saying, "Welcome to Orange City." It was a happy as well as symbolic color, and we all smiled as we pedaled by.

Orange City was settled by Dutch pioneers who obviously worked to maintain their Dutch heritage. It was named after William of

Orange (a Dutchman). The Chamber of Commerce brochure was titled "Welkom to Orange City" and listed the town's services in both languages: Education (Onderwijs), Worship (Kerken), Industry (Bedrijven), etc. A tulip festival is held on the third week in May every year, and a windmill houses a drive-in branch of the Northwestern Bank. Northwestern College, the pride of the town, has a Reformed Church Seminary. The Dutch Colony Inn, our home for the night, was as clean as a pin, with hand-painted flowers on the shutters adding a special touch.

After such an introduction, we were anxious to see the rest of town and to find a place to eat, and we were not disappointed. The Sioux County courthouse was a beautiful stone structure that looked like it was built to last centuries, and the old downtown was like a real Dutch village. We chose The Hatchery restaurant for dinner. Further west, such a name would have inferred a fish hatchery. In Iowa it refers to chickens; fifty years earlier the building had been a chicken hatchery. Roger and I ordered a recommended dark beer before dinner. It was Leinenkugal, a Wisconsin brew with rich amber color and a tangy, but not too tart, taste, an excellent beer, the best I'd had since leaving the west coast. Most people in America still seem to prefer the popular, what I consider boring and bland, beers. After our son Mike introduced me to the richer, darker varieties, I much prefer them. Maybe the rest of the country will eventually catch on. And dinner at The Hatchery was great.

Orange City also had a publishing company with systems to read Mary Anna's disk and print out newsletter #5. One of the employees overheard her describing the bike trip and came over to find out more. The publishing company was his day job; his passion was bicycling, and his second job was at the local bicycle shop.

The TV news announced another tornado watch nearby. Rain poured from the sky later that evening. So far our luck with the weather had been uncanny; most of the hard rains had been at night when we were indoors. The nights we chose to camp were sometimes windy but never wet.

The publishing/bicycle store guy recommended that we ride on the "blue roads" as much as possible. These are the county roads that are shown in blue on Iowa's transportation map, and the route signs are bright blue with yellow numbers and letters. "Most are paved and traffic is very light," he promised. "The blue roads are the best way to bike across Iowa." We took his advice and were never sorry. The only problem we had was occasionally needing help from local folks when signs were infrequent. Non-cycling Iowans were not familiar with the term "blue roads," nor did they relate to the route numbers. They simply referred to them as the "blacktop" to Alta or Hanover or wherever. Once having bridged that communication gap we were fine.

The blue roads are laid out in cardinal (north-south and east-west) directions as are most of the other roads in Iowa. As you fly over the state and, in fact, most of the western two-thirds of the country, the farm fields and towns look like checkerboards with neat perpendicular boundaries. We can credit that to the Federal Land Ordinance of 1785.

The Checkered Landscape

Shortly after the Revolutionary War, the United States needed a method to quickly define and subdivide the lands being acquired from the Indians in the Northwest Territories (between the Ohio River and the Canadian border). A rectangular system of surveys was established, originally in ten-mile squares and later standardized to six-mile-square townships. The system was later used throughout all western territories, with the exception of Texas. Some have criticized the system for dividing irregular terrain into regular squares. But it served its purpose well, facilitating the transfer of an area larger than western Europe from public to private ownership in less than one hundred years. In Iowa it took less than thirty years.

The process was meant to be orderly: 1) Land was acquired from the Indians, usually by treaty. Negotiations and security were assigned to the Army; 2) Surveyors laid out the townships and subdivided each township into thirty-six one-mile-square sections of 640 acres each, with maps drawn for each township. Property was set aside for Indian reservations, towns, and schools, and later for railroads, national parks, national forests, and other public needs; 3) Government land offices were set up in the newly opened territories to serve the new settlers and document their claims; 4) Settlers occupied their claims and, after verifying their ability to live off the land, acquired title to it; 5) Roads were built on the section-line boundaries between claims to provide access to and minimize impact on the private property.

The process never worked perfectly. Sometimes Indians were reluctant to leave; sometimes settlers squatted on land before it was surveyed (as did the first citizen of Le Mars, Iowa); and sometimes cattlemen who had grazed their herds freely on the public land were reluctant to leave when settlers came and legally claimed it (as happened to Jules Sandoz in Nebraska). But overall, the system worked effectively, as evidenced by the square cornfields in Iowa and roads that follow section lines between those fields.

We stopped for B-2 in Sutherland (population 897) that morning. The van arrived ahead of us and parked in front of a building with "Café" painted on the window, so we figured it must be the place. Mary Anna was in the van getting ready to leave and pointed out where the café actually was. It was not in the building in front of the van or in the other one down the block with another café sign; rather, it was in a building halfway between, with no sign at all.

In the café, some farmers were discussing the recent hail storm and the crop conditions on their farms. Periodically one of them would get up and help himself to coffee from the pot on the counter. A sign read, "Freida Miller's Birthday Coffee." It seems that on someone's birthday, he or she is expected to provide coffee at the café for the day. The waitress told us that it was almost always someone's birthday in town so people rarely had to pay for coffee (897 people divided by 365 days per year equals over two birthdays per day). "Don't be shy," she said. "Just help yourself to the second cup and you'll fit right in."

A sign above the counter reminded us of a similar one in Baker City at Oregon's Blue and White Café:

COFFEE PRICES

One cup with refill	$0.40
One hour, same chair	$0.70
Half the morning (includes rest room visit)	$1.50
All day (bring your own lunch)	$3.00
All day (lunch at home)	$2.50
Spoon knockers, whistlers, cup wavers, thumb snappers, fanny pinchers, and liars all pay double	

We gladly helped ourselves to coffee and will always remember the hospitality and the scorn for advertising at Sutherland's "no name" café.

It was a fine day on the blue roads: flat, cool, and sunny, with little wind after the storms of the previous few days. I was humming and whistling a lot, without thinking about it. Maybe it was just a natural, involuntary reaction to being so relaxed in such a peaceful setting and the tunes just rolled out. I began to notice then that some of the mailboxes along the way were quite creative. They were mounted in unique ways, using various parts of old farm implements and painted to emphasize the farm's name or the farmer's products or hobbies. They were works of art; I began to photograph some that appeared to be custom-made and wished I had started earlier. Maybe that will be another book someday.

With towns so small and infrequent along the blue roads, we packed sandwiches for lunch, just in case. We nearly pedaled right by Rossie (population 72), that was one hundred yards or so off County Road B-53, but an unusual sign caught our eye. It was mostly black, and the name "Rossie" stood out with an arrow pointing to the town. A closer look revealed rear-view silhouettes of three horses and the words "More Than a One-Horse Town." With a sign like that, how could we pass up Rossie?

Turning right at the grain elevators, we noticed a small metal building with a gas pump outside. It was the town grocery, gas station, café, and general store. Kirby went in to ask if there was a place in town where we could picnic. The proprietor pointed out the picnic area just down the street but warned us of the mosquitoes and invited us to come back and eat in her store if they were too bad. They were too bad, so we quickly retreated to the store. She motioned us to a table and made us feel at home even though we were not ordering food.

In the only other booth in the store a farmer and his three young sons were enjoying ice cream cones. Roger asked him about his farm and how his crops were doing compared to the previous year when the Midwest was so terribly flooded. His farm was nearly seven hundred acres in size (a little over one section, or just over one square mile), which he said was about average for Iowa. His corn and soybeans were doing well so far that year and would be fine if no hail or wind storms came by. He had no cattle. Beef was too risky, he said. Some farmers were losing $100 per head that year, but on a good year they could make $200 per head. He had a few hogs, but he was not sure if he would the next year. Hogs had done well in the past, but then "out-of-town" doctors and lawyers began investing in hogs. So too many hogs were being raised, and the price was dropping (we had noticed quite a few pig sties under construction that morning). The kids sat patiently as their dad filled us in on the rigors of Iowa farming. But he smiled through it all and likely never dreamed of doing anything else.

We each bought a dessert snack and, before leaving, asked about water to fill our bottles. The proprietor insisted on collecting all of our bottles and filling them from her personal supply of ice water in her back-room apartment. She even added ice cubes to each bottle. We thanked her and commented that, indeed, Rossie is far more than a one-horse town.

Mary Anna also thoroughly enjoyed Iowa's blue roads, with a routine down pat and more time to herself. She found classical music stations on the radio most of the time and enjoyed being immersed in the corn and soybean fields, clear air, and music. The van was like a freighter on an ocean voyage that stopped a couple of times a day to feed and nourish lone sailors in their dinghies. She had been busier further west due to the great distances between towns, lodging uncertainty, and concern for our safety. And further east there would be many route options and a need to stay in closer touch with us. Iowa was in between and just right for her.

Except for a few little right-angle jogs, Route B-53 continued dead east for the rest of the day. Those little jogs were due to adjustments in the section lines. As perfectly square sections could not be continually laid on a round earth, every so often adjustments had to be made. Thus the sections were not always perfectly square and the roads not always perfectly straight.

Roger and I were lagging behind as we pedaled into Emmetsburg, our home for the night. As we approached the town square, we saw Kirby sitting on a park bench talking to an older man who appeared to be a retired farmer. We waved and went by, as Mary Anna had made reservations at the Suburban Motel and had given us directions to it. I couldn't help but smile at the sight of Kirby in his colorful bicycle clothes sitting next to that man in his bib overalls and straw hat. Kirby had lived all over the country at various times and seemed to feel at home everywhere and with everyone. Kirby told us later that the conversation was primarily one way as the farmer was quizzing him about our trip and didn't volunteer much about life in Emmetsburg. I regret not stopping to take a picture of them, the Californian cyclist and Iowa farmer chatting on a park bench.

The Suburban Motel had a nice pool, and the large, clean rooms were probably our best of the trip and definitely worth a repeat stay. Kirby attended a high school baseball game that evening while Roger, Mary Anna, and I toured the town and the adjoining Five Island Lake. Northern central Iowa is known as the lakes region of the state and looks a lot like Minnesota. The lakes add variety to the rich farm landscape, but they cause a few more jogs in the roads.

Skies were gray the next morning so we carried rain gear, but fortunately we didn't need it. We certainly got wet all right but only from the inside. High humidity would be with us the rest of the way, and our clothes were damp with sweat after just the first few miles.

It was 10:00 a.m. and Fenton (population 394) looked like it ought to have a café, but the only place open with hot food was the North Star Bar and Grill. They didn't serve breakfast but were happy to fix us some hamburgers. The only other patron in the bar was interested in our trip as he was a Boston Red Sox fan and had a sister living in Novato, California. He asked if we were going to ride in the RAGBRAI while we were in Iowa. The annual bike tour that crosses Iowa had come by Fenton a couple of times, and he'd watched the thousands of cyclists stream by. We'd heard of the RAGBRAI but were not sure of the exact initials or what they stood for. He cleared that up for us: "Register's (the *Des Moines Register* sponsors the ride) Annual Great Bicycle Ride Across Iowa." He chuckled and said, "You can always tell where RAGBRAI has gone by looking for the yellow cornstalks along the road." He explained that the corn is tall enough during the July ride to offer privacy for those riders who need to relieve themselves.

Despite the unusual breakfast food, we have fond memories of the friendly conversation at Fenton's North Star Bar and Grill. Mary Anna had a hamburger with us and then left to find lodging in Forest City.

The rain was still holding off, but just barely, as we pedaled into Titonka (population 648), looking for food and drink. The grocery store looked like our best bet. There was plenty of food but a limited assortment of drinks. We chose a one-liter soft drink bottle but couldn't find any cups. Sensitive to our plight, the proprietor offered to call her daughter at home and have her bring us some cups. We were somewhat embarrassed that she would even propose such a generous act as there were other individual drinks in the store. We thanked her but decided to buy other drinks. Hearing about our trip, she described Titonka's primary tourist attraction, an old silo that has been converted into a five-story house. It was just south of town, and she offered to call the owner and arrange a private tour for us. As it was in the wrong direction, we declined but left with smiles, once again amazed at the friendliness of people in small-town America.

When Mary Anna left us, our plan was to take Route B-16 east to U.S. Highway 69, then north to Forest City. In mid-afternoon we decided to jog north earlier and come into town on B-14, going by Crystal Lake and staying on the blue roads all the way. If we lost touch with Mary Anna, we were confident she would just leave us a pink Post-It note at the post office (little did we know at the time that Post-It notes come from the 3M Company's distribution center in Forest City). We were oblivious to the darkening sky, as it was warm and humid and we couldn't get much wetter than we already were. But this time Mary Anna was concerned. At one of the motels she checked out someone mentioned that a tornado had been sighted ten miles south of town, and a tornado watch was in effect for the general area. So off she went down Highway 69, but she could find no cyclists. Then she drove west on B-16 and still no cyclists. By this time she was concerned about herself as well as us as the van was probably more vulnerable than we were. We could always find a ditch to lie in, but it would have been hard to hide the van, so she headed back to Forest City to seek shelter. But her motherly instinct kicked in again, and she made one more effort to find us on B-14 (on the Forest City map it was called the "Blacktop to Crystal Lake"). She saw us just west of town, poking along by the Winnebago RV plant. After hearing the weather status, we hustled on to the Chateau Motor Inn and arrived just before the skies opened. Kirby said it was the hardest rain he had ever seen. It was falling sideways, with visibility at less than twenty feet. Someone had to be watching out for us as not only had we just missed a tornado, but the rain held off, again, until after we'd finished the day's ride and were comfortably indoors.

Forest City was on our itinerary because we wanted to visit the Winnebago Industries plant. Winnebago is one of America's first major producers of motor homes and is still an industry leader. Friends of ours work for Winnebago, leading tours around the country, so we had heard about Forest City for a long time. The company was founded in the late

1950s while the town was in the midst of an economic crisis. Railroad traffic had declined, and nearby Mason City was drawing away farm-support business. A commission was formed to seek new industries for the town. One of its members, John Hanson, a local furniture dealer, had just returned from a trip to California and was convinced that Americans still loved mobility. He started Winnebago Industries in his home town, led its growth, and, by 1968, Forest City had more millionaires per population than any other town in the Midwest. The town's population was 2,900 and dropping when John Hanson started his company. By 1994, nearly that many worked at the Winnebago plant and the town had grown to 4300.

Our tour of the Winnebago plant was limited, as the production line was closed down for annual maintenance. We saw all of the facilities and partially built motor homes but no assembly-line activity. Several completed models were open for inspection, some with price tags over $100,000. One of the couples in our tour were Winnebago owners who left their motor home at the plant for repairs and were enjoying a couple of days of Forest City hospitality.

We were back on our bikes at 11:00 a.m. and heading east with a strong tail wind. It was another one of those days when it was just fun to go fast, and we covered the forty-two miles to Osage in two and a half hours. Kirby had arranged for us to spend the next couple of nights with the Roods, his relatives in Mason City. Mason City was a little south of our route so we planned to stop at some point north of town, load up the bikes, and drive there. Kirby and I were ready to load up in Osage, while Roger wanted to take advantage of the favorable winds and go further. He was outvoted though, and, after one more milkshake, we were off to Mason City.

Mary Dean Miller's cousin Janis and her husband Jed are actually natives of Nebraska but longtime residents of Mason City. Jed teaches junior high social studies and driver's education. He played football at the University of Nebraska, coached for awhile, and looks like he could still make an open-field tackle if he had to. Janis is obviously from the same stock as her cousin Mary Dean--bright, warm, and inquisitive. She made us all feel like part of her family, a treat after six weeks of campgrounds and motels.

A town tour was the first order of business. Mason City is the home of Meredith Wilson. His play *The Music Man* was written about his hometown Mason City, nicknamed River City. Our first stops were the footbridge and library that were written into the musical. The footbridge crosses one of the several rivers and creeks that pass through town, thus the nickname. Next stop was a group of familiar-looking contemporary homes near the footbridge. They were designed by students of Frank Lloyd Wright and look a bit like Wright's home, Taliesen, in Wisconsin. A bank and hotel in town were designed by Wright himself. The last and best stop was Birdsalls' ice cream parlor where Kirby had his third milkshake of the day.

That evening the Roods explained why we had seen some teenagers in town with muddy shoes and legs: they had probably been de-tasseling hybrid-seed corn. Silk from selected rows must be pulled off by hand before pollination can contaminate the hybrid strain. The going rate for de-tasseling was $100 per acre, a great summer job for Iowa's young people and in the Rood's case, their entire family. Two people could do one acre per day, and if it had rained recently, they would come home muddy from the knees down. The surrounding corn and soybean fields keep a lot of folks occupied in and around Mason City.

Railroads, Concrete, and Cars

Things were quiet around Mason City until the Milwaukee Railroad laid tracks through town in 1869. From then on, farmers had a fast and efficient way to transport their crops to the eastern states and around the world. By 1909 five lines converged at Mason City: the Iowa Central, the Great Western, the Chicago and North Western, and the St. Paul and Des Moines. More emigrants came, and concrete and tile companies grew. Those corn fields needed drainage tile; Mason City companies produced it. And the first mile of concrete rural road in Iowa was constructed in 1911 between Mason City and Clear Lake, just a year after the first Colby automobile rolled out of the factory.

Automobiles were invented in Europe in the 1880s and for the first twenty years the majority of those sold in America were imports. But by 1912 the majority were made here. The Colby Motor Company, founded in Mason City in 1910, was one of a wave of new companies that made America the leading automobile manufacturer in the world. Like so many of the non-Detroit based companies, however, Colby didn't last, closing its doors in 1915. It was located a long way from raw materials, its production methods were inefficient, and its race car crashed, killing the driver and seriously damaging its reputation. But Colby had built a high-quality automobile and had been part of a revolution that helped lead America to industrial prominence. And it happened in River City.

It was day forty-three, the 9th of July, and time for a rest. Kirby rode his bike to the library to read up on the local flora while Mary Anna, Roger, and I ran some errands, including a stop at a bike store. I was still looking for the part that had broken when I rear-ended Roger in South Dakota, and I found it in Mason City. The young salesman beamed when he heard our story, said he thought he had the part, and went to the back room to look for it. That usually means rummaging around in boxes of miscellaneous parts and hoping to eventually find a reasonable match. Instead, he came back immediately with a box containing a new set of profile bars, identical to mine. "I don't have any individual pads, so I'll just pull them out of this set," he said, tearing open the box and the plastic wrappers around the pads and refusing any payment. "Just have a safe trip and tell people about River City," he said as we left. I promised we would.

Jed and Janis fueled us well that evening with a delicious meal of barbecued hamburgers, salad, baked beans, and ice cream sundaes. And a package of Lynn's chocolate chip cookies arrived by Express Mail, enough to keep us well stocked for the next few days. After a multi-course breakfast the next morning, we said our grateful farewells, loaded the bikes on the van, and drove back to Osage. It was another quiet drive as we thought about how lucky we were to encounter so many good people.

Riding from Osage to Decorah was so-so. The corn, soy beans, and blue-road traffic were fine, but it was a little bumpier, hillier, and windier than usual. Maybe there was also a little let-down after our great day in Mason City. It was good to see the outskirts of Decorah. The city is named for Wauken Decorah, a Winnebago Indian chief, who assisted white settlers during the Black Hawk Indian War.

Home for the night was the Will Baker City Park campground, located in a rustic, wooded area well outside of town, with an atmosphere more like a mountain retreat than a city park. The weather was fine, and we were ready to camp again. The campground host promised no mosquitoes, and he was right. There was also shade, a nice stream nearby, and hot showers. After setting up camp and showering, a couple in the adjoining campsite waved and asked where we were headed. They were from central Iowa and stated proudly that there was "no need to leave Iowa for vacations." They come to Decorah every summer to enjoy the hills, trout fishing, and serenity of this spacious, quiet city park. Part of me wanted to say, "But wait 'till you see the Rocky Mountains or the Pacific Ocean. Those are far more beautiful." But another voice inside said, "Shut up and listen." They were not terribly impressed by our trip, probably wondering why we would go any further when we had already found the nicest spot in Iowa. I just listened and told them how much we enjoyed Iowa's people and blue roads and corn. As we talked, I thought about how relative beauty and serenity are and how those folks had clearly found it in their own backyard. Their love of Decorah and contentment with Iowa was real, something to admire rather than argue about.

Mary Anna had scouted the town and spent most of the afternoon in the Vesterheim Museum, the largest museum in the United States devoted to a single immigrant group (Norwegian). The museum includes fifteen historic buildings and covers most of a city block. The

Vesterheim (Norwegian for western home) depicts life in Norway and the ocean crossings, as well as the pioneer days in Iowa.

Norwegian and American flags lined the main street and posters prominently announced "Nordic Fest," to be held in Decorah on July 29th through the 31st; we would just miss it. Roger commented that it would have been fun to be in Decorah the day before when the Norwegian World Cup soccer team was playing. I wondered how and when all these Norwegians came to Iowa, and about Chief Decorah and Chief Black Hawk. I remembered my Grandfather McCully telling about the Black Hawk Indian War and why his grandfather had settled in Ontario, Canada, rather than Illinois.

Indians, Norwegians, and McCullys: Moving West

At the time of the Louisiana Purchase in 1804, President Jefferson believed that there was enough land east of the Mississippi to satisfy the white man for one thousand years. The vast area west of the river was valued primarily for its fur and would be left to the Indians. His vision was soon proven unacceptable to both peoples. In 1830, present-day Iowa was still officially occupied only by Indians, many of whom had migrated from the East. By 1860, most of the Indians were gone, 600,000 white emigrants had arrived, and most of Iowa's black soil was under cultivation. Rapid change is certainly not new to the twentieth century.

Prior to the westward movement of Americans and Europeans, Iowa's Indian population was relatively small. The grass was too coarse to support large buffalo herds, so it was not the choice of plains Indians, and eastern tribes preferred more wooded areas. Some tribes lived along the Mississippi and Missouri Rivers, but few ventured inland. By 1830 some Winnebago families, including Chief Decorah, had left their native Wisconsin and settled near present-day Decorah. Chief Black Hawk and his Sauk tribe were still in Illinois where tension with the whites was growing.

Black Hawk had fought with the British in the War of 1812 and retained bad feelings toward Americans. (The British had wanted to trade with the Indians, while Americans wanted to occupy their lands.) In 1831 Black Hawk was forced to leave his tribal lands along Illinois' Rock River and to move across the Mississippi to Iowa. When he arrived at the designated site along the Iowa River, a few white squatters were already there. Angry and desperate, Black Hawk turned to his British friends in Canada for help. He heard a rumor that they would cross the border into the United States, meet him in Wisconsin, and, together with the Winnebagos, drive the Americans out of Wisconsin and Illinois. Wanting to believe the rumor, Black Hawk led his tribe back across the Mississippi and north to the Wisconsin River, skirmishing with white settlers along the way. The rumor proved false; neither the British nor Winnebagos came to his aide. The Illinois militia (including Lieutenant Abraham Lincoln) and the U.S. Army (including Captain Jefferson Davis) drove Black Hawk and his followers back across the Mississippi. Chief Black Hawk was imprisoned but later released to return to his people in Iowa.

By 1836 Iowa was open to white settlement. Most Indians were forced to re-settle further west, and almost overnight, ten thousand Americans arrived. In the 1850s the first Norwegians settled near Decorah. They wrote glowing reports back to their relatives and friends in Norway and soon became the predominant nationality in the area. Americans, Europeans, and Indians kept moving west.

There is a connection between Chief Black Hawk and my McCully ancestors. Great-great Grandfather Cyrus McCully, his wife Mary, and baby Cyrus II were migrating from Nova Scotia, Canada, to Illinois in 1831-32. They traveled by boat via the Erie Canal and Lake Erie to Cleveland and then by covered wagon as far as Indiana. Hearing of the Indian troubles in Illinois (led by Black Hawk) they decided to return to Canada, eventually settling in southern Ontario just east of Detroit. Oliver McCully (son of Cyrus II) emigrated to Ohio in the 1890s and later became a U.S. citizen and my maternal grandfather.

We all slept well next to that cool Iowa trout stream. Scores of lifetime memories and two thousand miles were behind us. Tomorrow we would leave Iowa, cut across the southeast tip of Minnesota, and cross the Mississippi into Wisconsin. More milestones and experiences lay ahead.

12

FAMILY, FRIENDS, AND RAILS-TO-TRAILS

(Days 45-49)

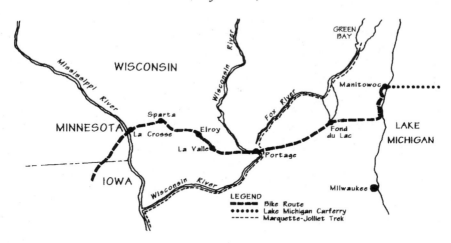

Our route plan for Wisconsin had firm anchors on the Mississippi River and Lake Michigan. On the eastern border, Manitowoc was the destination as it was the only Wisconsin port for the ferry across Lake Michigan. On the west side, the Elroy-Sparta and other connecting bike trails were a must. They had been constructed on abandoned railroad beds in 1967, the first such rail-to-trail conversions to become part of a national trail network. Beginning at La Crosse, the trail system extends seventy-five miles through Sparta and Elroy to Reedsburg. As a member of the Rails-to-Trails Conservancy, I had heard about the Elroy-Sparta trail for years and wanted very much to include it on our route. Roger had done the route planning for Wisconsin and came to the same conclusion.

So La Crosse it would be, but how would we get there? La Crosse was sixty-five miles northeast of Decorah. We could have continued east to Lansing, Iowa, on the Mississippi River, and then headed north to La Crosse on either side of the river. Highway 35 on the Wisconsin side was shown as unsuitable on the state bicycle map and Route 26 on the Iowa and Minnesota side was also questionable. We took the advice of neighbors at the campground and headed northeast on Route 76 through Caledonia and La Crescent, Minnesota, and then across the Mississippi to La Crosse.

There were a few hills in that glacial-moraine country along the Mississippi, but it was cool, the traffic, road surface, and winds were favorable, and the landscape was beautiful--a great biking day. Just fifteen miles north of Decorah we barely noticed the state border. No signs announced our departure from Iowa or entrance to Minnesota, only the subtle change in road surface and a cross road on the border named "State Border." Apparently the blue roads don't justify a more prominent sign. That corner of Minnesota reminded me of Virginia's Shenandoah Valley: soft forested hills and rich, cultivated valleys.

After a lunch stop in Caledonia, we started the final leg to La Crosse. Riding close together and in good spirits, we were all anxious to see the river and wanted to enjoy it together. A sign told us it was two miles to La Crescent, and just a few minutes later we could see the river. There was something magical about reaching the Mississippi, the largest body of water we had seen since the Pacific Ocean. Hundreds of birds were on and above the water, scores of boats lined its shores and plied its current, and there was so much history.

Steamboats, Railroads--and the Turks

The first steamboats reached the upper Mississippi in 1823, carrying supplies to Fort Snelling, near present-day Minneapolis. By 1842, several companies were operating steamboats in the region when the first settlers arrived in what would become La Crescent. A decade later, La Crosse, across the river in Wisconsin, was a booming frontier town, with two hundred steamboats a day landing there and railroad lines approaching from the East. Landowners on the Minnesota side needed a strategy to catch and surpass La Crosse as the area's premier city. First they needed a sophisticated name. The bluffs nearby formed a partial circle around the town site, and there was historic precedence for the term "crescent." During the Crusades the Turks rallied behind the crescent on their banners when fighting the Christians and their symbolic cross. So La Crescent it would be, and competition with La Crosse was underway.

La Crescent citizens chose to establish a ferry to La Crosse rather than vie for a steamboat landing, but the exorbitant rates discouraged many migrants from coming their way. They also lost out on the locations of the early railroads and railroad bridges across the Mississippi. The railway came through La Crosse but then headed north for seventy-five miles on the Wisconsin side before crossing the river. La Crescent would later get its railroad and a bridge to La Crosse, but by then the main lines had been established elsewhere. La Crescent is a nice town in a beautiful setting, but it never caught up to La Crosse in size or industrial importance. Today, barges and tug boats have replaced the steamboats on the river, and most of them still land in La Crosse.

We walked our bikes across the bridge, enjoying and photographing the scene. Just south of the bridge on the Wisconsin side, some prominent towers dominated the skyline; they looked like grain elevators from our distance. But closer inspection revealed the owner: G. Heileman Brewing Company.

Wisconsin Beer

Wisconsin is known for its dairy products, the Green Bay Packers, and Harley-Davidson motorcycles. But beer and beer makers are what many of us identify with Wisconsin as well. German immigrants brought their brewing skills to Wisconsin in the 1850s. Most of them settled in Milwaukee, and their businesses grew after many Chicago breweries were destroyed in the great Chicago Fire of 1871. By the early 1900s nearly every town in Wisconsin had a small brewery. They would be called micro-breweries today. Gottlieb Heileman started his brewery in La Crosse in 1858. His was one of the few small breweries that survived the period of national Prohibition (1920-1933). They temporarily converted to other products, then returned to beer-making after Prohibition was lifted, and today own and operate breweries in several states.

La Crosse was also where we would meet our son Matt, his wife Cindy, and their children Shane, age four, and Katie, age two. They were vacationing with friends in Minneapolis and wanted to meet and bike with us for a day. The Elroy-Sparta bike trail made La Crosse the logical rendezvous point. Matt and Cindy are both active cyclists, and they wanted to share in our adventure, as well as stop by for a visit.

Matt and family had not arrived yet when we got to La Crosse, so Roger and I took advantage of the brewery tour. It was an impressive, highly automated operation and included the "Largest Six Pack in the World." The towers we had seen from the bridge were six large aging vats arranged and dimensioned to look like giant beer cans. We browsed through the gift shop after the tour and tasting, and I considered buying a Heileman T-shirt. Roger talked me out of it.

Roger's Rule No. 10 - "Never pay to advertise for a private company."

He rationalized that a company should pay us to advertise their product, or at least they should give away their advertising items such as T-shirts. He felt it was okay to pay for a T-shirt that advertised a public or non-profit institution or place, but he didn't believe in subsidizing a for-profit company. I was not totally convinced but decided to heed Roger's advice that evening.

Matt, Cindy, and the kids had arrived by the time we got back to the motel, and after dinner we found a park near the river where Shane and Katie could run off some steam. It was great to see them. Matt was doing well as a sales executive with Travelers Insurance Company. He and Cindy had met during her senior year in high school, then went to the same university, and have been together ever since. Cindy was our first daughter-in-law, Shane our first grandchild, Katie our first granddaughter--and we all like each other. Everyone was trying to talk at once, with so much to catch up on. Smiles were broad and long-lasting that evening.

We shared some exciting news from our son, Bob. His job as a salesman for a yearbook publishing firm was not going well, so he decided to follow his passion and get back into golf. After college Bob played professionally in Canada for two years but was not doing well enough to continue. Now his idea was to start an indoor golf instruction business with video and computerized swing analysis. Penny Framstead, his fiancee, was as excited as Bob about the idea, and so were we.

Matt biked with us on the La Crosse River State Trail the next morning. He adjusted the seat on Lynn's bike and made the best of it. This twenty-two-mile trail was developed on a segment of the abandoned Chicago & North Western Railroad. We first rode right past the trail entrance, just east of La Crosse, but Matt thought he had seen the sign and talked us into going back to check it out. He was right--must have picked up that trait from his mother.

The trail was even better than we expected with a fine, well-bonded gravel surface, few road crossings, and gentle grades. Kirby compared the surface to a good clay tennis court. Small, unobtrusive signs, like miniature road signs and billboards, informed us of road crossings, bridges, towns, and services ahead. Occasionally an advertisement was painted on the side of a barn like those along rural roads in the East and Midwest, but these were directed at cyclists rather than car and truck drivers. The railroad, and now the trail, bisected small towns every ten to twelve miles. In Bangor, a large sign painted on the back of a commercial building, facing the trail, said, "Welcome Trail Users." A list of services such as restaurants, lodgings, and bike shops was keyed to a map of the town. People on the trail waved and smiled. It was the most bicycle-friendly atmosphere any of us had ever seen. As it is also used for snow-mobiling in the winter, the trail has been a year-around economic asset for those towns, so they smile at customers as well as guests. Whatever their motivation, it worked, and we were very happy to be there.

The landscape changed gradually from cultivated fields to pastures full of well-fed dairy cows to meandering streams and forests. A farmer on a tractor in an adjoining field waved as we pedaled by. While we were snapping pictures of a bridge, some cyclists, coming from the other direction, stopped and told us of the tunnels ahead on the Elroy-Sparta section. "You'll need flashlights," they said. "It's dark and wet in the tunnels, and the surface is pretty rough." Kirby and I had lights so we figured we could get by. "But you'll love it!" they yelled back as they started across the bridge.

Mary Anna, Cindy, and the kids joined us for lunch in Sparta at a 1950s-style A&W drive-in. Sparta seems to be the commercial hub for these trails with several bike rental stores and lodging catering to cyclists. If there was a heaven for cyclists, it would probably be something like Sparta, Wisconsin, and those trails. The old railroad station has been converted to an administrative office for the state's Department of Natural Resources (DNR), the agency that manages the trail. We stopped in to picked up some literature and buy our daily bike passes, as there are no entry gates along the trail. Passes are available at most public and commercial facilities nearby, and they just trust the honor system.

Cindy joined us on Mary Anna's bike for the thirty-two-mile ride to Elroy, while Mary Anna had a full afternoon with her grandchildren. Cindy is also an avid photographer, so we had a lot of fun looking for just the right scene or pose. "Oh, you've got to see this one," she exclaimed as she knelt down so that branches and wildflowers perfectly framed some cows, a fence line, and a distant barn. Soon we could see an Amish family moving slowly down a nearby road in their horse-drawn buggy. We honored their desire not to be photographed but were curious about their beliefs and lifestyle. We were in no hurry that afternoon; we just wanted to savor it all.

Signs indicating a tunnel ahead surprised us. We knew it was close, but the gentle grade and forest cover disguised the approaching hills. An artistic stone archway framed the tunnel entrance. Huge wooden doors that would be closed during heavy snowstorms were open for the summer. It was a definite photo opportunity and time for a maxi-butt-break. About twenty cyclists were milling about the entrance, taking pictures, looking for, or putting away, their flashlights, and swapping trail stories. Most of them were junior high kids on a church outing, sort of contained chaos. They were going our way and would be with us for the next several miles. Oh well, we thought, nothing stays perfect forever.

The cyclists we talked to in the morning were right about the tunnel. It was cool inside from the constantly dripping water. Little streams and puddles soaked our feet as we picked our way along the rough surface. Flashlights were a must as it was pitch black within the first one hundred feet of the quarter-mile-long tunnel. Flashlight beams, directed by the junior high kids, were pointed more at the ceiling than the trail surface. And the kids competed to see who could generate the loudest echo. But it was still a lot more fun than the freeway tunnel in Oregon, and in a few minutes we could see light at the other end.

The rest of the afternoon was perfect: two more shorter tunnels, three small towns, good company, and beautiful countryside. Kirby identified a woodchuck and several birds and flowers and relished the traffic-free environment. Roger is not one to show emotions easily, but he was smiling inside and out all day. He admitted, "This is the only five-star day of the trip so far; biking today is as good as it gets."

As we approached the trail head near Elroy, Shane and Katie saw us and came running. They had been "helping" grandma in her support duties by finding a place to stay and scouting out the town, including a couple of stops at playgrounds. Matt, Cindy, and the kids were returning to Minneapolis that night, so after we all showered, I drove them back to Sparta, where they had left their car. It was tough to say good-bye; it had been a six-star day for me, because they had been part of it.

But it wasn't quite over. Before starting back to Elroy I stopped by the A&W drive-in for a milkshake. Forgetting there were two bikes on top, I pulled under an overhang to place my order, and I heard a gruesome crunch. Fortunately, only the car rack and the saddle on Lynn's bike were damaged, and Mary Anna was able to find replacement parts the next day. I'm glad Shane and Katie didn't see me do that.

Back in Elroy things did not go well either. All of the restaurants and grocery stores were closed by the time Mary Anna and the guys were ready to eat, so it was canned beef stew and stale bread for supper.

Skies were gray the next morning, so we took along our rain gear, as well as the daily supply of trail mix and water. Cafés were open in Elroy, so we got an early hot breakfast, but the pancakes were of mediocre quality. Moreover, a strong wind was coming out of the east and the bike trail (the "400" trail segment) was not up to the previous day's standard. This was not a good start. And in just a few miles we ran into an obstruction on the trail. A tree had been blown down by the previous night's heavy winds, and we had to got off of our bikes and walk them around it. Roger and I mounted up to continue riding, but Kirby stopped to move the tree off the trail. Although we turned back to help, Kirby managed to move it by himself. Roger got a picture of Kirby moving that tree and of me observing, not one of my proudest moments but a gold star for Kirby.

Further on some horses and riders came our way. The stretch between Wonewoc and La Valle has a parallel horse trail. Those folks in Wisconsin were making full use of that abandoned railroad grade. As we entered La Valle, an old high-wheeled bicycle caught our attention. It was permanently mounted on a stand with a sign that read, "Trail Break--Refreshments," with an arrow pointing to a small café/bar/pizza parlor. How could we not investigate? There was only one other customer in the café, so the owner had time to chat over coffee. He had been in business for over a year and was doing okay, catering primarily to the folks on the trail. La Valle's 450 citizens provided some business but not enough to keep him afloat. We were there on a cool, wet Wednesday. He said the place was busy all day on warmer summer days and weekends, and winter was the best season. Apparently snowmobilers love pizza and beer. I have a feeling that some of them spend as much time in that café as they do on their machines.

The Trail Break Café also has a colorful logo by the entrance with images of a bicycle, a snowmobile, and a horse arrayed around the words "Trail Break" and a list of services. I noticed some T-shirts on a shelf in the corner with the same logo embossed on the front. Did I dare incur Roger's ridicule and pay to advertise for a private enterprise? Yes! They were high quality T-shirts, the logo was beautiful, and I wanted to support such an enterprise. Roger just smiled and even helped me pick one out, but he didn't go so far as to buy one himself.

The trail ended at Reedsburg, and we were back on the road and learning to cope with traffic. After a day and a half on the trails, we were spoiled forever. It took awhile to comfortably share the road with cars and trucks again. Fortunately the transition was gradual, as over the next fifteen miles to Baraboo, traffic was light, the road was okay, and the farms were beautiful. But the final fifteen-mile leg to Portage was a nightmare: heavy traffic, no shoulder, and very rough surface. Unfortunately we had not carefully studied our *Wisconsin Bicycle Map*. This terrific map, published by the state, classifies roads for cyclists and lists services, restrictions, etc. It recommends a different route from Reedsburg to Portage and classifies the road we were on as "unsuitable." Now we had a taste of what much of the remaining trip would be like: lots of roads to choose from, of widely varying quality for cycling. Navigation would be more complicated from now on.

Memories of the lousy road faded, and our spirits lifted as we approached the Wisconsin River. It was clear and wide, and Portage lay just across the bridge. A colorful hand-carved sign welcomed us to the city. "Portage" was in large letters, with a picture on the side showing two men, one carrying a canoe and the other a large pack. One man appeared to be an early European explorer and the other an Indian. Apparently they were portaging their canoe and supplies around rapids or maybe between bodies of water.

Louis Jolliet and Father Marquette Passed This Way

Until defeated by the British and American forces in the French and Indian War, France controlled most of the territory around the Great Lakes and between the Mississippi River and Rocky Mountains. In 1672 Louis Jolliet was instructed to find a route between the Great Lakes and the Mississippi, taking Father Marquette with him. Marquette had modest success in bringing Christianity to the Indians but had been more successful in gaining their friendship. Setting foot in Wisconsin near present-day Green Bay, they followed the Fox River to a point where a well-traveled Indian trail heads west. They investigated, and within a mile and a half found a larger river, the Wisconsin, flowing westward toward the Mississippi.

The Fox-Wisconsin transportation route was heavily used by fur traders and others under three flags: the French until 1763, the British until after the War of 1812, and finally the Americans. Fort Winnebago was built by the U.S. Army, and later the town of Portage was developed near the site where Jolliet and Marquette first encountered that westward flowing river, the Wisconsin.

At population 8,600, Portage is big enough to get lost in, and the post office was too out of the way for leaving us a note, so Mary Anna came back and met us at the edge of town with directions to the motel. She was again biking the trip in her head and finding a way to help.

We had more than one reason to smile about arriving in Portage. Bob and Rachel Fox, friends from California now living near Chicago, were driving up to meet us that evening, and Bob would be biking to Fond du Lac with us the next day. Mary Anna had success reaching Bob and Rachel on the cell-phone that afternoon, calling them while they were driving with directions to our motel. We hadn't had much luck with the phone in remote areas further west. They arrived about the same time we did, and we had a great evening catching up with each other's lives and enjoying Roger's red wine and the Foxes' Chicago bagels.

A light rain delayed our departure the next morning. Bob hadn't brought any rain gear and explained that summer showers in the midwest are usually brief and warm and that he never bothers with rain gear. It wasn't so brief that morning, so Bob reluctantly borrowed Mary Anna's rain jacket, and we were on our way. Bob had a new, up-scale racing bike. We accused him of cheating; he could probably coast uphill on that machine. It stopped raining in a little while, and Roger, Kirby, and I stopped to take off our rain gear. Bob left his on, confident that it would probably shower again soon, and it did, so we stopped again to put the rain gear back on. After another couple of stops to change, Bob started kidding us about how it was a miracle that we ever got that far when we were spending so much time changing clothes. So we kidded him about those "brief midwestern showers that never last very long." The friendly bantering went on all day. It was the most continuous conversation we'd had in weeks, and we loved it all. Bob liked to talk a lot. He rode and talked with us one at a time until that conversation slowed, then he would move on to the next...and the next...and then back to the first one. He was never boring and he listened as well as talked. He added a new spirit and enthusiasm to our group at a good time. We had been together for seven weeks and had nearly run out of things to talk about. Bob set a whole new agenda and kept us smiling all day, despite the rain.

We were on Wisconsin's blue roads, and the towns were small and widely spaced. We rode twenty-one miles to the first one, Dalton, where there were a few stores but no food or even a cup of coffee. Apparently some Amish folks lived nearby. A man with traditional beard, plain clothes, and broad-brimmed hat was talking on a pay phone while his horse and buggy waited patiently across the street. We watched briefly and then rode on another eight miles before finding a café for B-2. Although it was 11:00 a.m., Mary Anna and Rachel had talked the waitress and cook into continuing their hot breakfast menu until we arrived. The French toast and pancakes smelled awfully good as we were drying off.

The sun came out again in the early afternoon, and we took some more ribbing from Bob when we stopped to shed our rain gear. It stayed out this time, though; finally Bob said he just had to stop and take off his jacket. We were ready for him with appropriate boos and hisses.

The final twenty miles to Fond du Lac were ideal, on flat, quiet country roads with no wind--a nice way to finish another memorable day. Fond du Lac, located at the south end of Lake Winnebago, is not one of the Great Lakes, but it looked pretty great to us, about fifty miles long and twenty-five miles wide. Bob and Rachel were returning to Chicago that evening, but Roger's daughter Karen was to arrive. Karen had been in Chicago on a business trip and drove up to see her dad and bike with us for part of a day. She came with a recommendation from a Wisconsin friend that we have beer and brats (bratwurst sausage) in Fond du Lac. The town may have a French name but the population is now largely of Polish and German origin, and beer and brats are the local favorites. Bob and Rachel stayed over for dinner, and, with Karen, our crowd of seven enjoyed an early "Oktoberfest" at the Petries Bavarian House restaurant. And the beer, brats, and polish sausage were outstanding.

Changing the Guard at the "Foot of the Lake"

Winnebago Indians were the predominant tribe in southern Wisconsin in the mid-1600s, occupying three villages near the present-day site of Fond du Lac. The first white man in the area was probably Father Claude Allouez, a French Jesuit missionary, who visited the site during his explorations of southern Wisconsin between 1669 and 1672. For the French, access to Fond du Lac was from the north via Green Bay, the Fox River, and

Lake Winnebago, thus the name "Fond du Lac," meaning "far end of the lake" or "foot of the lake." The site would soon become a major fur trading center and would remain under French control for nearly one hundred years.

Like Portage, Fond du Lac was under British control from 1763 until after the War of 1812, when the area became part of the United States. And, like Iowa, immigration to Wisconsin was slow until the railroad reached the territory in the 1850s, exploding its growth from 20,000 to 750,000 between 1836 and 1860. By then, one third of the population was made up of European immigrants, most of those coming from Germany and bringing along their beer and bratwurst recipes. Fond du Lac grew with the state as a railroad, cheese-making, and recreation center, and today 38,000 citizens are thriving there.

There were hugs and farewells after dinner for Bob and Rachel. Somehow it didn't seem fair to have them leave, as Bob had inspired us to make this trip, yet he could bike only one day with us.

Later we drove around town and especially enjoyed the four-hundred-acre Lakeside Park, featuring a Victorian bandstand (once pictured on the cover of *Saturday Evening Post*). A stylish lighthouse marks the entrance to the boat harbor; it is a first-class park for a city of any size.

Karen was only up to riding for half a day, so she and Mary Anna spent the next morning driving what they thought was our route and exploring Sheboygan, on the shores of Lake Michigan. They would meet us just north of Sheboygan where Playbird Road meets Route LS. Karen would then ride north with us along the lake shore to Manitowoc, from where, on the next day, we would take the ferry across Lake Michigan.

We eventually found that intersection but were not exactly sure how we got there. After pedaling north along the shore of Lake Winnebago for a few miles, we began looking for a particular county road. Not finding it, we just took the next road east, which took us straight up the steepest hill we had yet encountered. Within a few miles we stumbled upon a road that was signed and on our map--we were found again. But a few miles later we were lost again, and so on and so on. But in this case there was never any concern. By continuing east, we would eventually intersect Route LS just before running into Lake Michigan. Wisconsin's network of blue roads is even more dense than Iowa's and not as well signed. The bicycle map was also a little hard to read. But it didn't really matter, as we just kept heading east until we encountered a town, a road, or something else that was on the map. It was surprisingly hilly but sunny and calm, with good roads, light traffic, and beautiful dairy farms. So despite not knowing exactly where we were at every moment and the fact that we probably could never exactly retrace our route, Roger gave it a four-star rating, and I concurred.

Some of the farms have small commercial signs in their front lawns, indicating their affiliation with butter or cheese companies. We were definitely in dairy country.

Wisconsin's Cheese

Wheat was Wisconsin's primary crop until the 1870s when the railroads reached the western plains states. Wheat could be grown more efficiently in the wide-open country of Kansas, Oklahoma, and Nebraska, and the railroads provided rapid transportation. Thanks to refrigeration, a populace with cheese-making skills, and a visionary governor, Wisconsin avoided an economic disaster. Many of the German and Swiss immigrants knew how to make high-quality cheese. Governor William Hoard could see the potential for transporting cheese products to eastern markets, so he campaigned vigorously with Wisconsin's farmers to convert to dairy farming. The high cost of livestock and processing facilities slowed the transition, but convert they did. In 1890, ninety percent of Wisconsin's farmers had dairy cows. By the 1920s, Wisconsin was producing two-thirds of America's cheese.

Despite our wanderings, we rendezvoused with Karen and Mary Anna close to the scheduled time. After our maxi-butt-break, Karen donned Mary Anna's helmet, shoes, and gloves, hopped on her mom's bike, and headed north with us on the twenty-one-mile leg to Manitowoc.

Within a couple of miles we were along the edge of a bluff and could see Lake Michigan for the first time. It was a spectacular vista, like looking across an ocean; the opposite shore was beyond the horizon. This was Roger's first view of any of the Great Lakes, and he was awed by the sight, as were the rest of us. The colors were spectacular: a clear blue sky with scattered puffy clouds and the lake's varying shades of blue and turquoise--what an introduction to the Great Lakes. We stopped for photographs, with and without bikers in the foreground, and just enjoyed the scene. We'd reached another milestone.

After we shoved off, I was taking a lot of pictures and lagging behind the rest of the group when my rear tire seemed soft--flat tire #5. The others soon disappeared around a corner, but I was less concerned than when the same thing happened in Wyoming. It was a beautiful afternoon, and there was little chance of getting lost or dehydrated along the lake shore. But Roger was worried when he realized I was out of sight, and he turned back to find me. By then a new tube was in and I was on my way again but happy to see him nonetheless.

The road soon dropped down off the bluff, and we biked along the lake shore by waterfront homes and beaches and through small towns and farms. Karen chose a great section to ride, and she did well, keeping up with Roger all afternoon. We even had a slight tail wind and very light traffic. That stretch of Route LS is a cyclist's paradise.

Mary Anna found camping facilities at the county fairgrounds about a half-mile from our motel in Manitowoc, so Kirby chose to sleep under the stars. Before dinner, Roger and Karen drove the van back to retrieve her rental car which had been parked near where she started biking. Driving back on the interstate highway, they realized what a rich experience it is to travel on the backroads. They could not see the lake at all and were bored by the road signs and billboards that look the same everywhere. On the backroads we can see what is unique about the country, especially at 13 mph. The return drive to Manitowoc on Route LS, even at 40 mph, was far more interesting than the interstate.

The next day, the Lake Michigan ferry didn't leave until 1:00 p.m., so we had time to explore Manitowoc. Shipbuilding has been the city's main industry since before the Civil War. Schooners, fishing boats, pleasure craft, and submarines have all been launched from Manitowoc's shipyards. Yes, even submarines. During World War II, shipyards all over the country were converted in order to build military vessels. Manitowoc's subs steamed down Lake Michigan to Chicago, through the locks to the Illinois River, on to the Mississippi and New Orleans, and finally through the Panama Canal to the Pacific Ocean. Many of the Manitowoc subs saw action against the Japanese. One of them is docked and on display at the Maritime Museum.

13

THE GREATEST LAKES

(Days 50-56)

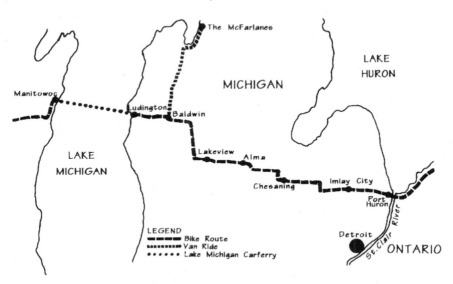

It was July 17th, a day off, and time to reflect on the 51 days, 2,600 miles, 6 states, and 56 counties that lay behind. The numbers were just that, numbers, but the names of every state and county brought back memories of what we had seen: the land and mountains and lemonade stands; the bridges and fireworks and blood-red skies; the great rivers and the greatest lakes. And who we had encountered: waitresses and cowboys; cyclists, teachers, and bums; farmers and ranchers; truckers, campers, and construction workers. And of what we had learned: of Indians and explorers and irrigation systems; of pioneers, railroads, battles, and steamboats; of fur traders, cattlemen, and homesteaders. Somehow all of these pieces formed a picture of America that was much more than fifty states on a map--and more than the evening news or a civics class or the "liberal press" or "conservative radio." It was a different kind of picture: more upbeat and solid yet continually changing, with variety, vitality, courage, and contentment. The roads we biked had taken us to quiet places where many others had left their marks and helped build our country, and where still others keep it humming today. And we still had a thousand miles to go.

We had also learned something about ourselves and each other, that we could do something far more physically demanding than we had ever done before, and we could enjoy it. We could compromise our sometimes conflicting interests and opinions to achieve a common goal. Roger was our captain and we his potentially mutinous crew. Roger lead simply because he had the strongest opinions about most issues we faced and expressed them clearly and immediately. Kirby and I also had opinions but about fewer issues, so we just followed Roger's lead most of the time. Kirby still preferred to ride hard and stop often to smell every rose along the way. I liked to smell every other rose, while Roger wanted to ride hard to reach our destination early, then intensely smell the roses nearby. Like in any partnership, finances were also a big issue. Kirby had budgeted about half as much for the trip (per person) as Roger and I, thus the frequent conflict over camping and cooking versus motels and restaurants. Mary Anna understood each of us and was the loving glue that kept us moving at a pace and in a way that pleased us all. With her help, somehow we worked everything out.

As we drove over to get in line for the ferry, Karen headed back to Chicago and her flight home. Roger was a happy guy the previous day; seeing Karen and catching up on family news was a special treat. Kirby, Mary Anna, and I were his friends, of course, but no substitute for family. Lynn Wedel and Mary Dean Miller would meet us in Michigan; then Kirby and Roger would be happier guys again.

The *SS Badger*, our ferry that day, is a coal-burning steamship that in the summer makes two round-trips daily (four hours each way) between Manitowoc, Wisconsin, and Ludington, Michigan. Built in 1952 by the Chesapeake & Ohio Railroad Company to carry railroad cars, it was later purchased by Charles Conrad, a Michigan entrepreneur, who converted it for auto, truck, and passenger service. The 410-foot-long *Badger* looks more like an ocean liner than a ferry boat, carrying up to 180 cars and trucks and 620 passengers. We noticed some other cyclists, with their fully loaded touring bikes, waiting to board.

We had to be in the ferry parking lot one hour before departure to allow time for loading by ferry company employees. There were only five or six drivers, so it took them the full hour to drive a car in, run back to get the next car, drive it in, etc. It seemed like a strange way to run a ferry; we never found out why self-loading was not allowed. Anyway, the whistle blew on schedule at 1:00 p.m., and the *SS Badger* was headed "out to sea." And it was more like a sea than a lake, as land was soon out of sight.

The first order of business was to explore the ship. And there was a lot to see: a museum, restaurants, a gift shop, a video arcade, bingo games, and even a movie theater, as well as comfortable seating inside and out on the deck. After our tour Mary Anna and I found a place on the deck and enjoyed the cool lake air. We noticed a young couple in cycling clothes and asked them about their trip. They'd left Bellingham, Washington, soon after we'd left Astoria, Oregon, and were also headed for Boston. Beven from Brooklyn and Kim from Boston had biked cross-country two years earlier with a touring group. This time they were on their own. We compared plans for the remainder of our trips and gave them one of our *New York Bicycle Touring Guides*. We asked Kim about a specific place to complete our trip in or near Boston. We wanted to dip our front wheels in the Atlantic at a scenic, uncongested location. Our maps indicated a bike path from the west side that goes all the way downtown. But that was the bay, not the ocean, and there was probably not an appropriate downtown site to dip our wheels and take pictures of the event. Kim was negative about the downtown idea as well and recommended Revere Beach, a few miles north of Boston. There were miles of uncrowded sandy beach, and it was easily accessible, so Revere Beach it would be. We exchanged addresses and phone numbers, and we promised to get in touch with Kim when we reached Boston. Their younger legs would no doubt get them there first.

It was exciting to see land again. Ludington's harbor was filled with commercial and pleasure boats, its shore lined with attractive Victorian homes. It felt a bit like we were entering a small New England town after an Atlantic crossing. A bright blue sign welcomed us to Michigan, and red, white, and blue petunias were in full bloom in the adjoining park, a warm and friendly sight.

But then came the unloading. Vehicles were brought out two or three at a time, left there until retrieved by their owners. Some owners were less attentive, so their vehicles waited there, blocking those behind. Passengers disembarked, weaving their way through moving and parked cars to the exit--and safety. Though chaotic, everyone seemed to bear it smiling, and eventually everyone found their friends and cars and whatever and headed down the road. After all, what was the rush, weren't we all on vacation? While waiting for our van to be unloaded, another cyclist from Sheboygan came by to chat. He had just completed a trip around Lake Superior (1,300 miles), winning a $1,000 bet that he could complete the trip in a month and spend no more than $700. He looked pretty ragged, but he still had $2 in his pocket, only twenty-one miles to go, and had finished in three weeks.

Cartier Park Campground, just north of the city, was home for the night. Kim and Beven (the cycling couple) had agreed to meet us there but did not show up for awhile. They came by later in the evening and explained that a resort owner had seen them in a grocery store and offered free lodging for the night. I guess their youth and fully-loaded bikes drew more sympathy than three older guys with lightly-loaded bikes and a support van. We wished them well and renewed our promise to see each other in Boston.

Heading over to my bike the next morning to prepare for the day's ride, I noticed flat tire #6. The rear tire was showing its age so I replaced the tire and tube and hoped to make it the rest of the way unscathed. Heading south back to town, we pedaled past miles of sandy beaches, filled with early morning bathers and many motels. Ludington attracts many tourists, deservedly so. But it has not always been a resort area.

Father Marquette, Forests, and Car Ferries

When Father Marquette made his trek across Wisconsin to the Mississippi River with Jolliet in 1673, he came to St. Ignace, his mission outpost in Michigan's upper peninsula, via present-day Illinois. The Indians in Illinois warmly accepted Marquette and asked him to return. He fulfilled their request the following year, but a serious illness caused him to shorten his visit. Returning north via Michigan's western shore, he felt he could go no further and went ashore in a protected cove to spend his last days. He died there and was buried nearby by his Indian companions. That cove was the same one that we had entered aboard the SS Badger the night before. The river that flows west into that cove was later named the Pere Marquette, in honor of the beloved and much-traveled Jesuit priest.

Like Wisconsin, Michigan had been French territory since the early 1600s. The western shore of Michigan's lower peninsula was a fruitful hunting ground for the French-Canadian fur traders, but no outposts or settlements were established there. Neither did the British occupy the area during their tenure from 1763 to 1812. Michigan became a U.S. territory in 1813, but early settlements were only in the southeast, near Detroit. The northern two-thirds of Michigan was heavily forested, inaccessible, and unsuitable for farming.

But with the growth of Chicago and other midwestern cities, the demand for lumber increased and woodsmen moved into Michigan's forests. They came to the Pere Marquette River and built a lumber mill in 1849. James Ludington bought that mill, a harbor was built to accommodate lake steamers, and the surrounding town took his name. Northern Michigan's forests were extensive but not inexhaustible; by 1893 they were largely depleted, so the woodsmen moved on. But Ludington was not ready to become a ghost town. A railroad announced plans to build a line from Flint to Ludington in 1859, largely to haul timber products. Construction progress was slow, but when the tracks reached Ludington in 1874, the town was given new life.

The idea of a ferry boat to carry railroad cars across Lake Michigan had been around since the Flint-Ludington railroad plan was first announced. Civic leaders in Manitowoc, Wisconsin, saw the advantage to their city of becoming an east-west railroad hub, so in 1859 they approached their peers in Ludington with the idea. Ludingtonians liked the idea as well and *successfully convinced the Flint & Pere Marquette Railroad officials to invest in a ferry fleet. In 1875, the side-wheel steamer* John Sherman *was leased to begin carrying passengers, grain, and freight between Ludington, Michigan, and Sheboygan, Wisconsin. A competing railroad, the Ann Arbor, carried the first railroad cars across the lake in 1892. Realizing its business potential, the reorganized Pere Marquette Railroad launched the first steel steamship, designed to carry railroad cars, in 1897, with service between Ludington and Manitowoc. The* SS Pere Marquette *was 350 feet long and carried thirty railroad cars and five passengers. Rail car ferry traffic grew steadily until the late 1950s when six ferries provided service from Ludington to Manitowoc, Milwaukee, and Kewaunee, Wisconsin. The* Badger, *launched in 1952, was one of the last boats added to the fleet. Railroad traffic began to decline in the 1950s, so rail car ferries were converted to handle automobiles as well. By the 1970s, rail car ferry service ceased and the railroad company sold off the ferries, some for scrap metal. But the* Badger *survived. She was purchased by Charles Conrad, who established the Lake Michigan Carferry Company and converted the* Badger *to her present classy form, hopefully to survive for a long time.*

  Much of the forty-two miles from Ludington to Baldwin are through remote, second-growth forests, so we fueled up on a hot breakfast before leaving. Mary Anna would meet us in Baldwin for the drive north to the McFarlanes' (Mary Dean Miller's parents) home near Eastport, Michigan. Mary Dean would be there visiting and would join us for the next two weeks. It was warm, muggy, and threatening rain so we carried rain gear again. Route 10 had a good shoulder, but the heavy traffic got to us, so we soon dropped a few miles south and continued east on a blue road but not without some uncertainty. Only some of Michigan's secondary roads are shown on their state highway maps, and the numbers or names for most of those are not shown. It was again clear that more detailed maps would be needed as we got into densely developed areas further east. Despite some head-scratching, false turns, and a short stretch of gravel road, we arrived in Baldwin (population 800) around noon and easily found Mary Anna. Small towns are ideal rendezvous points; bikers and a van with bike racks are easy to find.

  The rain held off for our morning ride, but it poured on the trip north to Traverse City and Eastport. Traverse City is on a large bay of Lake Michigan and is a major resort area. Traffic was heavy with RV's, cars, and motorcycles going to and from the large cities to the south. We were back into California-type crowds and traffic. Nearing Traverse City the forest and tree farms gave way to cherry orchards. We stopped at a roadside stand and bought some cherries for our hosts and for our own survival. I'm not sure what it takes to grow large, delicious cherries, but they surely have it in northern Michigan.

The traffic decreased nicely as we neared Torch Lake, Eastport, and the McFarlanes' home. Roger rejoiced as we arrived just before the World Cup soccer final match was beginning. Kirby was far happier because Mary Dean was there. Their fifty-day separation had been the longest of their thirty-five-year marriage. Mary Anna and I were just happy to be in another home and to get to know the McFarlanes a little better. We had met Mac and Dean McFarlane in California when they had spent the past few winters there with Kirby and Mary Dean. Mac had been a Disciples of Christ pastor before moving to their Torch Lake retirement home. He was an energetic eighty-nine and ever the optimist, having just purchased a new car. Dean was ninety-two, also full of life, and had the better ears of the two. So between them they could handle summers at the lake just fine. Mary Dean's Aunt Vera joined us for a delicious dinner, and we saw some of her finely detailed paintings of flowers and landscapes, many of which she sends to friends and family as Christmas cards. We had admired some of her paintings at the Roods in Mason City, so it was a treat to meet her. At seventy, she had just retired from her job at the nearby hospital. After dinner, we hiked down to the lake shore to watch the sunset. Water, sunsets, and good company are each a blessing; in combination they warm and relax the soul. We all slept well that night.

Mary Anna and I drove the van into Charlevoix the next morning and left it at the Plymouth dealer for routine maintenance. Surrounding water, an upscale marina, quaint shops, and a variety of condominiums and bed & breakfast inns make Charlevoix (located on an isthmus between Lake Michigan and Lake Charlevoix) a favorite vacation spot. We enjoyed watching and photographing a ferry and a variety of sail and power boats pass through the draw bridge and channel separating the lakes. Meanwhile, Kirby and Roger helped Mac clear away brush and small trees in the backyard.

Loading five people and their gear into our minivan was always a challenge; in a thunderstorm it was even more so. The rain continued the next morning, so we finally donned our rain gear, stuffed everything in, and headed back to Baldwin. Efficient packing would have to wait.

It was not a good cycling day. The rain had stopped by the time we reached Baldwin, but with the high humidity we were soon soaking wet anyway. Navigation on the blue roads was just as frustrating as it was from Ludington to Baldwin, but still better than dealing with Route 10's traffic. At one point we were in the middle of a very poor-looking rural neighborhood and got some unusual looks from the residents. We turned around and quickly got out of there, then found another route. The remaining roads to Reed City were narrow and rough, the forests and occasional farms looked scrubby, and there was a steady cross wind out of the south.

Our destination was Lake City, thirty miles south of Reed City. On our way there the conditions worsened. The southerly wind continued as we turned south on an old highway that parallels a modern freeway. It was the worst thirty miles of road to date: chuck holes, broken surface, and cracks as wide as our tires running in the direction of travel. We had to concentrate on the road continuously to avoid serious damage to our bikes and bodies. Kirby's eyes were so glued to the road immediately ahead that he went right through a red light at a major intersection without even realizing that the light was there, much less that it was red. He was very lucky that there was no cross traffic at the time. This was the only stretch of road on the trip so far that Roger ranked less than one-star; he just left the ranking blank.

Mary Anna and Mary Dean had gone ahead to find our lodging and to mail some boxes home, as we would need more space in the van when Lynn joined us. Mary Dean was getting a good workout on her first day as part of the sag team. They also stopped by an electronics store in Reed City looking for a place to print the newsletter. They were directed to the *Osceola County Newspaper*. The accommodating editor allowed them to plug the PowerBook computer directly into one of their printers and, like magic, out came newsletter #7. He was interested in our trip and told them about a new rails-to-trails conversion that was under development near Reed City. We'll be looking for it if we pass that way again.

The last few miles into Lakeview improved dramatically, and our spirits rose as we pedaled around a small lake and into town. We found the post office, but there was no sign of the van. No need to worry; a pink note waited on the door: "No lodging available in Lakeview. We're still looking nearby and will be back at 6:00 p.m." We were fully confident in Mary Anna and the pink note communication system by then, so we just relaxed and waited. They arrived thirty minutes later, on schedule, and we loaded the bikes on the van and headed to a campground twelve miles away at Edmore. The weather was still threatening and mosquitoes were in the air, but camping was the only choice that night.

The campground was great, spacious and grassy with nice showers and a small compound of goats, turkeys, and deer to entertain kids (of all ages). A nearby restaurant stayed open late for us, and a colorful sunset promised a bright ending to our mediocre day. And by helping to set up camp, Mary Dean became a fully qualified sag-wagon support team member on her very first day. Things were looking up, but only for a little while. About 1:00 a.m., thunder awakened us. I heard Roger shuffling around as he put the tarp over his tent. Then came lightning strikes less than a mile away, followed by some rain drops and wind gusts, and, finally, buckets of water pouring directly on our campground. Mary Anna and I could feel some moisture at the feet of our sleeping bags, but it was warm and the rain stopped in about an hour, so we just rolled over and went back to sleep. For the first time on the trip, Mary Anna and I were not the earliest risers. Our feet were wet and we knew it was wet outside, so it was not a day to arise and rejoice. Roger finally got us moving at 8:15 a.m., so we rolled out to survey the damage. The bottom half of our sleeping bags were soaked and there was water on the entire floor of the tent. Our air mattresses were nearly floating. The others had mysteriously remained dry in their tents. We had a rain tarp over the top, and our tent floor was treated with water repellent. However, we had failed to close the bottom zipper on the tent's front fly, and the storm had come from that direction. My feet had inadvertently forced open that crack just enough to let in a small gusher. Somehow we stuffed all that wet gear and our soggy bodies back in the van and drove back to Lakeview. We voted to look for a motel that night.

The roads, mosquitoes, wind, and humidity were lousy again. With heavy clouds in all directions, we loaded our rain gear on our bikes again. And the farms did not look prosperous. Iowa's deep black loam had given way to the sandy soil of central Michigan, and the once majestic white pine forests had become farms and small towns, satellites to Detroit's population and industry. Traffic was light on the bumpy blue roads to Alma, so we still made good time and arrived at the Triangle Motel at 2:00 p.m. The women had searched for a motel that was not only clean and moderately priced but also had clotheslines for drying our soggy clothes and camping gear. The Triangle's owners were most accommodating. By evening everything was dry. As there were only two rooms available, Roger stayed with Mary Anna and me that night so that Kirby and Mary Dean could have some long overdue privacy. The next night would be "catching-up" time for Roger, as Lynn would be back with us.

Alma is an industrial and a college town, settled originally by people from the Scottish Highlands. Alma College, founded in 1886, is a Presbyterian liberal arts college with an attractive campus on the western edge of town. An oil refinery provides the industrial base.

Though we had poor luck with Michigan's roads and weather, our encounters with people were much better. Folks on the streets and in the cafés and stores greeted us warmly. I needed some new pads for my helmet, and the owner of the local bicycle shop produced a handful and refused payment. "These ought to last all of you all the way to Boston," he said smiling. We could sense that much of Michigan was still hurting from the downturn in the auto and other "rust-belt" industries, but her people's spirits and generosity were still high. "I hope you are enjoying Michigan," was a comment we heard nearly every day.

Chesanning, Michigan, was our destination the next day. The Triangle Motel owners said we had to see Chesanning's "Showboat City." There were rooms available at the Colonial Motel, so Chesanning it was. Not surprisingly, the weather was rainy again with southerly winds, and

Michigan's monster mosquitoes were out in full force. They attacked us in hordes during a very brief butt-break. For awhile Roger varied his pace between a near stop and normal speed. He later explained that he was performing an experiment and wanted to be sure his results could be verified. He wanted to determine how fast he needed to go before mosquitoes could no longer hang onto his skin. The result was 5 mph, so we were hardly aware of the ornery bugs at our normal flat-land speed of 15-20 mph. I could just see the poor little guys landing on Roger and then having to hang on for dear life as he accelerated. As mosquitoes, gnats, and such are rare in California, Roger was fascinated as well as frustrated with the hordes that seemed to follow him everywhere in Michigan. And Kirby and I appreciated his research.

Roger's Rule No. 11 - "Keep moving in mosquito country."

We continued our dead-reckoning navigation south and east across Michigan's bumpy blue roads for another forty miles to Chesanning and arrived about noon. It was clearly a classy town. Stately brick Victorian homes and large hardwood trees lined the main street through town, adorned by ornate light posts and flower beds. It was definitely worth passing that way.

The first order of business was lunch; when we saw a sign in the window of the Showboat Restaurant advertising malts, we knew that was the place. While locking our bikes and taking off our helmets and gloves, a well-dressed man stopped by to ask where we were headed. He was not a cyclist, just interested and friendly. He was a food salesman and traveled through much of Michigan, and he assured us that Chesanning was one of his favorite spots.

The Marys (Anna and Dean) found us just ten minutes later. They spotted the "malt" sign before even seeing our bikes, and they knew they had found us. After checking into the Colonial Motel (mosquitoes and threatening rain were still driving us indoors), Roger dropped us off in town and left to pick up Lynn at the Detroit airport. We spent the afternoon exploring Chesanning. Showboat Park has an outdoor amphitheater and stage on the banks of the Shiawasee River, with a replica of a paddle boat steamer as a backdrop. During the show season in July, the town's population of three thousand swells to fifty thousand, and the churches and service clubs earn money by selling food to the visitors.

Before meeting us, the Marys discovered Sarah's Attic. In 1983, Sarah Johnson Shultz, a local woman, needed a new couch. And since one of her children was soon going to college, she was also looking for more income. She had long been encouraged by others to sell the sculptures she had created for years. So she designed some highly detailed resin figures of people doing "ordinary things." She has also developed a very popular line of African-American children and adults doing "ordinary things."

Her sales outlet was originally just the gift section of her husband's pharmacy; now half of the pharmacy's display area is devoted to the figurines. Sarah was away when Mary Anna and Mary Dean visited, but her husband was at the pharmacy and he graciously took time to tell about her business. She has received much appreciation from the African-American community for the reality of her figures (rather than the non-flattering caricatures that have often been done by others). A former grocery store has been converted into her factory, and over one hundred women (many of them single mothers) help her keep over three thousand outlets across the country supplied with her figurines.

Roger and Lynn returned from the airport with broad smiles. Lynn was glad to be part of the team again and looked forward to exploring some new country. Roger seemed to be on his best behavior. Lynn came bearing gifts: T-shirts with custom-designed emblems commemorating our trip. The emblem beautifully comprised a map, our route, three bicycles, and the words "Coast-to-Coast Cycling." We all loved the T-shirts and wore them to dinner that night, drawing lots of interest from other diners. And it was good to be six again.

Skies were clear the next morning, our first dry morning in Michigan. Roger had checked out the first fifteen miles of our route on his way to the airport the day before, and he predicted smooth riding. He was right. Traffic was light also, as we were well north of the industrial city of Flint. But we had not totally avoided Michigan's auto industry. While stopped for a red light I noticed a large industrial building, a quarter of a mile or so to the south, with a General Motors-Buick sign on top. Traffic was still light, so we must have avoided the shift change. As I thought more about it, I realized that the plant even could be closed or just operating with a skeleton work force. We had seen Michigan towns that appeared to be suffering from continued hard times in the automobile industry, but this was our first factory. I wondered how Detroit and southeast Michigan had become such an industrial giant. The French and British owned the area for two hundred years and could see little value in it beyond beaver fur. But in less than one hundred years under American tutelage, it had become the world's center for auto production.

From Carriages to Model-T's in a Decade

Americans and Europeans who flooded to the Northwest Territory (present states of Ohio, Indiana, Illinois, Wisconsin, and Michigan) in the last half of the nineteenth century believed in the importance of mobility. They had benefited from ships, steamboats, railroads, and canals in reaching that rugged land and understood there would be a continued hunger for improved transportation. Many had moved west more than once, seeking adventure, freedom, and riches. They were quick to exploit available opportunities: first the fur trade, then the great forests and ensuing farmlands, and finally the need for more flexible and mechanized land transportation.

Like the Oregon Trail migration, there was no grand plan to develop an auto industry in Detroit. But the time was right to develop it somewhere. Europeans had a head start, and at the turn of the century most autos in America were European imports. But America, Michigan, and Detroit had more of the ingredients to become the world's center for auto production. The area's industrial leaders had the vision and ability to convert their carriage, railroad car, ship, and stove factories to auto plants and to adopt efficient, production-line technology. Local political leaders had the strength to reduce political graft and utility rates and improve public services for urban dwellers. And there was an available, inexpensive, and hard-working labor pool that had moved from the depleted forests and sawmill towns to the Detroit area. Open shop was the tradition in Michigan. Labor unions had been suppressed by the lumber industry, and the newly arrived immigrants had no experience with labor organization--so labor wages were low. Finally, large quantities of the required natural resources were nearby, and a transportation system was in place with capability for great expansion.

While the French and British explorers and fur traders were tramping around Lake Superior, they had no idea that one of the world's largest deposits of iron ore lay beneath their feet. Americans made that discovery in 1844. Within twelve years a lock at Saulte Ste. Marie, Michigan, was completed, allowing efficient movement of iron ore from Lake Superior to the south-lakes industrial areas. Larger ships soon came off the production lines, and the locks were expanded...and expanded again. At the same time coal from Kentucky was moving by train to steel mills in Ohio and Pennsylvania. Those natural resources, industrial capacities, and transportation networks had been used to build war machines and railroads. In the twentieth century they would also feed Detroit's auto industry.

The first Model-T Ford came off the assembly line in 1908. By the 1920s, half of the world's automobiles were made in Detroit, and the rest is history.

It was somehow ironic that a state whose economy has been so dependent on the automobile would have such poor secondary roads. Recently the auto industry has had a comeback, so maybe on our next trip, Michigan's roads will finally be of the same high quality as its people.

With our first tail wind in Michigan, we covered the fifty-three miles to Lapeer by noon; within a few minutes the women found us having lunch on a pedestrian mall. We had not agreed before leaving that Lapeer would be our lunch stop, but they knew that it was about the right distance and went to the post office looking for the pink note. We had taped it to the front door ten minutes earlier, with directions to the café, and, like magic, they found us. The cellular phone was still not working, but pink notes and post offices were doing the job. The women had been a bit frustrated, though, until they found the pink note, as they had driven what they thought was our route (we had changed routes to avoid heavy traffic) and did not find us. This was another clue that the denser network of roads and towns in the East could complicate communication between the cyclists and the van.

After lunch Roger took his bike into a bike shop to have the front derailleur adjusted, as it would not shift to low gear. This maintenance, which took only a few minutes, was the only commercial maintenance any of us needed on the entire trip. Other mechanical problems were minor enough to fix ourselves.

Lynn decided to cycle with us the final fifteen miles to Imlay City. There was a brief rain shower during lunch, but as the sun came back out, she was ready to get some exercise. While cruising along on a quiet country road, we crested a hill and saw detour signs and barricades ahead. The detour pointed to the north, to who knows how far out of the way. While studying our maps and discussing options a local driver stopped by and said, "You can make it through the construction okay. They are just replacing a bridge, and then it's nice biking on into Imlay City." He was right--what a bonus it was to ignore that detour sign. There were no cars for the next four to five miles, and the river crossing was an adventure. The old bridge had been removed and only the footings for the new one were in place. Construction workers were amused to see us and said, "Sure, you can get across," pointing to a narrow steel beam just downstream from the construction site. That nine-inch-wide beam was about fifty feet long and six to eight feet above the water--not a life-threatening experience but challenging enough for us, a bit like walking the plank. Kirby and I chose to carry our bikes on our shoulders and walk across. Roger and Lynn somehow walked their bikes across. Lynn was not all that appreciative of me taking her picture while halfway across, but I couldn't miss the opportunity. It was a smooth ride the rest of the way to Imlay City, despite occasional showers and "rain-gear stops."

Lynn learned from the motel manager that Imlay City is the home of Vlassic Pickles, so she called to ask about tours. There were none so we spent a quiet, but dry, evening in the M-53 Motel while thunderstorms and an occasional small tornado passed nearby. The Michigan rains had not been heavy while riding and had not held us up, but they were getting tiresome and, no doubt, shaded our perspective on the state. The next day we would be leaving Michigan and the USA and, hopefully, those persistent storm fronts.

Skies were not clear the next morning, but patches of blue signaled improving weather. And we had a good road and a tail wind.

Yes, things were looking up. Riding through Emmett while looking for a café, we noticed several American flags flying, and, like many western and midwestern towns, the Veterans of Foreign Wars Post was very prominent. I never asked or pondered why, but in those small towns in mid-America, there is no question about what country we're in or about the residents' patriotism. Although we'd seen few familiar chain stores or restaurants, the ever-present flags assured us we were in America.

Coming into Port Huron, I stopped to take a picture of an elderly man on a riding lawn mower, a familiar scene in the Midwest that I had not yet photographed. One scene I'll always remember was a couple, perhaps in their eighties, he dressed in bib overalls, she in a cotton dress, and both wearing large straw hats, each riding a mower, in tandem, around their huge front lawn. I was too far behind and reluctant to stop for a picture that time, so I was not going to miss another opportunity.

The women met us near the Bluewater Bridge which crosses the St. Clair River into Canada. Cyclists are not allowed on the bridge, much to our dismay, so we loaded the bikes on the van and drove across. We beheld spectacular views of the river and Lake Huron, and it was a historic spot, a shame that we couldn't ride our bikes across and more fully take it in. Lake Huron was just to the north, bright turquoise and seemingly endless. Ships, boats, and barges of all types and sizes were moving to and from the lake and river (which leads south to Detroit and Lake Erie). We crossed what has been a major marine transportation route, under three flags, for over three hundred years.

Fur Bateaux, Lumber Schooners, and Ore Boats Passed This Way

In 1672, a year before he accompanied Father Marquette across Wisconsin to the Mississippi River, Louis Jolliet paddled a canoe from the northern tip of Michigan down Lake Huron to Lake Erie via the St. Clair River. He was the first white man to pass this way. In the ensuing years, French bateaux (boats that could be paddled or sailed) became a common sight on the river. The French were extending their beaver hunting throughout the Great Lakes. They wanted larger sailing ships to carry the immense cargoes of fur, so in 1679, Robert LaSalle built the forty-five-ton Griffin *on the shores of Lake Erie. He sailed the* Griffin *north through the St. Clair River and around to Lake Michigan and Green Bay. He then continued his explorations by land to the Mississippi River and floated down to New Orleans, while the* Griffin *began its return voyage with a full load of furs. Sadly, the ship was never seen again, lost in a storm somewhere in Lake Michigan.*

Timber replaced fur as Michigan's most valued natural resource in the nineteenth century, but water remained the principle method of transportation. Schooners loaded with lumber passed through the St. Clair River on their way south to the growing industrial cities of Detroit and Cleveland. On the return trip they were towed in groups by steam-powered tugboats up the south-flowing St. Clair to Lake Huron. Upon reaching this point they raised their sails and spread out across the lake. Some observers noted, "It was like watching a great hand release a flock of doves."

But as timber gave way to iron ore, sails gave way to coal-fired ore boats, and today, private cabin cruisers and sailing yachts also move gracefully through this river between the lakes.

14

OUR FRIENDS TO THE NORTH

(Days 57-62)

While waiting in line to get through Canadian customs in Sarnia, we mentally checked to determine if we had anything to declare. No worry, all they asked about was liquor, firearms, and drugs. We claimed to have none of those (forgetting about Roger's red wine). They smiled, asked us how long we planned to stay, welcomed us to Canada, and waved us through. They didn't even ask for our passports. What a friendly, painless process.

First stop was a nearby information center that was loaded with brochures, maps, displays, and more friendly, helpful people. We gave them our criteria for lodging (motel, as the weather was still threatening), they made some suggestions, we picked one, and they called to make our reservation. It was the finest information center we had yet visited on our trip and a great introduction to Canada.

Ontario's People and Economy

Most of the early white settlers in Ontario were Americans who had sided with the British during the American Revolutionary War. They moved north during and after the war, along with some Hessian soldiers (Germans who fought as mercenaries for the British) and some Pennsylvania Dutch, all of whom felt more comfortable under British sovereignty. A few French-Canadian fur trappers remained to bring the total population to about ten thousand whites in 1790. During the War of 1812, more Americans who were loyal to Britain fled north. American immigrants comprised half of

Ontario's seventy thousand whites at that time. Fearing their mixed loyalties and possible invasion from the U.S., immigration of Americans was stopped after the war, with the exception of runaway slaves who escaped to Canada via the Underground Railroad. By the mid-1800s, like America's Midwest, Ontario's population had exploded with European immigrants; sixty percent of their 900,000 people in 1850 had recently come from the British Isles.

Today Ontario's ten million people are nearly one third of the country's entire population and are far more ethnically diversified. African-Americans migrated there from the United States as well as people from eastern Europe and Asia. And fifty thousand native Indians live on 170 reservations.

Automobile production is now Ontario's primary industry, followed by agriculture and mining. As early as 1904, auto parts were ferried across the river from Detroit to assembly plants in Windsor. Today there are auto plants throughout southern Ontario. We avoided the big cities in Ontario, thus missing their auto production, but we would see plenty of their rich farmlands and appreciate how they have became a major exporter of farm products.

Sarnia is a pretty town with a distinctive look that's different from the Michigan side of the river. The brick homes, commercial buildings, and parks are a bit more formal, and some of the billboards advertise unfamiliar products and services; although not dramatically different, they clearly represent another country. Road signs in kilometers (distance and speed) were immediately noticeable. Fortunately the van's speedometer indicates both miles and kilometers per hour, so the transition was minimized. But those speed limit signs that said "80" (kilometers per hour) got our attention.

We headed for Arkona, Ontario, via Route 7 for twenty-five miles northeast near the shore of Lake Huron, then east on Route 12 for another sixteen miles. The ride along Route 7 was very nice: flat, good shoulders, modest traffic, and good weather. We pedaled through some upscale lake shore neighborhoods and country clubs, but we couldn't see the lake. Roger was particularly frustrated as he had been awed by Lake Michigan and wanted to see if Lake Huron was as awesome (we had only got a brief glimpse of it as we crossed the Bluewater Bridge). The van met us at the intersection with Route 12, and Lynn and Mary Anna were ready to ride inland with us to Arkona. But as far as Roger was concerned, we could not leave until he got a good look at Lake Huron.

So, while Mary Dean drove off to check out our motel in Arkona and Mary Anna, Kirby, and I headed that way on our bikes, Roger and Lynn went searching for Lake Huron. They turned off on a secondary road heading west and came near a bluff above the lake, but they could find no public access. They hailed a farmer on a lawn mower nearby and asked about getting to the lake. He gave them permission to cross his property bordering the lake, and he instructed them to tell anyone who might ask that "the boss" said it was okay. Sure enough as they neared the lake, they were approached, but the "the boss's" verbal approval was all it took to clear the way. They found a beautiful overlook above the lake shore and reported that Lake Huron was indeed as awesome as Lake Michigan. Lynn got a great picture of Roger staring out at the lake, with a look on his face probably not unlike that of Father Marquette when he first saw the Great Lakes.

The ride into Arkona was very pleasant, through immaculate corn, wheat, and barley fields and hardly a car on the road. Arkona (population 500) is named for a town in Germany, an indication of some of Ontario's German heritage that we would become more familiar with in the coming days. Mary Dean met us as we approached town with directions to the motel. She seemed to be enjoying her role as our sole sag-wagon supporter. The motel was surrounded by corn fields, and it had a pool and clean, reasonably priced rooms, one with a kitchenette. We quickly came to appreciate the favorable dollar exchange rate with Canada which was at thirty percent. Traveling in Canada is a real bargain for Americans, one of many good reasons to visit.

Roger and Lynn offered to cook pancakes in the morning but suggested we find a restaurant in town for dinner. That was a mistake (the dinner in town, not the homemade pancakes). Most of us ordered what appeared to be straight-forward, local items (following Roger's Rule No. 9) and did okay, but Lynn was tempted by the stir-fried dish. When it arrived, she didn't recognize the gooey assortment that appeared on her plate and reported that it tasted even worse. Arkona was delightful in many ways, but it gets the prize for serving the worst meal on our trip.

After dinner we drove around the countryside. This area of Ontario is known for its apples, cherries, and wild lands. We drove through some beautiful orchards, forests, and parks, and then to Rock Glen Falls on the Ausable River. Whatever Arkona lacks in restaurant food it more than makes up for with pastoral scenery.

We were in no rush to finish Lynn's pancakes the next morning as storm clouds were still with us. But by 8:45 a.m. the sky brightened and we headed off for Stratford on the Avon River, with rain gear on board. We traveled by maps from the Ontario Cycling Association, perhaps the best maps we had acquired so far. Nearly all roads were clearly signed on the ground as well as identified on the map. We had to leave their suggested bike route for awhile, however, to get to Stratford, so we just followed our instincts, taking blue roads in the right general direction until we got back on a suggested route. Navigation problems have been mentioned more than once in this book and will probably be mentioned again. Navigation is mentioned here because it was an opportunity rather than a problem. There are scores of routes to bike across southern Ontario, and I have a feeling that most of them would rate as "better" or "best." The combination of good, well-signed roads, light traffic, good cycling maps, gorgeous farmland, and quaint towns make this part of the world ideal for cycling.

The farms were immaculate, with strips of grass between fields mowed to the same precision as front lawns. Ontario's farmers seem to take great pride in appearance as well as productivity. We stopped for a butt-break next to a provincial experimental farm. It looked as much like a formal garden as a farm, complete with a fountain and flower garden in the front yard. Later we stopped to watch a young girl and her mother, dressed in equestrian outfits, practice jumping their horses. That morning I felt like we were on a casual ride through the English countryside rather than another leg of a cross-country ride.

We were ready for coffee (hot chocolate for Kirby) and found a clean grocery store/gas station/coffee shop at Nairn (population 241) that also serves as the post office. We learned that most post offices in Canada are in commercial facilities, rather than separate, publicly-owned buildings. The coffee, rolls, and conversation were as good as in any small town in the States. Although it was late July, they were already talking about their winter vacations, comparing Florida and Arizona. The weather probably gets a little brisk in Nairn in February.

Mary Anna, Mary Dean, and Lynn caught up to us in Alisa Craig. They'd had a full morning hiking to Rock Glen Falls and visiting the park's information center, which had a special display of locally-found fossils. Then they were off to explore Stratford and to find our night's lodging.

Even Ontario isn't perfect. We had to deal with a few miles of bumpy, busy Route 7 before we turned off on a quieter, smoother road; our map suggested Route 19 toward the Victorian-era town of St. Marys. We pedaled along the North Thames River as we rode toward Stratford, on the Avon River. There was no doubt that this area had once been part of the British Empire.

Captain Boerstler and General Tecumseh: War Comes to the Thames

Canadians and Americans were not always friendly neighbors. Early in the War of 1812 General William Hull, commander of the American garrison in Detroit, led his soldiers into Ontario with visions of occupying Canada. After a brief clash with British troops and their Indian allies, he retreated back to Detroit. One of the Americans killed in that failed invasion was Captain Jacob Boerstler, who had migrated to America from Germany with his parents and five brothers and sisters in 1784.

When they arrived, Jacob and his family settled near Hagerstown, Maryland, after an illegal escape from Germany and an eight-week ocean voyage fraught with storms, sickness, the death of a sister, and even an escape from being sold into slavery. Jacob, like many Americans, saw greener pastures further west and moved to Ohio, then part of the Northwest Territory. He twice floated down the Ohio and Mississippi Rivers with merchandise, bound for markets in New Orleans, barely making it each time after narrow escapes from hostile Indian attacks. When the War of 1812 broke out Jacob became a commander of a company of sharpshooters and went to Detroit with General Hull, never to return.

George Boerstler, Jacob's youngest brother, was born after the family emigrated to America and later followed Jacob to Ohio. George survived his tour of duty in the War of 1812 and settled down in Lancaster, Ohio. George Boerstler was my Grandmother Swinnerton's grandfather.

Later in the war, General William Henry Harrison led American troops back into southern Ontario and defeated the combined British and Indian forces in the Battle of the Thames. The Indian leader Tecumseh was killed in that battle. A Shawnee from Ohio, Tecumseh had traveled throughout the East and Midwest working to unite Indian tribes into a single alliance against invasion of their lands by Americans. He joined the British forces during the War of 1812 and was commissioned a general in command of the Indian forces. Tecumseh's death left a leadership void among midwestern tribes that was never filled; there would be no more Indian confederacies opposing America's movement into the old Northwest Territory.

St. Marys has a true touch of England with its Victorian homes and storefronts, pubs, and old stone churches, with the North Thames running through town. We had lunch at an upscale pub and strolled down to a bridge to see and photograph the river. What a contrast from central Wyoming where we had so recently been.

The final leg into Stratford via Routes 19 and 8 was as delightful as the morning ride; the last mile into town was between columns of old hardwood trees whose branches formed a canopy over the roadway. I expected to see the King's trumpeters welcome us as we entered the town. Well, it wasn't quite that spectacular, but we were happy to see the van parked ahead with the familiar pink note on a window.

The Alden House Bed and Breakfast was our home for the night. The attractive, Victorian-style brick home was pretty classy for us but seemed the right place to be in such a classy town. The owners were an interesting couple, he from Austria and she from the Netherlands. They came to Stratford to retire and seemed to be thriving on it. Mary Anna and I asked them for dinner recommendations, when they in turn asked, "Do you want to dine or just eat dinner?" Mary Anna and I chose moderate dining and were delighted with their recommendation: a cozy restaurant with crisp vegetables and delicious fish, within walking distance of the B&B, downtown, and the river.

The couples separated for dinner and for relaxing strolls around town through Upper Queen's Park and the Shakespeare Gardens along the Avon River. It was a warm, pleasant evening. The solid brick homes, well-trimmed yards and gardens, and large trees gave the whole scene a special ambiance. Stratford has three live theaters and hosts a summer Shakespeare festival that draws a worldwide audience, with contemporary plays running year-round. Kirby later described Stratford as having an "aura of distinction," one that he could sense but found difficult to explain.

The Huron Road, Railroad Barns, and Shakespeare

Transportation in the Great Lakes region was almost entirely by water until the early 1800s. One of Canada's early land routes between the lakes was the Huron Road, connecting the settlements on Lakes Ontario and Huron. The settlement of Stratford was established in 1832 about halfway between the lakes. A dam was built on the nearby creek (later to be named the Avon River), as well as a grist and saw mill--and the Shakespeare Hotel. The town was divided into five wards, each with its own school, named Avon, Falstaff, Hamlet, Romeo, and Shakespeare. The first Shakespearean celebration was held in 1864 to celebrate the bard's birthday, which firmly established the enduring connection. In 1856 the railroad came to town, and, in 1871, a repair shop was built, the beginning of a love-hate relationship between the railroad and Stratford's Shakespeare-oriented citizens. The railroad company was good for the economy but potentially bad for the environment, as they proposed building a line right next to the river, through what is now the Upper Queen's Park and Shakespearean Gardens. The park's board and the citizens resisted those proposals several times; today all of us that visit Stratford benefit from their vision and persistence.

As it was Sunday, no plays were performed in the evening, but the Guelph Concert Band was playing in the band shell by the Shakespeare Festival Theater. Sometime during the concert, all three couples found their way there. Kirby had called his cousin Elmo Miller in Kitchener (where we would spend the next two nights), and he and his wife Irmgard drove over to Stratford and found us at the concert. Kirby had spent boyhood summer vacations with Elmo and his family on their Ohio farm. They each had many fond memories but had not seen one another in years. After just a few minutes of Elmo's spirited welcome and his promise of TV news coverage, we knew there would be good times ahead in Kitchener.

A birthday party for Lynn at the B&B topped off the day, complete with ice cream sundaes, chocolate chip cookies (sent by Lynn's daughter Karen), gifts, and a crown of clover flowers, making Lynn "queen for a day." Then Roger reminded us that we had completed three thousand miles, another milestone and a special ending to a terrific day.

After a delicious deluxe continental breakfast served in the formal dining room, the cyclists said good-bye to the Alden House and were off to Kitchener. Lynn rode a few blocks with us and then toured the rest of Stratford on her bike; like the rest of us, she just couldn't get enough of that delightful town.

We were riding close together that morning, as we had been for the past week or two. Because there was more variety in the landscape, we all wanted to take it in rather than just get to the next destination. Moreover, I was probably in better shape and could keep up better. I felt we were finally more of a team than just three individuals meandering our way across the country, and it felt good.

As we traveled I noticed that many of the churches were Mennonite and that German was replacing English as the most common origin for street and town names. Elmo and Irmgard were Mennonites, of German heritage; it seemed they were among their people. Elmo was waiting a few miles outside Kitchener to welcome us, give us directions to his condominium, and let us know that the TV cameras should be poised as we entered town. Our wives had gotten a late start but had passed us about noon. They had already met Elmo, who had led them earlier through town to his home.

There were no TV cameras waiting for us on the edge of town, but they came to Elmo's condo shortly after our arrival. We met the cameramen outside and staged an entry by riding up and down a nearby street. I was elected spokesman and described the joys and rigors of our trip, with emphasis on how the wind in Nebraska was tougher to deal with than the Rocky Mountains. A small crowd gathered, and Elmo proudly described our trip and explained why we chose to come through Kitchener. "Watch for them on the six o'clock news," he told everyone. Although Elmo was a retired meat cutter, we all agreed he could have a second career in public relations. Sure enough, the evening news included an introduction of the "Three Kings of the Road" from California who had bicycled into town that day, having covered three thousand miles on their way to Boston. They included shots of the three of us pedaling down the road, my interview, and a close-up of the T-shirts designed by Lynn. We were thrilled. Elmo came through as he had promised and gave us a videotape of the segment for bragging rights when we got home.

Kitchener sounded to me like a German name, which seemed appropriate considering the number of ethnically German people in the area. Instead, the town was named after Horatio Kitchener, a British general who was killed in World War I. Like most of Ontario, Kitchener's earliest settlers were British and American emigrants, including some runaway slaves. The town was first called Ebytown, then Mount Pleasant. After a large number of Germans and Mennonites of German heritage settled in the area in the mid-1800s, the name was changed to Berlin. Then World War I made Germans as well as things German very unpopular in Canada; thus in 1916 it was renamed Kitchener.

We were all ready for a day off, but the Millers made sure it was not completely a day of rest. They were energetic and very proud of where they lived, and we would soon understand why. First stop was the Farmers' Market. Trucks and horse-drawn wagons were parked in a huge parking lot, and beautiful farm produce was on display. We noticed some of the horse-drawn wagons had rubber tires, while others had the old steel-rimmed wooden wheels. Many of the merchants were dressed in plain clothes, the men in black pants and white shirts and the women in long print dresses with bonnets over their hair. Other merchants were dressed conventionally, and the customers comprised the same mixture. Mary Anna bought some fruit from one of the Mennonite women.

Next stop was the quaint little town of St. Jacobs, a center for Mennonite culture and services. There were many horse-drawn buggies in town, some parked at a blacksmith's shop where horseshoes and buggy parts were being replaced or repaired. Noting our interest in Mennonite history, Irmgard suggested we visit a museum in town called The Meeting Place. Through a wealth of displays and audio-visual programs we learned how the Mennonites are part of the Reformation's Anabaptist movement in Germany and Switzerland. They do not believe in baptizing children or in military service and thus were in conflict with those governments as well as the state-recognized Roman Catholic and, later, the Lutheran Church. Because of persecutions in Europe most Mennonites migrated to North America. Today, of the 900,000 Mennonites worldwide, nearly 400,000 are in North America (115,000 in Canada), and the remainder are scattered throughout the world.

There are many different types or groups of Mennonites in Ontario, most of whom, like our hosts the Millers, are permitted to use all forms of modern technology and dress in conventional clothes. Those we saw dressed plainly were either Old Order Mennonites or Amish; both reside in Ontario and cling to the old ways. The different religious groups can be distinguished from each other by their meeting places. The Amish usually worship in small groups in their homes, while Old Order Mennonites have churches or meeting houses. Some of the Mennonite groups have adopted select forms of modern technology, thus the rubber-tired horse-drawn wagons we saw at the Farmers' Market. As we drove through the countryside, Elmo pointed out the Old Order or Amish farms, which had no power lines going to the houses or barns. We also saw a farmer cutting his grain with a horse-drawn mower and stacking it by hand to dry. Most roads there have wide gravel shoulders, just wide enough for a buggy. Some areas are almost exclusively Old Order or Amish, in which we felt like we had gone to sleep and awakened 150 years ago.

We asked the Millers about the stability of the Old Order communities, if the children were staying. Apparently the Old Order population is growing modestly. Each family usually has six or seven children and over half of them choose to stay, often after a brief period "in the world" before joining the church, which they must do before they marry.

Pacifism and resistance to military service is still common to all Mennonite and Amish groups. Elmo and Irmgard met in Washington, D.C., while performing alternate volunteer service during the Korean War.

Next stop was Anna Mae's Restaurant, famous for its pies--and other things you usually eat before pie. Anna Mae is a Mennonite, and most of her help are Old Order young people. Lunch and the pies were as good as advertised, and we all were intrigued by the Old Order atmosphere.

The day's final treat was a visit to Peter Etril Snyder's art gallery. Snyder is a well-known painter of Mennonite and Amish life and coincidentally, we discovered, a supporter of the Rails-to-Trails movement. In addition to the scores of beautiful Old Order farm scenes, he had painted a series of old railroad scenes of which he was donating the proceeds of these sales to the movement. And we learned of a recently completed trail that was along our next day's route.

Friends of the Millers, Henry and Marcella Martin, hosted us that evening. A great barbecue dinner and tales of Henry's youth in an Old Order family topped off a very special day. Henry's parents converted to a less conservative Mennonite group when he was a teenager, but he had a lot of memories of riding in black buggies.

Traffic was heavy the next morning as we left Kitchener and pedaled southeast through Cambridge to the trailhead. The Old Order farms were north of town and behind us, so we were back in a familiar world again and not so sure it was an improvement. We were happy to find the trail along the Grand River in Galt, one of the sub-districts of Cambridge. The Grand was flowing our way, southeast to Lake Erie, and even though the trail was not the best, it was a pleasure to get away from traffic for awhile. We took a break on a wooded bluff above the river and watched a group of canoeists. From their laughter and cheers, it was clear they were having as much fun as we were. Too soon it was traffic again, as only fifteen miles of the trail was completed. We were in Brantford without a good map. The Ontario Cycling Association maps were great in rural areas but lacked detail in cities, so we wandered around for awhile, like guys do before asking for help. Kirby finally hailed down a postman; coincidentally, he was also a cyclist and got us headed on the right road to Dunnville.

Somehow the women tracked us down in time for a picnic lunch in Onadaga, population 95, just our size of a town. The park comprised the front yard of the municipal building, which was a converted church. We enjoyed a shaded picnic table, water, a rest room inside, and no crowds; what more could we ask for? Although Dunnville was a little further than we needed to go that day, there was a motel (showers were predicted) and we could have a shorter trip to Niagara Falls the next day.

Roger had an encounter with a big dog that afternoon. He seemed friendly enough but just kept running at Roger's bike from the side and barking. We'd had a few incidents with barking dogs earlier, but this was the first time one of us had to get off his bike. The owner kept yelling at the dog to come home, and he finally did, with no harm done.

Later, we pulled into a restaurant parking lot to take a break, and a local guy in a pickup asked about our travels. He had grown up in New York City and moved to rural Ontario in his mid-twenties, primarily to get far away from urban violence. He loved the slow-paced life he'd found in the Grand River country and hoped that not many others from the States would discover it.

The back lawn of Dunnville's Riverview Motel reached down to the Grand River through a shaded picnic area. Lynn and Mary Dean volunteered to cook a meal outside on the camp stove, using some of the meat Elmo had sent along with us. There were some light showers on and off, but it was warm and relaxing and we were grateful for a home-cooked meal in that peaceful setting.

On to Niagara Falls! Although we were anxious to get there, we took a circuitous route to the south in order to see Lake Erie as well. The lake shore was lined with homes of all sizes, but it was unusually quiet, with little traffic and nothing open for coffee. I took a picture of Roger riding along the lake shore, documenting the visit to our third Great Lake. From there we planned to continue east to the Niagara River and then north to the falls.

While pedaling through the quiet streets of Port Colborne we could see a bridge ahead. "Must be a river entering Lake Erie," Kirby concluded as we approached what appeared to be a steel drawbridge. We scooted across the bridge just as a whistle blew and barriers came across the roadway, then we stopped on the other side to see what was going on. A boy who was biking the other way and didn't quite make it across pointed south toward Lake Erie and explained, "See, a big ship is coming through." It was big all right, like an ocean-going freighter. We had crossed the Welland Canal, a twenty-five-mile series of locks and canals that connects Lakes Erie and Ontario and bypasses Niagara Falls. With its completion by the Canadians in 1829, large vessels could navigate from Lake Ontario's eastern ports to Lake Erie, up through the Detroit and

Saint Clair Rivers to Lake Huron, through the Mackinac Straits to Lake Michigan, and on to Chicago. By 1856 Lake Superior was reachable via the locks at Sault Ste. Marie, and finally, the opening of the Saint Lawrence Seaway in 1959 provided access to the Atlantic Ocean. That ship we saw passing under the drawbridge that morning could have come from Duluth, Minnesota, and be headed toward Europe.

After a few more miles of quiet, flat back roads we sighted the Niagara River and New York state on the other side. The Niagara is only twenty-five miles long but is no small river. All of the waters of Lakes Superior, Michigan, Huron, and Erie eventually pass this way on their way to Niagara Falls, Lake Ontario, the Saint Lawrence River, and the Atlantic Ocean. Where we first saw it, the Niagara River was about a mile wide and moving quickly, though there was no white water in sight. A park with a picnic table by the river caught our eye, so we stopped to enjoy the view and have a sandwich. Three jet skiers were heading our way from the U.S. side. They didn't come ashore but easily could have, more evidence that the War of 1812 is long behind us. They just waved and headed back to America, unless they were Canadians going to America. I doubt if they carried visas.

The riverside park is actually a parkway along the Niagara River that reaches all the way to the falls. A paved bicycle trail meanders along the river for fifteen miles through parks and quiet residential areas. As we pedaled along, Kirby stopped to point out what appeared to be a large smoke plume on the horizon close to the falls. He thought it might be a wildfire or a large industrial fire. A pedestrian walking along the trail smiled and straightened us out. "It's just the mist rising above the falls," he said, probably thinking to himself, Tourists! The river was dropping fast by then, forming continuous rapids, and the quiet residential area gave way first to power plants and then to a much wider sidewalk with hordes of tourists. The road was crammed with tourist buses and taxis and the sidewalk filled with people from all over the world. That was the end of our biking for the day.

We walked our bikes through the crowd toward the falls and soon spotted Mary Anna. She waved us on, pointing to an area where we could see the full sweep of the falls and nearly touch the "Horseshoe." We secured our bikes and walked over to the rail right next to where the water from those four Great Lakes plunges over Horseshoe Falls. All of the well-worn words come to mind to describe the scene: awesome, frightening, beautiful, inspiring, spectacular, breathtaking. I had seen the falls once before but didn't take time then to get up close. It's nice to step back and look at the falls from several distant perspectives, but to understand their power and impact you need to be close, get wet, and feel the vibration. But not for too long. After a few minutes of being so close I almost felt like a wave would reach up and pull me over. For power, get close; for beauty, stand back! For the rest of our visit to Niagara Falls I chose beauty.

Mary Dean and Lynn opted to take the "Maid of the Mist" boat trip up to the bottom of Horseshoe Falls, while Mary Anna explored along the top and looked for us. Earlier, Lynn had found alternative lodging for herself and Roger. Kirby and I are youth hostel fans, as they are inexpensive, usually clean, and full of interesting people. Niagara Falls was the first place on our trip since Jackson, Wyoming, that had a hostel, and we were determined to use it. But when they checked it out, Lynn decided to look for other lodging, so she found a nice B&B just a few blocks away. The hostel was pretty crowded--but with the kind of folks we expected: students from Japan, China, and Korea, and an upscale couple from Montreal who just like hosteling. A woman who was our age, from Cincinnati, and her son were biking from Seattle to Maine, raising funds for a battered women's shelter. There is no place quite like a youth hostel to meet a cross section of the world's people.

Mary Anna and I spent the evening visiting her niece, Sarah Durbin, in nearby Buffalo, while the Millers and Wedels took in the sights and sounds on both sides of the border. Lynn and Roger considered taking one of the "up-close" tours, next to the American Falls, but decided against it after observing the wet and stressed looks of some folks who had just completed a tour. Kirby and Mary Dean enjoyed the visitor center and gardens on the American side (including flower beds in the shape of the five Great Lakes).

Several people recommended we visit the town of Niagara-on-the-Lake, just twelve miles north of the falls, where the Niagara River spills into Lake Ontario. Roger decided to sleep in and enjoy the second half of his B&B, while Lynn joined the rest of us for breakfast in the beautiful town that is two hundred years old. Strategically located, Niagara-on-the-Lake saw conflict during both of America's wars with Britain. It was a budding commercial center until the town of St. Catherines, a few miles further west, was selected as the northern termini for the Welland Canal. But Niagara-on-the-Lake's leaders saw its potential as a tourist destination, turning it into a jewel of a colonial-era village. Buildings have been authentically restored; a beautiful clock tower, flower beds, and hanging baskets grace Queen Elizabeth Way. And we found just the right café for breakfast.

On the way back to Niagara Falls we passed by old Fort George. I wanted to stop and investigate, but Roger was waiting and we were still slaves to our schedule. Later I learned more about Fort George and another family connection.

Fort George and Lieutenant-Colonel Charles Boerstler

In 1813 Niagara-on-the-Lake (then called Newark) was enemy territory to Americans, and Fort George guarded Canada's strategic entrance to the Niagara River. American troops lined the New York shore to fend off invasion by the British, and vice versa on the Ontario shore. Lieutenant-Colonel Charles Boerstler (older brother of Captain Jacob Boerstler, who had been killed the year before near Detroit) commanded six hundred American troops. He assisted in the Americans' capture of Fort George and later led an expedition further into Ontario to capture an enemy supply depot. Spies warned of his coming, and a British and Indian force met and defeated the Americans. Boerstler agreed to surrender, but as he drew his sword to present to his British counterpart he noticed an Indian about to take aim at him at close range. From a letter to his father we have an account of his next words to the commanding British officer: "Will you lose your head [Boerstler still held his sword] or prevent that Indian from shooting me?" The British officer motioned the Indian to drop his gun. Then he turned around and told Boerstler that he could not understand how he (Boerstler) was still alive as at least three hundred shots had been aimed at him. Boerstler answered, "I am under God's protection and your bullets cannot kill me."

Charles Boerstler survived his captivity in Quebec and, after the war, returned to Maryland and his mercantile business.

We walked our bikes across the Rainbow Bridge, enjoying our last views of Niagara Falls and the river below churning toward Lake Ontario. The U.S. Customs agents were about as casual and friendly as Canada's, and in a few minutes we said hello to New York.

15

ALONG THE ERIE CANAL

(Days 63-70)

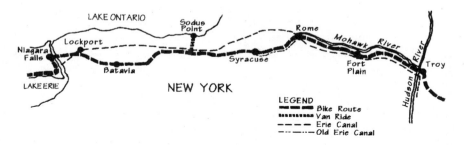

It was comforting to be back on American soil. Going through Ontario had been fascinating. It offered a new perspective on a neighbor we tend to know too little about, but it was still good to be home.

Our adrenaline was probably pumping a little more than usual that morning. New York is an east-coast state, and the highway map indicated only 490 miles to Boston (though our bike route would be a little longer). We were also anxious to see our friends the Fenns and to take a day off with them at their cottage on Lake Ontario.

Traversing upstate New York had been the eastern anchor of our route from the earliest planning. It was on a direct line to Boston and the easiest route across the eastern mountains. A relief map of the East reveals a natural notch across northern New York between the Allegheny and Adirondack Mountains. The Mohawk River flows eastward from its headwaters near Rome, New York, through that notch, and into the Hudson River just north of Troy. The Mohawk Valley has been a transportation corridor between the Great Lakes and the northeast coast for centuries, first used by the Indians, then French and British fur traders, then American and European migrants heading west. It was also New York's early western frontier and the site of key battles in the Revolutionary War. Today freeways, railroads, and the Erie Canal follow that same general route through the mountains, as well as lots of back roads.

We were especially interested in the Erie Canal. It was built prior to the railroads and was a major factor in America's westward movement. We all remembered the old folk ballad by Thomas S. Allen, with the familiar line, "fifteen miles on the Erie Canal." Though lacking complete information on the canal, we knew there were bike trails along portions of it and that it was navigable by barge and small commercial boats for its entire length. We were anxious to see it and learn more about it.

The New York Bicycle Touring Guide, produced by William N. Hoffman, was our primary map across New York. Its Route EM (Erie-Mohawk) seemed an ideal route for us, which it was for part of the way. We also had AAA maps for each of the states we traversed. They were okay in the West, but from eastern Nebraska on, they did not include enough back roads and therefore were useful only for general reference. For mountainous areas we had U.S. Geological Survey topographic maps, with a scale of 1:250,000. They were helpful in the western mountains, but in the East, they lacked road detail and were of minimum value for cycling.

Upstate New York has been much more than an important transportation corridor. It was the early frontier of the American colonies and was the site of critical conflicts during our Revolutionary War. The Kodak camera, women's suffrage, and several religious reform movements have their roots in upstate New York. We were eager to see those places and learn to appreciate those early New Yorkers who had passed this way.

It was in the low eighties with a westerly wind as we headed east toward the town of Lockport and had our first encounter with the Erie Canal. Within a couple of miles we were away from tourist congestion and passed a huge power distribution facility. We stopped for a minute on an overpass to view the power lines that brought electricity from generators at Niagara Falls and then fanned it out for delivery to homes and businesses in western New York. Then came flat farmlands and a smooth, quiet ride to the canal.

The van caught up to us, and the women agreed to wait a couple of miles ahead where our road dead-ended at a road that paralleled the canal (which was heading north and south at that point). Our first canal sighting was a little disappointing. We were south of Lockport, there was no towpath or trail along the canal, and no signs or indications of a parkway, just a big ditch through the woods. Our bicycle touring guide suggested we head south for a mile or so (away from Lockport), then cross the canal and continue east. We followed the suggested route but hoped we would see more of the canal soon. The women learned that there were canal locks at Lockport and headed back that way to investigate. We agreed to rendezvous in Batavia and most likely spend the night there.

While pedaling through Pendleton about lunch time Roger spotted a deli with a picnic table and motioned us to pull over. It was New York, where deli food was famous, and Roger was following his instincts (Roger's Rule No. 9). Lunch and conversation were both a treat as the owner joined us and told us of his earlier job operating a lock on what he called the "Barge Canal." In the 1960s he worked the graveyard shift (midnight to 8:00 a.m.) and spent much of his time sleeping on a cot in the lock control room. Only one boat came through during his shift, in two years, and he was sure it was some type of military vessel on a secret mission. Shortly thereafter the locks were only open during the day, his job was eliminated, and he got into the deli business.

Our afternoon ride to Batavia was delightful--quiet country roads with good shoulders and flat terrain, a nice welcome back to the U.S. and good marks for our bicycle guide. The van found us again a few miles west of Batavia and then went on to find a motel (rain was still a threat). As we didn't see them along the main road into town, we continued on to the post office, sure that there would be a pink note. No pink note; this was the first time on the trip that we didn't spot the van or a note on our first pass through town. "Oh well," said Kirby. "They must still be looking for a motel." So we headed for a café to get a cold drink. An hour later Mary Anna pulled up with a quizzical look on her face and asked, "Didn't you see the van parked by a motel on the western edge of town? You must have ridden right by it." This was our first communication breakdown, not a serious one and not the last either.

Lynn, Mary Anna, and Mary Dean were enthusiastic about their visit to Lockport. They'd been there most of the day watching boats pass through the canal locks. There were a series of modern locks in the middle of town that had been carved through solid rock, each with gates to control the water level. The remains of older, narrower locks were still there, right next to the newer ones. And there was a towpath and bike trail along the canal, heading northeast out of town.

You can always tell your neighbor,
You can always tell your pal,
If you've ever navigated on the Erie Canal.

Thomas S. Allen

America's westward movement started long before wagon trains left Missouri for Oregon. The first rush west began right after the Revolutionary War when rich and poor Americans, tired of rocky, expensive land in New England, weary of war, and looking for adventure and riches, began pushing over the Appalachian Mountains. The Mohawk Valley was the only real break in the mountain chain between Canada and Alabama, thus it was one of the most heavily traveled routes west. The people came first in boats, portaging around the many rapids, and soon a crude wagon road was built. Once they reached Buffalo, travelers moved further west easily via the Great Lakes, but getting to Buffalo took four to six weeks and was the toughest part of the trip.

George Washington, as a surveyor and engineer, understood the potential and importance of waterways for inland navigation. He was aware of the Mohawk and other rivers in central New York and encouraged their development. Private companies built the first navigation improvements on the Mohawk, beginning in the 1790s. The cities of Utica, Rome, Syracuse, Rochester, and Buffalo grew due to their location along the river/wagon route, but transportation to eastern markets was still a bottleneck to the kind of growth envisioned by New Yorkers. Governor DeWitt Clinton, dreaming of a cross-state canal, sold the controversial idea to the New York legislature, and in 1817 construction began. By his enemies, the canal was referred to as "Clinton's Folly" or "Clinton's Ditch," but to his supporters, and eventually all Americans, it is the Erie Canal.

Completed in 1825, using only state funds and primarily local labor (supplemented by recent Irish immigrants), the 363-mile long Erie Canal (and its eighty-three locks) was soon overwhelmed with traffic. Packet boats, carrying only passengers, made the trip in six days. Line boats carrying freight and a few passengers were a little slower but very efficient (freight prices were $4 per ton compared to $100 per ton by wagon). The boats were pulled by ropes attached to horses or mules walking along the towpath. Bridges allowing travel across the canal were built just barely high enough for boats to pass under, thus the refrain from Allen's ballad: "Low bridge, everybody down! Low bridge! We are coming into town!"

By 1836 enough tolls had been collected to pay off all construction costs, so a year later work began to widen the canal from forty to seventy feet, mostly in the same location as the original. (The old abandoned locks in Lockport, seen by our wives, were remnants of the enlarged canal.) A few years later railroads offered strong competition, and people recognized the need for a major enlargement if the canal was to remain economically viable. During that era many canals in America and around the world were abandoned--but not in New York. Newer canals linked Lakes Ontario, Cayuga, Champlain, and Seneca with the main east-west canal. And in 1905 work began on the Barge Canal, 127 feet wide and, in some sections, miles from the original location. There is no towpath on the relocated Barge Canal; steam, gasoline, and diesel engines replaced horse and mule power.

In 1918 the Barge Canal was completed, and the old Erie Canal passed out of existence. The canal we had first encountered was the Barge Canal, and in that section the old Erie Canal is buried under the reconstruction or is in a different location. In other sections, parts of the old canal were incorporated into the Barge Canal and the towpath was salvaged (thus the towpath seen in Lockport).

The Barge Canal, with its three-hundred-foot diesel-driven barges, is far more efficient than the old Erie Canal, with its horses plodding along between colorful canal towns. But what a lousy name. New Yorkers soon recognized the error of losing a colorful, historical name, and today the main east-west Barge Canal is again known as the Erie Canal.

We gathered some new information about the new and old Erie Canals, but we still lacked a good map showing where the old canal is intact and where the towpath or other trails along either of the canals are bikable. Although our *New York Bicycle Touring Guide* indicated the Erie Canal in a few places, we wondered if we were missing some of it.

Our motel in Batavia was borderline, even for us, but it was clean and had an air conditioner in each room, so we didn't question the selection. The proprietor seemed a little nervous and asked us to conserve electricity as much as we could; apparently the owner had pressured him to hold down utility costs. We were sympathetic but didn't take his request too seriously. It was hot and humid, so we immediately turned on the air conditioners. We left them on when we went to dinner, thinking we would turn them off later in the evening when it cooled down. However, when we got back to the motel, not only were the air conditioners not running, but the power was turned off. After some unfriendly words with the proprietor, Roger found the circuit breaker, and we were back in business. Dinner at an Italian restaurant had been great, but for us Batavia will always be remembered for its tightwad motel owner.

It rained hard again during the night and was foggy and cool the next morning, so rain gear was in order. But not for long; it became one of those perfect days after a rain storm: cool, with puffy clouds scattered across a bright blue sky. And the touring guide was still serving us well. There were a few mild hills, but traffic was light and the back roads were unusually good, probably the best we had seen so far. After lunch we left the touring guide's suggested route and jogged north toward the town of Lyons, where Al and Mary Jeanne Fenn were to meet us.

Mary Dean Miller was leaving us in Syracuse and needed to pick up a bus ticket in Rochester, so the women did some sightseeing there. They toured the George Eastman (founder of Eastman Kodak) house and the photography museum, then they were off to find the Fenns' cottage.

While pedaling over a bridge in Pitsford on Highway 31, we stopped and looked down on what appeared to be a canal. Sure enough it was our friend the Erie Canal, and there was a heavily-used trail on one side. We walked our bikes down to the trail and asked some folks for directions. "Lyons is that way," they said, pointing more or less easterly. "The trail continues for another ten miles and then runs into Route 31 again, just this side of Palmyra." We smiled gratefully, thanked them, and headed down the fairly-smooth gravel trail. We were on the new canal, over one hundred feet wide, but with the towpath intact and lots of recreation boaters on the water as well as walkers, joggers, and bikers on the path. The towpath resembled the one on the old Chesapeake & Ohio (C&O) Canal where I had spent a lot of time, both as a boy growing up near Washington, D.C., and later with my own family when we lived in northern Virginia. So riding along that towpath was more than just a respite from roads; it brought back many pleasant memories.

An hour later we were in a café in Palmyra enjoying a milkshake and the ambiance of an old canal town; the ten miles on the trail had gone by too quickly. I called Mary Anna's pager on the cellular phone, and she called back in a few minutes with a suggested meeting place in Lyons. The connection between the cellular phone and the pager worked like a charm--for the first time.

Route 31 is close to the canal for much of the way, and with wide smooth shoulders and a tailwind we flew the last twenty miles to Lyons. It was an eighty-mile day and, at that stage of our trip, a leisurely ride. Mary Anna and Mary Jeanne Fenn were there waiting for us in Lyons. We vanned the fifteen miles north to the cottage (it had been an easy day, but not that easy).

While we were in Palmyra, I reflected on why the name sounded familiar to me. I thought it had something to do with the Mormon Church.

Joseph Smith and the Angel Moroni

Mormons believe that Jesus Christ came to the American continent after his resurrection. Their beliefs are based on visions first seen by Joseph Smith in 1823, then a fourteen-year-old boy living in Palmyra, New York. Smith testified to being visited by the angel Moroni, who directed him to some golden plates that were buried just south of town. The text on the plates was translated and printed in Palmyra and is now known as The Book of Mormon. *Smith gathered a group of people who believed in him and in the book, forming the Church of Jesus Christ of Latter-day Saints, but they were persecuted by those who were threatened by the new religion. They moved west several times to escape persecution, eventually crossing much of the Oregon Trail on their way to Salt Lake City. There are now more than nine million members worldwide, and it all began in Palmyra.*

The Fenns had lived in California since the mid-1970s but continued to spend each summer vacation at their cottage on Lake Ontario. I was raised in the East but had grown to love the West, thus I could not understand at first why anyone from California would want to go all the way to New York every summer. As we drove through the informal complex of cottages on Lake Bluff I immediately understood. The view of Lake Ontario and Sodus Bay was spectacular, the bluff was isolated and very quiet, cottages were randomly placed among the trees, and the few people we saw seemed to be having a great time. The whole place was a picture of serenity and relaxation. We had planned to take only one day off at Lake Bluff but, with only minor encouragement from Al and Mary Jeanne, quickly decided that two days would be barely enough.

Most of the eight or ten cottages have belonged to Mary Jeanne's extended family since she was a child. Various aunts, uncles, and cousins come and go throughout the summer, and many of the wives and younger kids stay all summer. We joined their extended-family picnic the first night and enjoyed getting to know Mary Jeanne's clan, as well as corn on the cob cooked in a charcoal pit. Fresh apple and blueberry pie (with ice cream for all but Roger) awaited us later in the Fenns' cottage. This was definitely a five-star day.

The cycling crew stayed in a couple of unused cottages. Each day started slowly and unplanned over coffee and goodies on the Fenns' front porch. We eventually got moving, and we toured the area, lunched at a waterside restaurant in Sodus Point, and walked along the beach. Some went boating and water-skiing on Sodus Bay the second afternoon, while Mary Anna and I visited friends of hers who lived in nearby Seneca Falls (home of the women's suffrage movement). That night we celebrated Kirby's birthday, complete with cake and candles. These were our second and third five-star days in a row.

Near the restaurant in Sodus Point, I took a picture of an historic sign titled, "War of 1812, British Fleet at Sodus Point." The sign told only part of the story.

"The British are Landing!"

A British fleet controlled Lake Ontario in the early stages of the War of 1812 and often harassed villages along the New York shore looking for U.S. military supplies. The American Army was concentrated further east, so defense of the towns was left up to local militias. On June 19, 1813, British warships were sighted off Sodus Point and New York men on horseback spread the word to local militia and citizens: "Turn out! Turn out! The British are landing!"

About sixty men--militia and other citizens--arrived and by nightfall were ready for the invaders. The British landed with a far superior force but were stopped by a volley of shots from the Americans before they reached the town. The British retreated to their boats after the exchange of fire, as they were unable in the dark to determine the size of the American force. The Americans scattered after the fire-fight, knowing they were vastly outnumbered. Several casualties were taken by both sides. The British returned in the morning, seized the supplies, and burned the town.

However, not knowing what force they might face next time, they never again raided Sodus Point.

We left the Fenns on Tuesday, August 2nd, one of the few days on the trip when we were not anxious to get back on our bikes; it had been so nice there. Al showed no interest in joining us on the bike trip, so we made him an honorary member by having him fold, staple, and stamp newsletter #8. Mary Jeanne was a most gracious hostess; she made us feel like just a few more of her extended family. Lynn kept thinking of reasons for staying at least one more day but to no avail, for Boston was waiting. Al and Mary Jeanne drove down to see us off in Lyons when we made Al one more offer to join us. He laughed, quickly declined, and, after more hugs, handshakes, group photos, and well-wishes, we were off to Syracuse. The Fenns later mentioned that the reality of what we were doing sunk in as they watched us pedal away. They had driven to the bluff many times from the west coast--but couldn't imagine doing it on a bicycle!

It was a cool, damp, but quick twenty-eight-mile ride to Weedsport where we would have lunch with Carl Oney, one of Kirby's college classmates and best man in his wedding. It started raining pretty hard as we pedaled into town, so we took cover under a gas station canopy. Because the station was conveniently out of gas, we had all the pump/service area to ourselves as we waited for Carl to arrive and lead us to his home. Carl had recently retired from teaching biology and was restoring his two-hundred-year-old home. He was also selling a new kind of energy bar and gave us samples to take along. They were okay, but we still preferred our custom-made trail mix (nuts, dried fruit, and a few M&M's) for butt-break snacks.

Lightning was striking nearby when we returned to the gas station, forcing us to wait around the pumps awhile longer. Then it started pouring, so Lynn took a picture of Kirby and Roger sitting next to their bikes and the gas pumps, surrounded by flash-flood water. As soon as the rain let up we were ready to get going, but the women wanted us to wait a little longer. Boston was still calling, though, so we took off through the puddles--but not for long. In a few minutes lightning was striking very close again and we pulled off the road, just as the van caught up to us. "You were right," we all sheepishly admitted as we climbed in the van. Right again, Mary Anna probably thought to herself. This was the only time on the trip that we stopped cycling due to weather conditions.

The fifteen-mile ride to Syracuse was uneventful, with so-so road conditions and increasing traffic as we neared the largest city we had been through (population 200,000) since Portland, Oregon. The women found a motel on the east side of town so we pedaled right through downtown. Traffic was not bad for rush hour in a city, but it was definitely not a preferred cycling route. We had two reasons for being near Syracuse, rather than skirting well around it: one, to get Mary Dean to the bus station the next morning and two, to ride the Erie Canal towpath trail from Syracuse to Rome, New York.

Mary Dean left the next morning for her conference on Long Island. She had contributed far more than just being an additional member of the sag team. She supported Kirby's desire to make the trip, even though each of them had been in serious bicycling accidents. And we would ever be grateful to her for arranging visits with the Roods in Nebraska and with her parents in Michigan. She is a very caring person and a real trooper; we would all miss her. And Kirby had smiled more during the past two weeks than he had since we left Astoria.

Mary Anna had finished newsletter #9 the night before and stopped at the local Kinko's Copies to print it, make copies, and mail them. She had planned to meet us a couple of hours later where, according to the map, the canal crossed a main road near Oneida. Lynn biked with us and was anxious to see the canal again. The Old Erie Canal State Park is a thirty-six-mile section of the old canal, restored to its original condition and miles away from the new Erie Canal with its heavy boating traffic. The contrast was even more dramatic as the park entrance is next to an interstate highway. But the traffic noise was soon behind us as we pedaled easily down the towpath and into another world. There were no packet boats or horses plodding along the towpath, but the rest of the scene was vintage Erie Canal: a quiet waterway meandering through the trees, an occasional house or barn that looked older than the canal, and wildflowers and birds that seemed at home in the peaceful setting. Only another cyclist or walker occasionally broke the spell. I stopped and chatted with two young girls on horseback. The canal was no big deal to them, just a convenient place to ride.

Roger, Lynn, and Kirby had gone ahead when I was talking with the girls. Riding alone for awhile, I could envision a line boat coming my way and the captain shouting, "Low bridge!" My McCully ancestors had passed this way in 1832 on their way west to Illinois and on to Ontario, Canada. They were probably on a line boat, as the fare was less expensive than the faster packet boats, thus they were preferred by immigrants.

Ahead I could see a bridge across the canal, an attractive new, old-style building, and some other structures that seemed to be related to the canal. Roger, Lynn, and Kirby had dismounted their bikes and were waiting for me. "Let's go check this out," suggested Lynn. "It looks interesting." The new building was the Chittenango Landing Canal Boat Museum and was definitely worth the stop. A variety of photographs, paintings, and objects helped explain how the system worked on the old canal. Roger was curious about how the horse-drawn boats passed in opposite directions without getting their ropes tangled. He found the answer in the Chittenango Museum: boats going in a particular direction always had the right-of-way, while boats going the other way had to stop and let their ropes go slack until the other boat passed. Chittenango Landing had also been a boat-building and maintenance facility, complete with three dry docks. Archeological digs were still underway, with plans to completely restore the boatyard.

We lost track of time while in and around the museum and would be over an hour late for our rendezvous with Mary Anna, so Kirby took off in order to reach her as soon as possible. Suddenly we came to a break in the canal and towpath on the outskirts of Oneida; they just dead-ended on Route 46. The canal was not visible from the road, with no signs indicating where it continued. Neither was there any sign of Kirby or Mary Anna. The canal and towpath actually bypass downtown Oneida by two miles. We knew how to get to Rome from there but decided to wait for awhile. Mary Anna drove up thirty minutes later and was pretty frustrated. We were two hours late for a meeting which didn't have an existing location because of the unexpected loss of the canal. She had driven around for two hours looking for us after leaving a pink note at the downtown post office. When Kirby arrived earlier he headed for the post office, found Mary Anna's pink note, and remained there as instructed. We had fouled up by not calling Mary Anna's pager to let her know we would be late. She had planned to visit a silver museum in Oneida that morning but instead spent that time trying to find us.

Later we found a terrific map of the canal system, published by the New York State Canal Corporation, that showed all the bikable towpaths and connections between them. Good maps are a passion of mine; at home my personalized auto-license plate letters are "LUVMAPS." I would have loved to have better maps that day, as well as enough sense to call the pager. Mary Anna later said that the only good that came out of my foul-up that day was that I have been trying to make up for it ever since.

We agreed to meet at Fort Stanwix in downtown Rome, so Mary Anna took off. There was another canal museum on the way to Rome which she was not going to miss. We found the towpath again, but Kirby and I decided to dead-head into Rome on a nearby road. It felt good to just ride fast again, especially because I was determined to get there before Mary Anna did. Kirby and I were coolly standing by our bikes when Mary Anna drove up to the fort. She was in a much better mood and ready to explore the fort, but first, we needed to find a place to stay. Roger and Lynn arrived in a few minutes and we outvoted Kirby (who wanted to camp) and decided to find a motel. There was a nice one just across the street and no campground for miles.

Fort Stanwix, now a national monument, is well worth a visit. Live cannon fire, fife and drum demonstrations, a museum, and an audio-visual presentation of the fort's history were fascinating. This site was a vital link to America's western frontier in the summer of 1777.

Fort Stanwix and the Oneida Carry

If someone draws a straight line on a map between Troy, New York, on the Hudson River and Oswego, New York, on Lake Ontario, it closely follows water all the way up the Mohawk River to Rome, a mile overland to Wood Creek, down to Lake Oneida, and then the Oneida and Oswego Rivers to Oswego. That land (or portage) between the rivers, known by the British as the Oneida Carry, was a well-traveled Indian and fur-trader route for centuries. It gained strategic importance initially during the French and Indian War and later during the Revolutionary War.

Fort Stanwix was first built by the British in 1758 to defend the Oneida Carry and the Mohawk Valley from French incursions from Canada. After their victory over the French the British abandoned the fort, but eighteen years later in 1776, the Americans occupied and rebuilt the ruins of the fort, using it against them. The Americans under Colonel Peter Gansevoort, who arrived at the fort in the summer of 1777, prepared the fort for the impending siege. The British Army Regulars and their loyalist Indian and colonist allies, under the command of Lieutenant-Colonel Barry St. Leger, were coming down Lake Ontario and up Wood Creek from Canada. As the British arrived in August, a crudely sewn red, white, and blue flag was raised above the fort for the first time, the "Grand Union." As the three-week siege of Fort Stanwix began, a group of American militia and Indian allies led by General Nicholas Herkimer was forming fifty miles east of the fort in the Mohawk Valley. They were sent to reinforce the fort, but they never got there. Along the way, they were ambushed near present-day Oriskany by a contingent of St. Leger's loyalist Indians and colonists. Herkimer's militia took heavy losses, including Herkimer who was mortally wounded during one of the bloodiest battles of the war, but their valor was not wasted. During the battle at Oriskany some American troops from the fort raided the British camp and collected all the supplies and personal items they could carry. On August 22nd, after receiving word that overwhelming American forces under the command of General Benedict Arnold were on their way, the loyalist Indians scattered, joined by the British and Tory troops. Fort Stanwix would stand and never be attacked again.

A hearty pasta dinner at the Plaza Italian Restaurant fueled us for the next day's ride. The combination of the Italian restaurant and New York conjured up discussions of the Mafia. Roger and Lynn were convinced that we might see some gangsters enter anytime with machine guns blazing. The waitress assured us it had not happened in the Plaza since its opening in 1906, so not to worry.

Mary Anna and I got up early and biked eight miles to the town of Oriskany for breakfast. It was a little tricky getting out of Rome: too much traffic and a nasty cloverleaf intersection to negotiate. But then Route 69 mellowed to a quiet country lane. Oriskany is off the main highway, a pleasant little town with a good coffee shop. It was nice to have some time to ourselves.

The others reached Oriskany by 9:00 a.m., and we were on our way down the Mohawk Valley. Lynn and Mary Anna visited the Oriskany battlefield site and General Herkimer's home in Little Falls, immersing themselves in Revolutionary War history and lifestyles. (General Herkimer had been taken to his home after being wounded and died there two days later.) The cyclists continued east on Route 69, but it was soon no longer a country lane. Utica (population 100,000) was just ahead. Like Syracuse and Rome, Utica looks a bit like it is struggling economically: lots of old brick buildings with no sign of new construction. We moved right along through the industrial section, by the railroad tracks and near the river. The air was getting hot and muggy, and we were just glad to get through town. We soon noticed that people were talking differently. Our waitress at the coffee shop in Frankfort referred to us as "youse" rather then "you guys," but she was friendly and efficient so we just enjoyed it. She no doubt thought we were the ones that talked differently.

Mary Anna and Lynn were going to meet us in St. Johnsville for lunch after their sightseeing. The bicycle touring guide and other maps showed a turnoff to St. Johnsville from our Route 5S, but we missed it, possibly because we were distracted by some other touring cyclists we rode along with for awhile. They were from Detroit on their way to Mystic, Connecticut, to attend a bicycling conference and were self-contained (carrying their own gear). One was riding a recumbent bicycle: a low-slung machine in which the rider sits in a chair-like seat with legs stretched out in front to reach the pedals. We finally pulled away from them on a steep hill. The Mohawk River was well below us, so we knew we had missed our turnoff. I tried to call the pager but couldn't get through. Oh no, not again, I thought. All we could do was continue on to the next town, Fort Plain, thus beginning the great phone chase. We didn't see a pay phone on the first pass through town, so we stopped at a diner, asked to use their phone, and were refused. On to a pay phone outside a convenience store, but it had no posted number and the people inside didn't know what it was, meaning Mary Anna would not know where to call us back. The nice folks inside the convenience store let us use their private phone. Finally I got through to the pager, but after thirty minutes and repeat calls, there was still no response. Roger called Lynn's business number at home and left a message on the recorder and still no response. Kirby'd had enough by then and took off on his bike to find another pay phone (with a number). I considered riding back the five miles to St. Johnsville. In the meantime Mary Anna and Lynn had also missed the turnoff to St. Johnsville and spent two hours trying to figure out where we were. At one point they passed a farm produce stand that, among other things, had some home-baked goodies. They had planned to buy some after lunch, but because we never showed up they never got the goodies. We'd fouled up in more ways than one. Finally Kirby came back with good news: "I got through to them. They should be here in a few minutes," he said smiling. I guess this is the rule we learned: when in densely populated, unknown territory, have a backup rendezvous location and detailed maps. And remember to check the battery in the cellular phone; ours had died the night before. Before separating again we made our lodging decision. As it was still threatening rain, a motel/truck stop in Fultonville sounded just fine.

Route 5S clings to the Mohawk Valley into Fultonville. The valley is surely no longer the wilderness faced by the early Dutch and German settlers. The bordering hills have not changed, but frequent towns, an interstate highway, power lines, dams, and factories have changed the valley forever, still a pretty place but humming with human activity. A sign pointed across the river to the town of Palatine Bridge.

Georg and Magdalena Hirchmer Come to the Mohawk Valley

The Hirchmers fled the tyranny of German kings and came to America in the early 1700s, like the Boerstlers (my ancestors) would sixty years later. Georg and Magdalena were from the Palatinate (origin of the name "Palatine Bridge") area on the lower Rhine River and settled in the Mohawk Valley near many of their countrymen. Despite the constant threat of Indian attacks and harassment by the British government's tax collectors, they raised a large family and acquired thousands of acres of land. General Nicholas Herkimer was one of their grandchildren.

Nicholas Herkimer (his father Johan, Georg's son, changed the spelling) was born into wealth and influence and naturally assumed leadership in the Mohawk's Palatine community. The militia he led to rescue the defenders of Fort Stanwix were Palatines. Today a town and a county in the Mohawk Valley honor Herkimer's name.

The Cloverleaf Motel had more trucks in the parking lot than we had ever seen in one place; Interstate 90 goes right through town. The motel office is nestled in the corner of an all-service truck stop, including a bar, restaurant, video arcade, truck parts store, laundromat, showers, and "macho" magazine rack. We had to elbow our way through a crowd of muscular truck drivers to get to the registration counter. They were not unfriendly, but, in our cycling gear, we were clearly not one of their own.

The Detroit-to-Mystic cycling group also stayed at the Cloverleaf that night, and we talked "shop" and exchanged "war stories" for awhile. They had cycled down the Mohawk Valley before and told us of a bike trail that would be on our route the next day. Mary Anna had just found some detailed maps of the valley, so we spread them out on a bed. The JIMAPCO (a private mapping company) maps show every road and trail and were a great help on the rest of our way across New York. They are available in most drug and grocery stores and gas stations. "Right there," said one of them, pointing to the faint trail symbol. "Pick it up right there and follow the trail signs for about thirty miles down through Schenectady and on to Cohos, on the Hudson River. Then it's just a short trip on city streets to the bridge over to Troy. Most of it's a separate paved trail. Although some sections are along back roads, they are well signed." That was good news. We were not looking forward to pedaling through more urban areas. Despite the truck-stop hubbub, we slept well that night.

Rain was predicted for that night, supposedly clearing in the morning. Wrong! It was raining lightly when we got up and continued as we pedaled away. A secondary road headed down toward the river. It looked on the map to be a little longer than the main road, but we felt it might be worth trying. It definitely was. I stopped to photograph an eighteenth-century stone house that was being restored when the van pulled up--they'd made the same navigational decision we had. We agreed to meet at the river where there were some old Erie Canal locks. But in a few minutes we saw them headed back our way. "There's a paved bike trail just below you. Take the next left." This was a bonus as the bike trail we planned to ride was supposed to be another ten miles downriver. This trail was brand new and not yet on the JIMAPCO map. It led us right to the locks on the remnants of the old canal, which parallels the river a hundred yards or so from the water. There was no sign of any new locks.

Stopping at a visitor center to get out of the rain for awhile, we met the leader of a work crew of girls from the New York Center for Delinquent Girls (juvenile offenders ages thirteen to eighteen who show some promise of going straight). This is the only such center in the state, and it has been very successful. The center was even scheduled to be covered in a *48 Hours* TV segment in September. The leader was enthusiastic and energetic; we wished him and the girls well as we headed back into the rain.

The new trail ended in a couple of miles where the road (Route 5S again) still hugs the Mohawk River. Just ahead there appeared to be a dam and some locks, so we pulled over to investigate. The dam is constructed mostly of steel and the locks are huge--part of the new Erie

Canal system. The engineering strategy in building the new system was to use the rivers and lakes as much as possible. Dams were built to raise the water level in shallow, cascading sections, with adjoining locks to raise and lower boats past the dams. During winter months when the canal is not navigable, the movable dams are rotated out of the water and the river runs free. The new canal is an engineering marvel and has been serving New York for over seventy years, but it sure lacks the charm of the old one.

We had to get back on the streets for awhile in Rotterdam and soon saw the van parked by a café. The hot soup hit the spot, along with dry clothing, the first time we changed clothes mid-day. Despite the continuing light rain, Mary Anna joined us on the trail for the next twenty-five miles. She wore a good rain jacket, but her lower half was soon soaked. But never a complaint, she was just glad to be out of the van for awhile. The trail was paved and wide, as good as any we had seen, particularly good in contrast to the surrounding urban area.

At one high point on the trail we could see the Mohawk River flowing into the Hudson Valley in the distance, the eastern terminus of the Erie Canal. Troy, New York, is just beyond, where it becomes tidewater from there south to Albany and on down to New York City. Commercial traffic has declined on the canal in recent years, but recreation boating is on the rise, as well as hiking and biking along the sections of existing towpath. Recognizing its recreation potential, a State Canal Recreationway Commission was recently tasked to prepare a master plan for revitalizing the canal system. The plan will propose marinas, ports, motels, restaurants, and recreation trails. Hopefully, on our next trip to New York, we can bike on a trail all the way from Buffalo to Troy.

That view of the merging Mohawk and Hudson Valleys reminded me of those troubled years prior to the Civil War when runaway slaves passed this way via the Underground Railroad.

North to Freedom

New York hung on to slavery longer than other northern states, but after it was outlawed there in 1827, New Yorkers were adamant in their opposition. Their political leaders were outspoken foes of slavery as a national practice, and many New Yorkers assisted runaway slaves as they fled to the northern United States and Canada. A favorite route came up the Hudson Valley to Albany and Troy, then split into two forks: one, further up the Hudson and Champlain Valleys to Vermont and Quebec and the other, up the Mohawk Valley to Niagara and Ontario. Troy, Schenectady, Utica,

Syracuse, and Lockport were all important links in the escape route that became known as the Underground Railroad. Many of today's black citizens in New York, New England, and Canada are proud descendants of those brave slaves who risked their lives for freedom.

Thanks to good maps and a well-marked trail we rendezvoused with Lynn on schedule. On the way to the rendezvous point she checked out the neighborhood in Schenectady where she and Roger had lived for the first year of their married life. She had planned to bike the last leg into Troy with us, but the continuing rain discouraged her. Mary Anna opted for the van as well, so they took off to find lodging, as there was no question about camping that night. Roger gave this route a four-star rating. (Remember, weather is not a factor in his rating system.)

The Super 8 Motel lived up to its name as the registrar gave us a good dinner recommendation. Holmes and Watson Ltd. is in a quiet old neighborhood within walking distance, and their fine food was followed by piano music, courtesy of Kirby. An old player piano was sitting idle near our table, so Kirby got permission from the waitress to play a tune. His family had a player piano when he was growing up. We and the other customers loved the "golden oldies," and he enthusiastically played some encores. Kirby was finally back in his musical element.

16

RELIGION, EDUCATION, AND REVOLUTION

(Days 70-75)

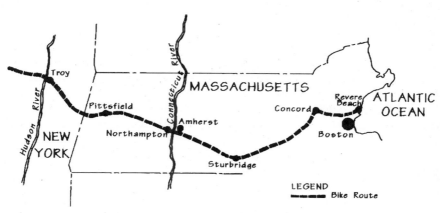

LEGEND
▬▬▬ Bike Route

Mary Anna and I were up early the next morning and, seeing a bright sunrise, decided to check out the area. Some whiffs of fog along the Hudson River were all that remained from the wet, gray skies of the day before. We found a great little café with a huge coffee pot hanging above the door, a welcome sight to early risers. After breakfast we walked along the river parkway and watched a barge move slowly through a drawbridge on its way to the Mohawk River and the Erie Canal--or maybe to other ports further up the Hudson.

British, Dutch, and American Landlords

Henry Hudson, the adventurous British sea captain, was employed by the Dutch East India Company when he sailed up the river that would take his name. He traveled as far as Albany and Troy, looking for the Northwest Passage. He never found a shortcut to the Far East, but his description of the river valley gave the Dutch claim to the territory and would stimulate further exploration and settlement. First came Dutch fur traders, then a few colonists who by 1626 established permanent settlements in present-day Albany, Manhattan Island, and Schenectady. But volunteers to settle the new land were scarce, so a "patroon" (landowner) system was set up as an incentive. Members of the Dutch East India Company were offered huge tracts of land in what they called "New Netherland" if they could recruit farmers to rent parcels of land within their tracts. Kiliaen Van Rensselaer, an Amsterdam diamond merchant, acquired 700,000 acres of land in the Hudson Valley, and one of those parcels became the city of Troy.

While Dutch colonists slowly migrated to New Netherland, the British moved faster to populate surrounding colonies, anxious to expand their empire. In 1664 a British fleet sailed into New Amsterdam's harbor and demanded that the Dutch governor surrender, which he did without a shot fired. Thus New Netherland became New York and New Amsterdam, New York City.

Descendants of the original patroons and their landlords retained ownership of their property through British and American administrations, but resistance among their tenant farmers steadily grew. In 1846 the farmers had enough political clout to convince the New York legislature to amend the constitution and transfer to them ownership of the farms they had worked for generations.

Rensselaer's was the most prosperous and long-lasting of the patroonships, and today a city and county in New York, as well as the Rensselaer Polytechnic Institute in Troy, honor his name.

Troy's Uncle Sam Wilson

Samuel Wilson and his brother Ebenezer were in the meat-packing business in Troy in the early 1800s. They sold supplies to the Army through Elbert Anderson, Jr., a New York City contractor. Casks of supplies were marked "E.A.-U.S." When one of Wilson's workmen was asked what the initials stood for he said he didn't know, unless they meant "Elbert Anderson" and "Uncle Sam." The letters "U.S." for United States were not yet familiar to them, and Sam Wilson was known locally as "Uncle Sam." When the War of 1812 broke out, some of those workmen joined the Army and spread the word that Uncle Sam Wilson was providing their supplies. Gradually the name "Wilson" was dropped and "Uncle Sam" became the accepted term for the United States of America.

In 1931 descendants of Uncle Sam Wilson dedicated a statue of him at his gravesite in Troy, and his memory lives on.

Pittsfield, Massachusetts, lies just over the Berkshires and not far beyond, Boston and the Atlantic Ocean. It was our last leg, our last state, and soon the last of our odyssey. Like earlier long hills, the climb out of the Hudson River Valley was not that difficult: grades were gentle, traffic was light, the road surface was smooth, and we were anxious to cross the last mountains of our trip. I kept having mixed feelings, eager to reach the ocean but not wanting to miss anything along the way. And though Massachusetts is relatively small in size, it is huge in American history and culture.

But there was a little more of New York before we crested the Berkshires. Kirby had a flat tire a mile or so from the top, so Roger and I waited while he repaired it; we were going over the top together. The van pulled up as we were about to climb on our bikes. Seeing that we were all right, they drove down the side road to turn around and soon came back to suggest we visit the Mount Lebanon Shaker Village at the end of the road. A gentleman they spoke to in the parking lot had visited the larger Hancock Shaker Village a few miles away in Massachusetts and said he felt this one was more authentic and less commercial.

We coasted down a short hill to a scene out of the eighteenth century. The shell of a huge old stone barn is held up by large steel girders. Another twenty or so buildings look much like they did when built in the 1780s. A handful of other tourists were the only thing out of sync with the scene. As Shakers no longer live in the village, it is managed by the Mount Lebanon Shaker Village, a not-for-profit educational organization. In the following couple of hours we learned a lot more about the Shakers.

The Shakers Passed This Way

Originally named the United Society of Believers in Christ's Second Appearing, the sect became known as the Shakers because of their violent movements during worship services. Members of a movement started in England by disgruntled Quakers, the Shakers came to America under the leadership of Ann Lee and established their first village at Mount Lebanon. Through their missionary efforts they grew to six thousand members and occupied eighteen villages at their peak in the 1850s. Only one community of Shakers remains today at Sabbathday Lake in Maine. Like the Quakers, Amish, and Old Order Mennonites, Shakers are pacifists and believe in plainness of dress and lifestyle. They all oppose slavery and respect the land, and the Shakers, Amish, and Old Order Mennonites withdrew from the world to live in their own communities. But there are differences. Unlike their brethren of other religions, Shakers are celibate, believing their movement grows through conversion of adults and adoption of orphans. In the past they made full use of modern technology; their furniture-making, water-power development, and agriculture were considered world-class in their time. And they believe in equality of the sexes; men and women are equally represented in all leadership positions. Some Shaker women were leaders in the women's suffrage movement.

Shakerism declined in the later nineteenth century along with many other religious revivals. Families sought economic opportunity out west rather than the comfort of a communal lifestyle. Women found jobs in the growing industrial cities and did not need the protection of a Shaker village. Mass production in factories was more efficient, drawing business away. And the most fervent leaders all died off. A unique religious expression and lifestyle had bloomed for awhile in the new world, when it could not in the old.

The 1500-foot summit was just ahead with a "Welcome to Massachusetts" sign. Needless to say this border-crossing was another on Roger's list of memorable milestones. We were feeling awfully good, it was a beautiful day, and we had climbed the highest remaining hill on our trip with ease. And there's nothing like a long downhill run and a little tail wind to top off the day. We cruised by the Hancock Shaker Village, noted a large, full parking lot, and were glad we had stopped at Mount Lebanon.

When we arrived at the post office we had to wait awhile for the van. Roger got impatient and left to find a phone. The pay phones in Pittsfield had no numbers either (according to the operator, to discourage their use by drug dealers). He found a bar with a generous bartender, called the pager, and then tried to leave, but not before a rough-looking patron got very unfriendly. We never knew what bothered the guy about Roger. Fortunately the bartender calmed him down and Roger escaped, ruffled but unharmed. Mary Anna showed up at the post office a few minutes later.

As there was no sign of rain or mosquitoes, a campground north of Pittsfield was our home for the night. This is resort country with lots of lakes nearby, as well as the famous Tanglewood Music Festival. Everything was full--motels, restaurants, and our campground--but we squeezed our three small tents onto the last available campsite and were sound asleep shortly after dark. We're in Massachusetts and we're going to make it, I thought, as I snuggled against Mary Anna and peacefully dozed off.

Our route across Massachusetts would take us through the five-college area of Northampton and Amherst, then a bit south to visit the vintage nineteenth-century Sturbridge Village, northeast to Concord and Lexington, and finally, through the northern outskirts of Boston to Revere Beach. We were in for a full dose of excitement; hopefully the traffic level would cooperate.

Massachusetts' blue roads are generally good for biking, and, until the last day, traffic was not bad. But finding the right road was another question. Although western Massachusetts is still mostly rural, there are scores of roads, many not well-signed or not on our maps. The situation got tougher as we approached Boston. Unlike the western states, most of the roads in the East do not go in cardinal directions. Instead they follow ridges or valleys or simply connect two towns in a straight line regardless of the hills in between. A typical problem was a Y in the road with no indication of which leg of the Y was our route. At one point we were stopped at a Y, scratching our heads, and studying the maps, when the van came by. Lynn smiled and asked, "Which fork do we take? We tried this one for awhile and are still not sure." We smiled back and responded, "Then let's try that one." Though semi-lost across parts of Massachusetts, we never worried; there are so many roads that we could always make a course correction within a mile or two. We learned to relax and enjoy it. We just stuck close together and had a few extra butt-breaks to study our maps and ask directions--and to more fully absorb the quaint towns and splendid rolling countryside.

Our blue road to Northampton was Route 143. It meandered a bit and was a little hilly, but it gave us a good taste of old Massachusetts: low-lying rock walls between fields, large deciduous trees, and houses that look centuries old. Except for the pavement and a rare car, the landscape had probably not changed much since Paul Revere's day. But despite the pleasant surroundings, two hours in the saddle was enough, and we were ready for coffee.

Worthington Corners was just ahead; surely they would have a coffee shop. The scene was right out of a Norman Rockwell painting: fine old houses clustered around a single commercial building. A sign indicated the following services: post office, groceries, deli, bakery, and meat market, with gas pumps out front. But what about coffee? Mary Anna and Lynn had arrived at the same time, and Mary Anna went inside to check it out. She came out shaking her head. "No café or coffee, just groceries," she said. Roger found that hard to believe, so he went back in to investigate further. In a few minutes he waved us in. "It's in the back," he said, "in the storeroom." An area of the storeroom had some old benches arranged around a table, a coffee pot nearby, and a variety of donuts and bagels. An elderly gentleman was filling his coffee cup. "Help yourself," he said. We asked about prices, and he chuckled and said, "Just put whatever you feel it's worth in the basket. This is a community coffee house. We don't have many rules." I asked if he was sure it was okay for out-of-towners to drink their coffee. He chuckled again. "Well, they let me drink it and I'm an outsider, even though I've been here forty-five years," he replied. "How about people from California?" I asked apologetically but with a little twinkle in my eye, knowing that Californians aren't the most highly regarded in some areas of the country. That stopped him for a few seconds as he carefully looked us over. "Oh, I guess I'll take a chance on you folks," he said. "Make yourselves at home."

Roger and Lynn got their coffee, wandered around, and chatted with the storekeeper while Mary Anna, Kirby, and I spent some quality time quizzing our host. He explained that he is in the 10:30 a.m. coffee group, and the others had apparently not made it that morning. There is a 7:00 a.m. group of "youngsters" (in their forties and fifties) and an 8:30 a.m. group of ladies. They all take turns taking care of the coffee and bringing goodies. He is a retired college professor, as are most of the others in his group; one is a retired judge (a little different than the cowboys we met in the Wagon Wheel Café in Durkee, Oregon). I glanced at a nearby bulletin board and noticed some handwritten notes and post cards. Apparently when people are out of town they send notes and post cards to the coffee groups. One of the 7:00 a.m. "youngsters" is an airline pilot, and while in Paris he sent a postcard of a topless girl posing on the Riviera. When the 8:30 ladies saw it they drew some upper garments on the girl. So there are some rules after all.

Our host asked if we had noticed any mulberry trees as we came into town. He explained that they are remnants of the silk industry that thrived in the early 1800s. Special varieties were planted, the leaves of which were fed to the silk worms. Spinning and weaving mills flourished in this area for ten to fifteen years in the early 1800s and then succumbed to competition from China and Japan (sounds familiar). But many of the mulberry trees live on.

He also volunteered his opinion on coed education: he is against it. His daughters had all gone to Smith College in Northampton, "a fine school where the girls can concentrate on academic learning and building self-confidence," he blustered. He was not interested in discussing that subject; he just wanted us to know how strongly he felt about it. Then came a story about one of his ancestors who was tried as a witch but acquitted.

We could have spent all day listening to more stories of Massachusetts' heritage, but Boston still called, so we diplomatically asked for directions to the rest room. "Just up the stairs, you can't miss it. But be careful you don't trip over anything," he chuckled. The only toilet sat alone in the middle of the attic, surrounded by mops, shovels, lumber, and other odds and ends, with a few cobwebs overhead. But it worked fine. Finally, we thanked our host and asked for directions out of town. "You have one hill to climb, and then it's downhill all the way to Northampton." We'd heard something like that before.

As we were mounting our bikes Kirby smiled and said, "Yep, we're in New England all right." He had gone to graduate school in Boston, so the morning discussions had brought back a lot of memories. Roger mentioned that he had always envisioned an old Yankee country store with folks sitting around a pot-bellied stove watching the snow fall. Now, except for the snow, he had seen it. Lynn had heard the reference to "downhill" and announced she would meet us at the top of the hill and bike down to Northampton.

Our host had also recommended that we have lunch at the Woodside Restaurant in Williamsburg (a national historic site that used to be a blacksmith shop in its earlier life). We followed his recommendation, and it was great. I could almost see a carriage and fine horses waiting outside to take us home.

Population density and traffic picked up as we pedaled down along Mill River toward Northampton, This was where some of the silk mills had been. In 1855 there were seventy-four mills of various kinds along Mill River, all powered by water or steam. Most were destroyed in the 1870s by flood waters and were never replaced. Currently, industry in the area is more dispersed.

Mary Anna got to the Northampton Post Office about the same time we did and gave us directions to our motel, across the Connecticut River near Amherst. Kirby and I took the most direct route, stopping only to view the Connecticut River from the bridge. The Connecticut's headwaters are in New Hampshire and it flows south, bisecting Massachusetts and Connecticut on its way to Long Island Sound. The earliest white fur traders and settlers came into the area by moving up the river from Connecticut. By the mid-1600s farmers arrived and built crude roads to Albany and Boston. Northampton became a crossroads. Industry thrived along the Connecticut River in the nineteenth and twentieth centuries, bringing prosperity to the area but pollution to the river. The river appeared to us to be running clean again; the pollution abatement programs of the past twenty years must have been effective as boaters, water skiers, and fisherman were enjoying the river on that clear August day.

Roger and Lynn found a bike trail that headed toward our motel, the Five College Trail that connects Smith College in Northampton with the University of Massachusetts and Amherst, Mt. Holyoke, and Hampshire Colleges in Amherst. The schools are connected by more than a trail; we learned that they are all members of a consortium where a student can register at one of them and take courses at any of the five. The trail was first-class, so Mary Anna and I got up early and took a breakfast ride on it the next morning.

We went separate ways that evening. Mary Anna and I drove into downtown Amherst, had dinner, and walked around the Amherst College campus. Few students were around in August, but we could feel the tradition. It made me think of how many gifts we have as Americans, and how many came from those early pilgrims in the Massachusetts Bay Colony. The stories of their coming to Massachusetts from England in the Mayflower and the first Thanksgiving are so familiar that it's easy to forget who these people were and why they came here.

The Pilgrims' Vision for America

The pilgrims that came to America in 1620 were members of the Puritan or Separatist religious sect that was attempting to purify the Church of England of its institutional trappings and ceremonies such as music, colored windows, and other symbols. They also believed in the equal rank of all clergyman and thus refused to accept the authority of a bishop. After decades of abuse in England and a twelve-year stint in Holland they set sail for America. Here in Massachusetts they set up the first democratic system of government in America, under the terms of the Mayflower Compact, which bound all to conform to the will of the majority. Initially the principles of self-government were endorsed by English authorities but then gradually reduced over the next 150 years. The pilgrims' vision remained strong, however, and their beliefs in self-government, education, and high moral values became embedded in Massachusetts and in American daily life. Massachusetts is famous for its many "first's" in America: first University (Harvard in 1636), first free public schools (1639), first public library (1653), first regularly issued newspaper (1704), first battle of the Revolution (1775), first church built for free blacks (1806), and even the first basketball game (in Springfield in 1891).

Life in early Massachusetts was not always pristine for all of its citizens. For a period theocracy in England was replaced by a Puritanical version in Massachusetts. All voters had to be members of the church; non-members were discriminated against in other ways. The witch trials may be hard to believe today, but they happened in Massachusetts as well as Europe. Theocracy was abolished in 1691, but the more enlightened elements of Massachusetts' Puritanical roots remain and still serve us well.

August 8th broke clear and cool, and Sturbridge was only forty miles away. There were a few hills, and we still stopped often to figure out where we were, but we reached Sturbridge shortly after noon. A highlight of the morning was seeing a road sign that indicated, "Boston - 76 miles." Roger saw it as another milestone (less than one hundred miles to go), while Kirby and I chuckled at the symbolism (1776). After camping in Pittsfield we had decided by majority vote to complete our trip in modest luxury: motels and good meals the rest of the way. The women were waiting for us at the Sturbridge Heritage Motel, ready to be tourists for the afternoon.

Old Sturbridge Village is a re-created 1830s-style New England village. The buildings, brought from all over the region, and the authentically dressed "citizens" portray aspects of life from spinning, weaving, and gardening to blacksmithing, shoemaking, and banking. Water power drives a sawmill, gristmill, and wool carding operation. Farmers harvest hay with horses and hand implements. A banker explained how each bank prints its own money and often has difficulty maintaining its credibility. They each keep lists of banks with unreliable currency (similar to today's lists of invalid credit cards). One of the tour guides mentioned that 1830 was a period of industrial transition. By then most furniture and textiles were being produced in factories rather than by families in small villages. In that sense Old Sturbridge Village is incomplete, but we wouldn't have wanted to visit an old factory. We all loved it. Lynn returned the next morning to get more pictures of village scenes before the rush of tourists ruined their authenticity.

The previous seventy-three days had been the experience of a lifetime for each of us. In many ways we had grown closer, learning to compromise and tolerate each other's idiosyncrasies in order to safely reach Boston together. But seventy-three days is a long time to be together, day and night. When you know the color and brand of each other's underwear, you're pretty close. Some built-up tensions surfaced that evening in Sturbridge as we planned our next day's ride to Concord. For the last third or so of our trip we spent time in the evening planning the next day's route; there were just so many choices. I usually took the lead on the map work, Roger sometimes sat in, and Kirby was usually happy to just be briefed on our plans the next morning. It was different that night in Sturbridge. We all studied the maps, and Roger and Kirby developed strong preferences for different routes. Roger had expressed strong opinions on many issues between Astoria and Sturbridge; Kirby and I often went along, relying on a vote to settle our differences. But it was not clear that a vote would settle things this night. Differences that might never have surfaced in our previous relationship came out that night. Kirby and Roger each pointed emphatically at the map with a pencil, raising their voices while arguing their sides. I could see benefits in both routes and was reluctant to take sides. So Mary Anna finally stepped in. After a couple of questions she said, "Okay, you're going this way. Lynn and I will see you in Concord. Let's go to bed." And we did.

Kirby and Roger talked quietly the next morning and apologized to each other, realizing that we had come too far together to let personality differences dampen our pending celebration. It was the 9th of August, and we were off on a circuitous route to Concord. As it turned out we followed no one's planned route for much of the day, just kept avoiding the larger cities and heading in the general direction of Concord on nameless roads. We even swallowed our male pride and asked for directions a couple of times. In one town we asked a policeman for directions. He laughed and said, "It might help if we put up a few more street signs." We rolled our eyes, smiled, and made no comment. Kirby was convinced that Massachusetts only signs its roads at each end and that we always intersected them in the middle. A lady in a garden supply store was very helpful, offering fresh water, directions, and a brief tour of her nursery.

Our B-2 stop in Milbury was classic. It was an old converted trolley car that was packed with men from the neighborhood, talking shop (a textile mill was nearby). One of the waitresses was partially deaf, so both waitresses were constantly shouting at each other. The local customers just smiled and took it in stride. We asked about a rest room and were told it was in the basement, the door to which was in the back behind the garbage cans. After moving the garbage cans we climbed down a narrow spiral staircase to a dark, damp cellar filled with supplies and a few cobwebs. A tiny enclosure stood in the center of the cellar with a toilet inside, raised on blocks a foot above the floor. So we literally "sat on the throne."

Notwithstanding our navigational problems, a few potholes to dodge, and increasing traffic, it was another fascinating day through quiet old villages and suburban neighborhoods, by textile mills, small farms, and "gentlemen's" estates. Despite the frequent stops and starts, I enjoyed it all. We reached Concord in mid-afternoon and found the motel easily. Our final pink note was taped on the post office door. As we pedaled toward the Howard Johnson's Motel the cellular phone rang. Mary Anna had learned the local access code for the phone and was making sure we got the message. As we turned into the motel's access road we could see Mary Anna and Lynn by the front door, smiling. "Only thirty miles to Revere Beach!" Lynn shouted.

Concord was a perfect place to stage our final run to the sea. If all went well we could finish by noon the next day, and the Concord area was a slow-paced, fascinating place to visit. After exploring Concord we would return the next night to celebrate and make final departure arrangements.

It was exciting to be where Emerson, Hawthorne, the Alcotts, and Thoreau had lived, where they had been inspired to make such rich contributions to America's literature. Walden Pond was just out of town, where Thoreau had spent two years in semi-seclusion in order to better understand the most basic elements of life. And so much history here-- the North Bridge was nearby where American minutemen fired on British soldiers and sparked the Revolutionary War.

Roger and Lynn visited some of the sites that afternoon while Mary Anna, Kirby, and I relaxed and quietly prepared for the next day. Kirby had seen the sites during earlier visits and was making arrangements for his circuitous route home. Mary Anna and I would be staying a third night in Concord and had plenty of time to see things later.

Our final day's ride would follow the old "Battle Road" to Lexington, then the Minuteman Bikeway for a few miles before heading northeast through Medford and Malden to the beach. Somehow, as I was dozing off, thoughts of the "Battle Road" and Lexington Green were as much on my mind as reaching the Atlantic Ocean. The process was still more interesting than just getting there.

Mary Anna and I awoke at our usual early hour and decided to drive over to see the North Bridge before breakfast. It was not on our bike route, and Lynn and Roger had raved about the visitor displays there. We were not disappointed. The bridge had been reconstructed exactly as it stood in 1775, and the dirt road, low stone walls, and open fields lent credibility to the scene. Audio tapes added to the text and graphic displays. It was very dramatic; this was where a few American militia men decided to take on the most powerful army in the world.

🚲   🚲   🚲

"The Shot Heard 'Round The World"

American militia men gathered across the Concord River after warnings the night before from William Dawes. Paul Revere and Dawes had reached Lexington to warn John Adams, John Hancock, and the local citizens that the British were coming, but Revere was captured as they continued west toward Concord. Seven hundred British troops arrived in Lexington at dawn on April 19, 1775, and faced Captain John Parker and his seventy-seven militia men. Parker was only showing resolve, having no thought of trying to stop the overwhelming British force. He began to disperse his men when ordered to do so, but a shot was fired, then many more as the Americans fled. Eight patriots lay dead, and the British marched on to Concord. News of the shooting at Lexington spread rapidly. Other militia men flocked to the British line of march between Boston and Concord.

The British came to Concord to find and destroy American military supplies. They were successful. Fires from the burning supplies alarmed the Americans gathering across North Bridge. Thinking that their homes were being destroyed, the Americans started across the bridge, and the British fired a volley into their ranks. "Fire, fellow soldiers, for God's sake, fire!" yelled Concord's Major Buttrick. For the first time Americans fired into the ranks of British soldiers.

Revere Beach beckoned, so we checked our tires, filled our water bottles and trail mix bags for the last time, and headed down Lexington Road. Signs indicating "Battle Road" and the Minuteman National Historical Park were just ahead. In places the road was rough and unpaved, much as it was when the American militia men fired on the British troops as they marched back to Boston. We stopped at the Battle Road Visitor Center, the site where Paul Revere was captured, and again in Lexington at the spot where Captain Parker's men were riddled with British gunfire. We biked slowly through those beautifully preserved historic places and took time to read every sign and marker.

After a pleasant five miles on the Minuteman Bikeway, which heads into downtown Boston, we were back into the hubbub of city streets. We soon encountered what may be a Boston phenomenon: cars parallel-parked with their doors left open on the driver's side. We didn't think much about it the first time, but after three or four more, we figured it was just the way to make a quick stop. Narrow streets, open doors in our pathway, roundabouts, heavy traffic, and a lack of street signs did not enhance our final miles to the beach, but at that stage we could handle most anything. Then we saw it: water on the horizon--lots of it--and a beach. We could coast the rest of the way.

Mary Anna and Lynn were waiting at the designated spot with cameras in hand. We wanted to take some "wheel-dipping" photos but were in no hurry. It was a beautiful day, and we wanted to call our kids, eat lunch, and savor the moment for awhile. Lynn had made a large sign that read, "WE DID IT, Pacific to Atlantic, 75 days, 3,794 miles." We posed in various combinations: with and without the sign, with and without the front wheels of our bikes in the water, and with and without the special T-shirts Lynn had made for us. I nearly fell over with my bike after standing so long in the wet, shifting sand, but I wouldn't have cared. A nice lady came by and took pictures of our entire group with each camera. A couple of other passersby asked what was going on. Too soon our celebration was over. We loaded the bikes onto the van and headed back to Concord.

THE SEND OFF, *above*. We embarked on a stormy day from Fort Stevens State Park on the Pacific Ocean near Astoria, Oregon—an immediate test for our rain gear. This group includes cyclists and supporters (left to right): Roger Wedel, Lynn Wedel, Mary Dean Miller, Kirby Miller, Robbi Swinnerton, Mike Swinnerton, Andy Swinnerton, Dick Swinnerton, Mary Anna Swinnerton, and Juli Swinnerton (kneeling).

BLUE MOUNTAIN CROSSING ON THE OREGON TRAIL, *above*. Near La Grande, Oregon, we stumbled upon a living-history program sponsored by the U.S. Forest Service. "Have you seen John?" asked the young woman dressed in a plain nineteenth-century dress. She remained in character as she told her pioneer story. Her husband John had returned to the last settlement to seek help for their sick child, now dead and buried nearby. She showed us the authentic contents of the wagon as she talked about the rigors of life on the trail.

This Tractor Is No Toy, *above*. These young boys near Emmett, Idaho, had work to do and would not be distracted by three bicyclists who stopped to watch and take pictures. The newly plowed furrows were straight as a string, and there was no adult in sight, just two steely-eyed boys with a job to do. And they meant to do it right.

Calf-feeding Time at the Hopwoods' Ranch, *above*. The Hopwoods kindly invited us to stay with them at the ranch just south of Hansen, Idaho. Wes Hopwood (pictured) is an old hand at this twice-a-day chore and patiently showed us how to help out. At the onset the feisty calves roared with hunger; later, it was very quiet when all the calves had been fed. This silence told us that it was okay to head back to the house for a real ranch breakfast.

BUFFALO VALLEY AND THE TETON RANGE, *above.* This breathtaking view from the front porch of our motel northeast of Jackson, Wyoming, made all the headwinds, hills, and bumps worthwhile. Horses from the dude ranch next door are having supper after a hard day. The sharp crest of the Teton Mountains looms in the distance. Mary Anna and I relaxed here the next day while Kirby, Roger, and Lynn toured Yellowstone National Park.

WARMED-OVER SPAGHETTI FOR BREAKFAST, *above.* On a gloomy morning near Muddy Gap, Wyoming, Mary Anna came to our rescue after twenty-five miles and no coffee shop in sight. She pulled into this Devils Gate overlook, cranked up the camp stove, and had spaghetti and hot chocolate ready when we arrived. Throughout the trip, this van was always a welcomed sight.

Finishing Up the Weekly Newsletter, *above.* Mary Anna is plugged into the electrical outlet at our Lusk, Wyoming, campsite. Every evening she quizzed us for news and then went to work with Roger's laptop computer. She was determined to keep friends and relatives up to date on our progress and highlights.

Roll On, Round Bale, *above.* Near Chadron, Nebraska, Kirby is pushing as hard as he can, but the 1,400-pound bale will not budge. These huge bales are now a common sight on Nebraska's farms and ranches, replacing the traditional, smaller rectangular bales. It takes a pretty stout tractor with a front-end loader to move these bales.

LE MARS CELEBRATES THE FOURTH OF JULY, *above.* This is true Americana. Everyone in Le Mars, Iowa, seems to be proud of America and enjoys her birthday. Entertainment in the town square continued throughout the day; later at the fairgrounds, fireworks lit up the sky.

BLUE ROADS ACROSS IOWA, *above.* On Iowa's road maps, blue is the color for paved secondary roads and the background color on the route signs. Traffic is rare, corn, soy beans, hogs, and people are full of life, and mail boxes are creative along the "blue roads," the best way to see Iowa.

IGNORING THE DETOUR SIGN,
above. Near Imlay City, Michigan, we took a chance and went right on through. The construction workers used this steel beam to cross the stream while building a new bridge. It worked well for us, too.

FLOWERS BLOOM WHERE AMERICANS ONCE FOUGHT THE BRITISH, *right.* Now a quaint and beautiful resort community, Niagara-on-the-Lake, Ontario, is where Americans clashed with the British, the Canadians, and their Indian allies during the War of 1812. The city was a strategic spot where the Niagara River enters Lake Ontario.

THE ERIE CANAL LIVES ON, *above.* In Lockport, New York, the old and the new remain side by side. Boats currently transit the modern locks (right) under their own power, but in the early 1800's, horse-drawn packet boats passed through the old locks (left), moving people and cargo from Albany to Buffalo. The canal was once known as "Clinton's Folly," named for the man who governed New York state at the time.

WE'RE SIX AGAIN, *above.* Mary Dean Miller and Lynn Wedel rejoined us in Michigan. Here In Lyons, New York, we are about to pedal east again after two restful days with our friends, the Fenns, at their summer place on Lake Ontario.

To Arms, To Arms, *left.* In Rome, New York, we saw this living-history demonstration at Fort Stanwix National Monument. During the Revolutionary War, various fife and drum calls were used to direct the soldiers' activities. Americans held off the invading British Army here at Fort Stanwix and prevented them from moving further south.

Iron Butt, Tail Gunner, and Wind Slayer Reach the Atlantic, *below.* We had mixed feelings when we reached Revere Beach, Massachusetts. Where is the next blue road? I wanted to say. The sense of accomplishment was terrific, but I was sorry to see the experience of my lifetime come to an end.

17

REVERE BEACH REFLECTIONS

Several months later, when hearing about our trip, a friend commented, "You must have felt ecstatic when you first saw the Atlantic Ocean." My answer was, "Happy, yes, but ecstatic, no. In fact in many ways I was sorry it was over." Sure it felt great to make it, with all of us in good health, but in a way I was disappointed not to see a blue road stretching out across the ocean, with a café ahead filled with the local crowd. Or some kids on bikes riding out to greet us, yelling, "Where are you guys going?" Or a tall stranger in a black cowboy hat whose frown melts into a smile as we ride by.

For the past seventy-five days the schedule and goal of getting to Boston had been our constant companion. Without the discipline associated with the schedule we might never have completed the trip. Yes, I was anxious to announce to family and friends that we had made it, but something was missing. The celebration at the beach was nice but not wonderful. It was not the exultation of winning a race or kicking a game-winning field goal, more like finishing a cruise or walking out of a theater after a great show. Perhaps we learned again that the show, not the final curtain, is the important part. And the show was over.

It was quiet on the drive back to Concord. There was some talk about heading home: Kirby needed a ride to the bus station the next morning to begin his circuitous route to California; Roger and Lynn would spend a few days sight-seeing and visiting friends in Boston, then fly home; Mary Anna and I would drive the van home across the southern states, visiting her mom and other relatives, friends, and places along the way.

That evening we had a delicious four-star celebration dinner together. After placing our dinner orders, Mary Anna asked for our reflections on the entire trip. A section of her newsletter was titled, "Reflections," and she needed input for the final edition. Of course we were unanimous in our enthusiasm for having bicycled across the country, but no one mentioned being thrilled over simply reaching the Atlantic Ocean. Apparently I was not the only one who considered it an anti-climax.

We were thankful for the miraculous weather; nearly all the rain came at night, and the temperature seldom exceeded ninety degrees. Roger commented that he would never bike across the country again, as the law of averages would come into play and next time it would be much hotter and always rain during the day.

We realized how little we need to survive and still have stimulating lives. We each had only one suitcase for nearly three months and seldom missed a thing (though Lynn missed having a choice of ethnic foods in the Rocky Mountain and midwestern states). "Why do we accumulate so much stuff?" Mary Anna and I had often asked ourselves during the trip. Without the "stuff," we took more time to meet new people, read, and just enjoy each place and each other.

And we had some advice for others who plan to take an extended bicycle tour like ours (a self-planned and supported trip with more than one person):

• <u>Route plan and schedule</u> - Have one but stay flexible; otherwise you miss surprise opportunities and spend too much effort on just grinding down the road and not enough on "smelling the roses." Take time off from riding. One day per week worked well for us; one and a half or two might be even better.

• <u>Lodging and food</u> - Be sure that you have consensus on how much camping and cooking versus motels and restaurants. These are the biggest budget items and can cause conflict if not clearly agreed upon.

• <u>Separation in the evening</u> - Eat and socialize some together, but don't get locked into it. Plan to occasionally get away individually or in smaller groups.

• <u>Laundry</u> - Each person brought enough clothes and underwear so that we could do laundry about every four to five days. Taking turns with this responsibility worked for us (although Kirby was best at giving us back the right clothes, neatly folded).

• <u>Biking together</u> - We overdid our "stay in sight" rule. There are times when it is important to stay together for security reasons or to celebrate reaching milestones, but in most areas, if everyone has a map and a rendezvous is agreed upon, it's more pleasant and relaxing for the bikers to pedal at their own pace and be free to separate.

• <u>Maps</u> - You can never have too many of them. We had two maps for each area, one for the van and one for the cyclists. We should have had a set for each cyclist; then separation would have been more comfortable. Also, seek out detailed maps for every city you go through or near. While the city insets on state maps are fine for driving right through town, they do not show enough secondary roads, and they never show suggested bike routes, lanes, or trails. The same goes for special features or places like the Oregon Trail, national parks, or the Erie Canal. Do your homework; get good maps in advance if you can or know where to get them along the way. Local drug, grocery, and convenience stores, as well as bike shops, often have county or area maps that give more detailed information.

• <u>Communication</u> - This is partly a question of devices: cellular phones, pagers, a phone mail box, and pink Post-It notes. These all worked well for us at times (as long as batteries were checked and local phone codes known). The other side of communication--and just as important--is simply talking about issues and concerns on a regular basis.

Important issues include whether to ride together or separately, when to take an extra day off, whether to clarify or change the route or schedule, and concerns about what happened the previous day. Daily meetings of all parties is recommended. Take time to work out any minor problems before they grow. And take advantage of everyone's good ideas.

• The sag wagon - Having a vehicle carry the gear, extra parts, etc. makes the actual riding a little easier. It also gives you more options as to where you can stay, as it was necessary at times to van ahead or back in order to find lodging. Organizing the vehicle so that each person has his/her own "spot" and takes care of seeing that their gear is loaded and unloaded makes life easier for the sag wagon driver, and the van doesn't have to be reorganized each day. Our pattern entailed the sag wagon catching up in mid-morning, checking to see that all was okay, and then driving ahead to find the night's lodging. (The day's destination was generally determined each morning.) Once lodging was found, a note at the post office or the van waiting at the edge of town seemed to suffice. (At our pace of 10 mph including stops, the van driver could usually determine our time of arrival at the end of the day.) Originally, we thought the sag wagon driver would have lots of extra time, but the reality was different. Writing a weekly newsletter, finding the cyclists, and then driving ahead to the night's destination took the entire morning. Often much time was spent calling or visiting various motels to find the best price, as most were not listed in a AAA or motel chain directory. As the men finished their day between 3:30 and 4:30 p.m., there was usually not much extra time in the afternoon. Each day was an adventure (especially on the blue roads) for we never knew what we would find at the day's destination. The trip for the sag wagon driver was certainly different from that of the cyclists but equally rewarding.

Finally, we all were deeply impressed with the quality and diversity of our country: its geography, vegetation, architecture, commerce, agriculture, transportation systems, and people. Kirby mentioned that he had been taught all of these things since he was a kid and had driven across the country several times, but they all appear far more real from the seat of a bicycle. Lynn said she would always remember the grandeur of the Grand Tetons, Yellowstone, Niagara Falls, the Great Lakes, and the amazing contrast in vegetation and culture between eastern Wyoming and Massachusetts. Mary Anna was impressed by the very different "frames of reference" people have across the country. She learned how difficult it is for a farmer to understand the problems of people in the cities, and vice versa. We talked about how most Americans now live in urban areas, few understanding how milk, meat, and potatoes are grown or understanding the farmers and ranchers who grow them. Those farmers and ranchers who frequently use guns to protect their crops and livestock from predators do not understand why city folks support gun control. In our nation's "tapestry" the colors of geography and people are often very different, but somehow they blend gradually from one region to another to form a beautiful, strong, and dynamic country. Like Kirby, I had read such words and had seen much of the country before, but when passing through it slowly and stopping often to examine its pieces, the miracle that is America truly sinks in.

It's been over two years since we dipped our wheels in the water at Revere Beach, and I still cannot get the trip out of my system. It was a grand adventure, but it was not the excitement of it that has lasted. Rather it has been the deeper understanding of and appreciation for our country that came as we slowly absorbed it farm by farm, town by town, and county by county--how it got to this point and how it works today. This appreciation bloomed as I later learned more about the history of the areas we passed through:

- How the America of thirteen colonies expanded to the Pacific Ocean in less than a hundred years;
- Why South Pass was the doorway to the West on the Oregon Trail;
- Why the Erie Canal survived and so many others failed when railroads came along;
- Why a railroad was in a particular location and why it was carrying coal;
- How so much of the arid West became lush and green;
- Why there is so much corn in Iowa and so many dairy cows in Wisconsin;
- Why so many towns in the Midwest have strong ethnic identities;
- Why Model-T Fords were built in Detroit.

It's a pretty long list, but I've observed some common elements running through it all: personal initiative, private enterprise, and effective government. All three seem to be present in so many of our country's great leaps forward, for example in the following:

• The Erie Canal - Venture capitalists started the idea by risking their resources to build isolated canal and lock segments on the Mohawk River. Some were washed away by flood waters or failed economically, but they inspired Governor Clinton and the New York state legislature to build a well-engineered waterway from the Hudson River to the Great Lakes, both opening the doorway to westward migration and assuring the future of New York City as a major economic center.

• The railroads - Workers came from Asia and Europe, as well as America, to build the railroads, hoping to build better lives for themselves. With the government providing a legislative framework, financial resources, and a military escort, capitalists stepped forward to risk huge investments. Some became wealthier, but many went bankrupt. Government-owned land and mineral rights were offered to the railroad companies, as well as funds to subsidize construction costs.

While it took the three-way partnership to allow the Erie Canal and the railroads to take their major place in history, it is still continuing today to the benefit of cyclists. With recent actions by private and public institutions and with the support of individuals, the number of trails along old railroad beds and places like the Erie Canal is increasing.

Somehow when looking back it's easy to see the roles that individuals, capitalists, and the government have played in our country's development. While there is some tension between them today we must remember that as this three-way interaction worked well in the past, so it may be the key to our future. There have always been problems to address and tension between the three elements, but new alliances evolved to help us solve the problems and become a greater nation. After seeing so much of it from the seat of a bicycle, I feel very optimistic about the future of our country, that through continuous, and at times painful, debate, new solutions will continue to emerge, and far brighter days lie ahead. Who knows but that someday cyclists, government, and commercial sponsors will form alliances to build coast-to-coast and border-to-border bicycle trails. I look forward to riding on them.

ACKNOWLEDGMENTS

I deeply appreciate the generous assistance of the following historical societies and other institutions that provided source material for the historical sections of this book: Bowring Ranch State Historical Park (Nebraska); Bonneville County Historical Society (Idaho), Mary Jane Fritzen; Chittenango Landing Canal Boat Museum (New York), Joan DiChristina; Concord Museum (Massachusetts), Carol Haines; Fond du Lac County Historical Society (Wisconsin), John J. Ebert; Fort Caspar Museum (Wyoming), Richard Young; Fort Robinson Museum (Nebraska), Thomas R. Buecker; Fort Stanwix National Monument (New York), Michael R. Kusch; Herkimer County Historical Society (New York), Susan R. Perkins; Historic Northampton (Massachusetts), Marie Panik; Jackson Hole Historical Society and Museum (Wyoming), Ronald E. Diener; Kinney Pioneer Museum (Iowa), Fran Tagesen; La Crosse County Historical Society (Wisconsin), Brenda R. Jordan; Lake Michigan Carferry Service, Thomas Hawley; Lexington Historical Society (Massachusetts), Christine Ellis; Maryhill Museum of Art (Washington), Lee Musgrave; Mason County Historical Society (Michigan), Kay E. Stakenas; Massachusetts Historical Society, Jennifer Tolpa; National Park Service; Niagara Historical Museum (Ontario, Canada), Bill Severin; Oregon Department of Transportation, Carolyn Philp; Pendleton Underground Tours (Oregon), Pamela Severe-Bruton; Pendleton Woolen Mills (Oregon); Plymouth County Historical Museum (Iowa), Delores Burkard; Port Huron Museum (Michigan), Michelle Measel; Rensselaer County Historical Society (New York), Robert N. Andersen; Rome Historical Society (New York), Kathleen Hynes-Bouska; Museum of the Fur Trade (Nebraska), Charles E. Hanson, Jr.; The State Historical Society of Wisconsin, Geraldine Strey; Vesterheim Norwegian-American Musuem (Iowa); Wayne County Office of Tourism/History (New York), Deborah Ferrell; Winnebago Industries (Iowa), Sheila M. Davis.

Old Jules, copyright ©1935, 1963 by Mari Sandoz. Synopsis by permission of McIntosh and Otis, Inc., New York.

Photographs are by Lynn Wedel, Dick Swinnerton, Mary Anna Swinnerton, Cindy Swinnerton, and Al Fenn. The maps for each chapter heading are by Brenda Pallemaerts.

And I especially thank the following individuals who offered suggestions, criticism, and encouragement along the way: Peggy and Karen Choate, Jim and Connie Cochran, Elizabeth Davidson, Rodney and Carol Hopwood, Mary Jaskower, Debbie Lindberg, Ralph and Janet Litchfield, Kirby and Mary Dean Miller, Anna Pritchett, Dorothy Pritchett, Dick and Pat Schoof, Roger and Elizabeth Stephan, Roger and

Lynn Wedel, my four children Mike, Matt, Bob, and Juli Swinnerton, and daughters-in-law Robbi, Cindy, and Penny Swinnerton.

Andrist, Ralph E., ed. *The American Heritage History of the Making of the Nation*. New York: American Publishing Company, 1987.

Bateman, Richard. *The Outer Coast*. San Diego: Harcourt Brace Jovanovich, 1985.

Brown, Dee. *Hear That Lonesome Whistle Blow: Railroads in the West*. New York: Touchstone, 1977.

---. *Bury My Heart at Wounded Knee*. New York: Holt, Rinehart and Winston,Inc., 1971.

Bullard, Oral. *Lancaster's Road: The Historic Columbia River Highway*. J. K. Gill Company, 1929

Catton, Bruce. *Michigan: A Bicentennial History*. New York: W. W. Norton & Company, Inc., 1976.

Creigh, Dorothy Weyer. *Nebraska: A History*. New York: W. W. Norton & Company, Inc., 1976.

Cross, Whitney R. *The Burned-Over District: The Social and Intellectual History of Enthusiastic Religion in Western New York, 1800-1850*. Ithaca, NY: Cornell University Press, 1950.

Crutchfield, James A. *It Happened in Oregon*. Helena, MT: Falcon Press Publishing Company, Inc., 1994.

Frazier, Joseph. *Iowa: A History*. New York: W. W. Norton & Company, Inc., 1976.

Garrett, Wilber E., ed. *Historical Atlas of the United States: Centennial Edition*. Washington, D.C.: National Geographic Society, 1988.

Gilbert, Bill, et al. *The Trailblazers*. New York: Time, Inc., 1973.

Havighurst, Walter. *Land of Promise: The Story of the Northwest Territory*. New York: The Macmillan Company, 1946.

Hostetler, John A. *Mennonite Life*. Scottsdale, PA: Herald Press, 1983.

Jenkins, Peter and Barbara. *The Road Unseen*. New York: Ballantine Books, 1985.

---. *The Walk West: A Walk Across America 2*. New York: William Morrow & Company, Inc., 1981.

Kellar, Allan. *Life Along the Hudson*. Tarrytown, NY: Sleepy Hollow Restorations, 1976.

Larson, T. A. *Wyoming: A History*. New York: W. W. Norton & Company, Inc., 1976.

LeVert, Suzanne. *Let's Discover Canada: Ontario*. New York: Chelsea House, 1991.

Lovett, Richard A. *Free-Wheelin': A Solo Journey Across America*. Camden, ME: Ragged Mountain Press, 1992.

McDonald, Lucile. *Search for the Northwest Passage*. Portland, OR: Binfords & Mort, 1958.

Miller, Levi. *Our People: The Amish and Mennonites of Ohio*. Scottsdale, PA: Herald Press, 1983.

Murphy, Dan and Gary Ladd. *Oregon Trail: Voyage of Discovery*. KC Publications, Inc., 1992.

Newhouse, Elizabeth L., ed. *The Story of America: A National Geographic Picture Atlas*. Washington, D.C.: The National Geographic Society, 1984.

Parkman, Francis. *The Oregon Trail*. New York: Penguin Group, 1950.

Peterson, F. Ross. *Idaho: A Bicentennial History*. New York: W. W. Norton & Company Inc., 1976.

Schuster, Helen H. and Frank W. Porter III, eds. *Indians of North America: The Yakima*. New York: Chelsea House Publishers, 1990.

Snyder, Gerald S. *In the Footsteps of Lewis and Clark*. Washington, D.C.: National Geographic Society, 1970.

The World Book Encyclopedia. Chicago: Field Enterprises Educational Corporation, 1972.

Turner, Frederick. *Beyond Geography: The Western Spirit Against the Wilderness*. New Brunswick, NJ: Rutgers University Press, 1992.

Wellman, Paul I. *Death on the Prairie: The Thirty Years' Struggle for the Western Plains*. Lincoln, NE: University of Nebraska Press, 1934.

White, Richard. *The Middle Ground: Indians, Empires, and Republics in the Great Lakes Region, 1650-1815*. New York: Cambridge University Press, 1991.

Woodcock, George. *The Canadians*. Cambridge, MA: Harvard University Press, 1979.

Yoder, Doyle and Leslie A. Kelly. *America's Amish Country*. Berlin, OH: America's Amish Country Publications, 1992.

DAY	DESTINATION	ROUTE COMMENTS	MI/TOT	RATE
1	OR -Astoria to OR - Rainier	Lots of traffic, good shoulder.	30	**
	WA -Puget Island to WA -Longview	Very nice on island. WA4: rolling hills, nice road along river. This route avoids steep hill along OR30 before Longview.	25 - 55	****
2	OR -Troutdale	Cross Lewis & Clark Bridge back to OR, then OR30 to Portland (good road, some traffic). Bike trails from Portland to Troutdale.	72 - 127	***
3	OR -Multnomah Falls	Take old Oregon Highway to Crown Pt & then down to Falls	15 - 142	***
	OR -Cascade Locks	I84: dangerous, long narrow tunnel. AVOID.	15 - 157	-
	WA - Home Valley	Over Bridge of Gods, then WA14: good.	12 - 169	***
4	WA - Maryhill	WA14	54 - 223	***
5	WA - Crow Butte	WA14: good shoulder, light traffic, tailwind.	55 -278	****
6	OR - Echo	WA14 to Umatilla, OR, old HWY30 on Oregon side. Some traffic.	50 - 328	**
	OR - Pendleton	Beautiful along river, no traffic, scenic.	25 -353	****
7	OR - Pendleton	REST DAY		
	OR -Dead Man Gp	Old road, steep, but no traffic.	26 - 379	****
8	OR - La Grande	OR30: good, quiet, downhill. Last ten miles on I84.	23 - 402	***
9	OR -Baker City	OR30: good, quite, flat, little traffic.	50 - 452	***
10	OR -Baker City	REST DAY, VISIT MUSEUM		
11	OR -Ontario	Some hills through desert, then through range and wheat fields, pass Farewell Bend along Snake River.	85 - 537	***
12	ID - Eagle	New Plymouth, Emmett on ID16 to Eagle.	50 - 587	***
	ID - Boise	Eagle thru Boise: no shoulders, heavy traffic.	20 - 607	*
13	ID - Mountain Home	I84 except for last seven miles: wide shoulder, traffic.	40 - 647	**
	ID - Glenn's Ferry	Back roads, nice, long downhill, along Snake.	25 - 672	***
14	ID - Shoshone	Back roads to Bliss, then ID26 - high desert.	78 - 750	**
15	ID - Hansen	(Vanned from Shoshone to Hagerman) Hagerman to Buhl on US30, back roads to Twin Falls, US30 to Hansen.	45 - 795	****
16	ID -American Falls	US30 to Burley okay, ID81 to Delco, then I-84 which is very rough.	65 - 860	**
17	ID -Blackfoot	I-86 to Pocatello very good (best freeway).	72 - 932	***
		ID91 to Blackfoot: rough, no shoulder.		*
18	ID - Swan Valley	I-15 to Idaho Falls (good), then US26: okay.	65 - 997	**

DAY	DESTINATION	ROUTE COMMENTS	MI/TOT	RATE
19	WY - Alpine	US26 through Swan Valley: nice except for shoulder; rolling hills along Palisades Res.	34 - 1031	***
20	WY - Hobart Jct.	US26 along Snake River thru canyon, narrow shoulder.	18 - 1049	
	WY - Jackson	US91: wide shoulder, much traffic, boring.	23 - 1072	**
21	WY - Moran Jct.	Travel through Tetons, Jenny Lake bypass.	48 - 1120	****
22	WY - Moran Jct.	REST DAY		
23	WY - Dubois	US26: steady, gradual climb to Cont. Divide, nice long downhill to Wind River Valley.	55 - 1175	***
24	WY - Lander	US26, ID287: mostly flat land, elevation loss of 1500 feet, wide shoulders.	75 - 1250	**
25	WY - Jeffrey City	Mostly wide shoulders, some rough sections, steep six miles after thirty miles; mostly sagebrush, little farmland.	62 - 1312	**
26	WY - Alcova (stayed in Casper)	Rolling hills, two-lane road with wide shoulder, some parts very rough.	64 - 1376	**
27	WY - Casper	Downhill with tailwind, took 2.2 hours.	34 - 1410	***
28	WY - Douglas	WY26, then I25: good roads, wind at back.	49 - 1459	***
29	WY - Lusk	I-25 from Douglas, good; US20 is two lanes with shoulder, trucks.	59 - 1518	**
30	NE - Crawford,	US20 slightly improved in Nebraska, rolling hills, last eight miles steep downhill.	55 - 1573	**
31	NE - Rushville	US20: tailwind, okay to Chadron, beautiful ride, very good to Hay Springs.	61 - 1634	***
		Very rough road and shoulder to Rushville.		*
32	NE - Valentine	Rolling hills, some areas rough, others good.	107 - 1741	**
33	NE - Valentine	REST DAY		
34	NE -Stuart (stayed in O'Neil)	US20: rolling Sand Hills until Bassett, then flat, wide shoulders.	82 - 1823	**
35	NE - Niobrara	US20 to O'Neill, new pavement, flat.	27 - 1850	**
		NE51 to turn off to Niobrara, last thirty miles rolling hills, some steep.	34 - 1884	*
		NE14 to Niobrara, nice rolling hills, scenic.	20 - 1904	***
36	S.D. - Yankton	NE12 to Crofton, NE121 to Yankton: two-lane, little traffic, steep rolling hills to Crofton, flat most of way to Yankton.	46 - 1950	**
37	Iowa Border	SD50 okay to Vermillion, very rough shoulder to I-25, good thereafter.	50 - 2000	*
38	IA - LeMars	REST DAY		
39	IA - Paullina	IA3 and IA10: no shoulders, mostly flat, too much traffic for no shoulder.	62 - 2062	**
40	IA - Emmettsberg	Rolling country roads: no shoulders, no traffic	65 - 2127	***

DAY	DESTINATION	ROUTE COMMENTS	MI/TOT	RATE
41	IA - Forrestville	Rolling country roads: no shoulders, no traffic	72 - 2199	***
42	IA - Osage	IA9: fairly busy, not too interesting.	44 - 2243	**
43	IA - Mason City	REST DAY	0	
44	IA - Decorah	IA9 and blacktop IA48. IA9 rough, no shoulders, traffic; IA48 very good-little traffic, rolling hills.	60 - 2303	***
45	WI - La Crosse	Fairly steep rolling hills, scenic. IA38 to Minn. border. MI44 very good with wide, paved shoulders, traffic near Mississippi River.	59 - 2362	*
46	WI - Elroy	Rail-Trail entire way; Sparta to Elroy has three tunnels.	64 - 2426	*****
47	WI - Portage	Rail-Trail to Reedsberg.	20 - 2446	****
		WI33 from Baraboo to Portage very poor, no shoulder, traffic, rough.	38 - 2484	*
48	WI - Fond du Lac	Back roads all good, little traffic, no shoulders, rolling hills.	68 - 2552	****
49	WI - Manitowac	Rolling hills to Lake Michigan, good road along lake.	68 - 2620	****
50	MI - Ludington	REST DAY AND 4-HR FERRY TRIP		
51	MI - Baldwin	MI10 from Ludington: some rolling hills on back roads, mostly flat.	42 - 2662	***
52	MI - Eastport	REST DAY		
53	MI - Lakeview	Baldwin-Reed Cty: US10, shoulder, traffic.	62 - 2724	**
		Reed City: south thirty miles parallel to US131, worst yet, rough, no shoulder.		-
		East along back roads, good, not interesting.		**
54	MI - Alma	MI91: south bad, rest on back roads okay; rough, no shoulder or traffic.	43 - 2767	**
55	MI - Chesaning	Unmarked Michigan roads, no shoulder, not much traffic.	40 - 2807	**
56	MI - Imlay City	Back roads okay; main roads have no shoulder, rough pavement.	68 - 2875	**
57	CAN - Arkona,Ont	Parallel I69 to Pt. Huron: no traffic.	74 - 2949	*
		CA 7 from Sarnia: no shoulder, wide road with some traffic.		***
58	CAN - Stratford Ontario	Back roads leaving Arkona: good, no traffic, scenic.	58 - 3007	***
		CA7: among worst, no shoulder, traffic, potholes.		*
59	CAN - Kitchener Ontario	Okay, rolling hills, no shoulders, minimal traffic until Waterloo.	31 - 3038	**

DAY	DESTINATION	ROUTE COMMENTS	MI/TOT	RATE
60	CAN - Kitchener	REST DAY, VISIT		
61	CAN - Dunnville Ontario	Kitchener to Cambridge okay. R-T for eleven miles to Paris, boring for R-T. Brantford-Cayuga-Dunnville on Can 54: no shoulder, moderate traffic; along river is nice.	80 - 3118	**
62	CAN - Niagara Falls, Ontario	Along back roads and Lake Erie; no shoulders but no traffic; then bike path along Niagara River.	53 - 3171	****
63	NY - Batavia	Outside of Niagara Falls: New York backroads are good, flat, farmland.	68 - 3239	***
64	NY - Lyons	Back roads, Erie Canal Trail, NY31: all good with wide shoulders, flat, little traffic except for NY31.	80 - 3319	****
65	NY - Fenn's cottage	REST DAY at Lake Bluff near Sodus Bay		
66	NY - Fenn's cottage	REST DAY		
67	NY - Syracuse	Back roads to Weedsport: rough, no shoulder, city streets of Syracuse.	62 - 3381	**
68	NY - Rome	On Old Erie Canal Trail most of way, like R-T, more gravel, no locks.	43 - 3424	***
69	NY - Fultonville	NY69 to Utica: rolling hills, good shoulder; old NY5S along river: mostly flat to Mohawk; 5S to Ft Plain: very hilly, but river road would be flat.	69 - 3493	**
	Fultonville, better better route	5S to Fultonville along canal: flat, good shoulder, little traffic.		****
70	NY - Troy	Mostly bike trail along Mohawk River flat, paved.	58 - 3551	****
71	MA - Pittsfield	Good road with shoulders, hilly, over Berkshire Hills.	41 - 3592	***
72	MA -Amherst/ Northampton	MA143 to MA9: 143 very steep hills, scenic, little traffic, good roads.	61 - 3653	***
73	MA -Sturbridge	MA116 to MA181 to US20: some traffic, hilly but not as bad as MA143.	40 - 3693	**
74	MA - Concord	Along various roads: few street signs, varying levels of traffic, rolling hills, unsure of location much of time.	61 - 3754	*
75	MA -Revere Beach (Boston)	Along Battle Road to Lexington, then bike path, then city streets.	27 - 3781	*
		TOTAL MILES	3781	
		AVERAGE MILES PER DAY	50.41	

Note: Rating of four stars is a highly recommended road; low score of minus (-) means road should be avoided.